To my b
nurse Machine for a
day.

Manley

THE UNPAVED ROAD
An Incredible Journey

By Manley Kiefer

Credits/ Explanation

David Kiefer: for front and back cover, book design, graphics, photo work and formatting.

Yale Kiefer: for front cover photo taken from our property in Formentera.

Front Cover: Our house is on the cliff to the left. Dark hills in the background, Island of Ibiza.

Back Cover: Manley & Jyl, Villa Rosa, Madrid circa 1960.

To our beloved children: Yale, Linda and David

Yale, Linda and David   circa 1980

Contents

Preface

I've never been a writer nor have I attempted to write previously. My basic aim is to relate my story, not to create a work of artistic quality. Because of my interest and love of the Castilian language and Hispanic culture, this was first done in its entirety in that language to be translated ultimately to my American English.

Hopefully I will be able to carry out and complete this endeavor. My thanks to anyone who may have the interest and patience to read this in part or its entirety.

My heartfelt thanks to the many people and friends who have been in my life and those who have encouraged me in this endeavor. I am also thankful for my invaluable Oxford Spanish/English Dictionary whose contents continually impress me. After researching many English dictionaries and in spite of recommendations of friends knowledgeable, I chose this particular volume. Without doubt, since Spanish is my second language, the original work in Castilian is more academic than my American English translation.

I found trying to translate directly from my original version in Castilian to English was more difficult and complicated than I anticipated, therefore for this version, I started anew. Consequently there will be differences, some items and or events in one may be omitted in the other. (Had I another computer and monitor along side, I believe it would have been simpler to translate directly from the Spanish text rather than starting again from scratch).

Introduction

Madrid, Plaza Santa Ana – October 12, 2005, Fiesta Nacional de España. This day commemorates Christopher Columbus discovery of the Americas.

At eleven this morning, sitting on a bench in this plaza, I began, at last, starting something that I've contemplated doing for the past few years. I have always had a feeling of nostalgia for this city where I spent my first eight years in Spain. I am only staying a few days on my return home to San Pedro, California after spending a month in Formentera, my island home. At this point I have little idea of how I will continue and no assurance of doing so.

Plaza Santa Ana is just a few blocks from Madrid's center, Puerta del Sol. It is typical of many small plazas, the old Hotel Victoria on the west, Teatro Español on the east and bordering on the north and south are restaurants, cafes and other commercial entities. Even though there have been many changes in the fifty years plus since my first time in Madrid, Madrid will always be Madrid.

I wrote the first dozen pages of handwritten notes which I proceeded to trash. The following year I began anew, in earnest, after returning to Formentera in September of 2006

Chapter I
Family History & Neighborhood

I was born, Manley Charles Kieferstein, in Minneapolis, Minnesota on February 22nd 1927. Our last name was legally changed and shortened to Kiefer ten years after my birth. I only was aware of the name Kiefer and didn't realize when the official name change took place until seeing my birth certificate years later. My paternal grandfather was the only one who did not change his last name.

My parents, James and Anne Kiefer and two younger brothers, Yale, three years my junior, who died at 21 in the Korean war, and the youngest, Dick (Richard) who is six years younger than I. My parents fled the Ukraine, with their parents, as very young children with other family members, and settled in Minneapolis. When I was about eight or nine years old, my maternal grandfather told me that he and his younger brother deserted the Russian army during maneuvers in the North Sea fleeing to Argentina where they worked in the wheat fields in the region of Santa Fe and Rosario for three years to save the money necessary to bribe the Russian officials in order to smuggle the family out of Russia, after which he left Argentina to join the family in Minneapolis. He lost all contact with his younger brother who remained in Argentina. Life in the Ukraine was very difficult for Jews during the "pogroms". I assume it was during the last few years of the century when they left for Argentina. I will comment later about my trips to Buenos Aires related to contact with my grandfather's nephews, the offspring of his younger brother.

My maternal grandmother was named Fanny and her husband was named Michael. Their six children, oldest to youngest, Pauline, Johnny, Anne, Irving, Jack and Betty, and my paternal grandfather was named William and his wife, Raisel. Their children were Sue, James, Paul and Martin. I am certain that my grandparents and possibly some of the older children born outside of the United States had their original names, that were probably either Russian or Yiddish, anglicized. I don't have any information of any family lineage before my grandparents, except to assume they originated from the same geographical region in the Ukraine. The paternal clan were from the vicinity of Kiev and the maternal from Nikoliev, near Odessa.

I am called "Manny" by my family and by many of my friends (in Hebrew, Menachem). Until in my late teens I didn't like my name, so different and unusual as a first name, but through the years I appreciate the difference; when someone says, John, Joe, Harry, etc a few may answer, but to Manley, I doubt it.

As a baby and as an infant my parents and relatives commented on my light brown curly hair. As a young boy I was small and thin and grew slowly in height. A few years later in the doctor's office, I heard my mother while I was in the waiting room, "Dr. Siperstein, he is so skinny I'm afraid he might die." The doctor answered, "Anne, does he have a good appetite, is he active and does he have good bowel movements?" My mother said definitely yes to all and the doctor replied, "Anne, don't worry."

Whenever we went to the Medical Arts Building, I would run up and down the eighteen flights of stairs. I had no shortage of energy as a boy. The Medical Arts building was nineteen stories, one of the taller buildings in Minneapolis. The tallest was the Foshay Tower at 32 stories and a height of 607 feet including the antenna.

Chapter II
Childhood Memories

Top L to R -my father, uncles Irving and Hymie, aunt Betty, uncles Elmer, Jack and Johnny
Center – my brother Yale, me and my cousin Irwin
Front – My mother, aunt Florence, my grandmother (holding cousin Lynne), my grandfather (holding my brother Richard), aunts Pauline and Esther (holding her daughter Carole).
Circa 1935

Anne and James Kiefer's
Wedding Day

My first memories were when we lived upstairs of my maternal grandparent's house at 1620 6th Avenue North in Minneapolis. We were the only house within a hundred yards of another building except for our barn and garage and a few houses across the street. Along Sixth Avenue toward downtown there were many small businesses and stores with vehicles and horse drawn carts for the most part. There was a streetcar line along the avenue. One of the shops had piles of baled hay on the street in front of the shop with other animal products and feed inside.

Another half mile further, on 6th near Lyndale, there was a small outlet shop that sold food items received from retail food stores that were sold for a fraction of the retail price. They were referred to as "one day old," but I'm sure that was a gross exaggeration. The items consisted of potato chips, popcorn, peanuts, donuts, candy bars, small fruit pies, etc., all in the original wrapping, package or bag. Two or three of us would each pitch in a nickel or a dime for a large shopping bag full of whatever we chose or was available - - - talk about junk food.

I didn't really like some of the typical Jewish foods but later appreciated many of the delicacies, especially the cheese bagel my mother and so few others knew how to make, the paper thin dough wrapped and stuffed with filling of hoop cheese and other ingredients in the shape of a large letter "S" and baked then with a big glob of sour cream on top (some add jam). It doesn't get much better than that.

The neighborhood was mainly Jewish with a mix of Scandinavians. There was an empty store that some non Jewish religious organization set up for crafts etc. for young people with intentions of indoctrinating the non believers. We all took advantage of their offerings, knowing from the beginning what was really going on and without paying attention to the religious talks they constantly gave.

I was probably around four or five years old, alone in the bedroom, while my mother, Aunt Florence and a few of their female friends were playing cards or mah-jong in the adjoining living room. When I came out, everyone was horrified. I looked like a bloody mess until they discovered that it was lipstick I put all over my face. At about the same age, I recall having sensual feelings seeing my Aunt Florence who was well endowed and Rubenesque.

There was a hill in the rear of our back yard, on top of which we had a large structure consisting of a chicken coop, large barn and garage with access to them either from the alley or the stairs up the hill from the rear of the house. It was an eerie feeling as a boy coming home at night seeing the chicken coop with openings that resembled a ghostly, sinister face. To make matters worse, a few years later when the large garage barn was no longer used for cattle, a man held a woman captive there. I didn't know any of the details as I was young and only heard the adults speak about it. To the west was an empty lot on which the neighborhood lads, largely of Scandinavian heritage, would build a ski jump with barrels each winter at the bottom of the hill. At the time our homemade jumping skis and bindings consisted of barrel staves and rubber bands cut from inner tubes. Later US Army surplus ski equipment was available at low cost, such as ski boots, ridge-top steel-edged downhill skis, etc. My father bought me a pair of touring skis from Lund, one of the few local commercial companies that made skis. They were heavy and wide with two grooves on the bottom and definitely not for downhill skiing. I don't remember ever using them or what became of them.

I recall a few neighborhood gang fights where we threw bricks and stones and held used trash can covers as shields. I was never hurt and I think the threat of injury worried most of us so we abstained as we became a little older and wiser.

A childhood friend Harold "Hersh" Berkus and some of us kids would play at his dad's Phillips 66 gas station on the corner of our block. We delighted in climbing the iron pole with a large light on top. I don't know if the others got the same sexual sensation shimmying up the pole. Across the street on the opposite corner was old Charlie Silver's Pure Oil gas station. Those were the days when there was more space to play and less danger for children.

Most of the time, weather permitting, we played out of doors. During inclement weather or if it was dark outside, we often listened to our favorite radio programs; Jack Armstrong, Captain Midnight and The Shadow were a few that I remember. There was no television as yet.

My grandfather, Michael, dealt in cattle which often he would keep in the barn before taking them to the slaughter houses in South Saint Paul. He would start out at three or four in the morning to drive to farms in the countryside to buy cattle. A few times he took me along. First we would stop at a cafe or diner to order a cup of tea. He would pour a small amount in his saucer to cool before sipping it from the saucer. One evening we had a family dinner party in our dining room, normally we ate in the kitchen but this was a special occasion. When my tea was served I poured it into my saucer. My mother asked me what I was doing, apparently ashamed of this breach of etiquette. I said Zadie (Yiddish for grandfather) did it. I guess he didn't feel too good about that and maybe a little embarrassed.

We had another large formal family party at our house on Elwood Avenue. During the conversation at the table my father told a joke or two. Not to be outdone, my Uncle Johnny, my mother's older brother was telling a joke where the punch line was "fig plucker." Without realizing he inadvertently said "pig f- - - -r". There was an embarrassed silence for a few moments while others tried to change the subject. I'm not certain if he was ever aware of his faux pas.

Almost all my time was spent with my maternal grandfather Michael, who often baby sat me when my parents were out. My grandfather was not a large man but very wiry and strong. He was only about five seven in height and always accustomed to hard physical labor, unlike my paternal grandfather who was more learned and academic.

Before I was born, he ran a dairy farm in Hopkins just west of Minneapolis. I always envied his big black Cossack type boots he wore when buying cattle. Even though his feet were small, my feet swam in them when I used to put them on. Sometimes when I accompanied him buying cattle, there were a few occasions when the animals were so wild that the farmers wouldn't dare get near them and my grandfather would wrestle them into his truck. He made me sit in the cab, which was fine, as there were some frightening scenes for a young boy. I'm not certain of the reason, but later he stopped dealing in cattle and went into the junk business. I assume it was for economic reasons.

An unpleasant memory of being alone at night in my bed when I was seven or eight and was very frightened, knowing that the day would come and I would die. I went crying to my grandfather, who after talking to me, finally consoled me enough so I was able to go back to sleep.

One day he hit his big toe with a sledge hammer. It was horrible to see, all bloody and swollen and eventually turned red, blue and black. Everyone insisted he seek medical attention, but stubborn and proud, he refused and eventually it healed completely. Unfortunately, he was a heavy smoker of three to four packs of Lucky Strikes daily, which finally did strike. He died of emphysema at seventy six. I have always admired who and what he was.

With three young children, and my Dad traveling on the road working, we occasionally hired a maid to help out. When we were with the maid in public, I would subtly say, "When is my mother coming home?" or "Where did my mother go?" just so people would know that she wasn't my mother. I was about seven at the time.

Winter sports for many of the young kids consisted of throwing snowballs, making snowmen and other figures, putting snow or ice down one's back, licking icicles, lying on your back in the snow and waving your arms to make snow angels and mainly for the boys, getting your tongue frozen onto iron pipes on dares. The latter activity wasn't usually repeated. Some boys would throw snowballs at the girls until one or two of the girls would fight back and actually beat up on the boys.

A family of Italian descent, the Critellis, lived a few blocks from our house. One day one of the boys was riding a motorcycle going in tight circles in the street until he skidded and fell, skinning both legs. He wasn't hurt badly but that discouraged any ideas I might have had in the future of getting on a motorcycle. One of the sisters named Frances had the reputation of being wild and aggressive. She was in a street fight with another girl brutally bashing her head against the curb. I believe that many women can be more cruel and more violent than men.

I was about ten years old the first time I went fishing. I had a pole, string, cork, sinker and a hook baited with an earthworm. I went with my dad to Glenwood Lake, about a mile and a half from our house. I couldn't believe it, suddenly I caught a small sunfish. I was spellbound, in another world. I was hooked on fishing. One disadvantage of so many waterways is the menace of our state bird, the mosquito. When they are numerous, you don't want to be around. Aside from the bites and the irritating buzzing when you're trying to sleep, they let you know that sooner or later they will get you if you don't get them first. It was near this lake that I made a fire to roast wieners. Wanting to put out the fire, I spied a small dead pine tree lying on the ground and dragged it over the hot embers. The tree immediately became a torch and I panicked as the surrounding area was surrounded with dry grass and trees and I wasn't sure I would be able to put out the fire or keeping from spreading. Before I was able to put it out, I envisioned starting a forest fire and the fire department coming out and arresting me.

When I was much younger my father took my younger brother Yale and me to the north shore of Lake Superior. I prepared to fish from the shore with a worm as bait. At dawn Yale and I cautiously clambered down the rocky shore with both anticipation and trepidation, not knowing what monstrous fish, sharks, whales, etc., we might encounter and probably weren't strong enough to land on my meager equipment. It looked like an ocean to us as the other shore was out of sight and we weren't even in a very wide part of the lake. The widest part is 160 miles. On another trip to the north shore my father and I hired a guide and boat to fish for lake trout and cisco, encountered in very deep waters. We used a spindle with a few hundred feet of copper line. Instead of retrieving the hooked trout and rewinding the line as it was coming in, I just kept hauling it in, naturally the copper line ended up in a tangled heap in the bottom of the boat. None of us were thrilled at the prospect of doing the untangling, which ended up with the guide telling me to leave it and he would do this time consuming chore.

I loved to climb trees. I was about ten years old when I fell from a tree when I jumped from the roof of the barn to swing on a branch of the tree. When I arrived home and my mother saw my wrist, she immediately called Dr. Larson, who came to the house, set and cast the two compound fractured bones in my lower left forearm near the wrist. I had a rapid recovery, as most young people do, and even though I'm right handed, the left arm has been as strong and as muscular the right.

I recall having my tonsils removed at a tender age. This was a common practice at the time whether they were infected or not. Under the anesthesia I dreamt that my mother joined her index finger and thumb together forming an opening and I was continually floating through the opening. I was aware of the smell of the gas and the colors orange and brown. The only pleasure was the ice cream following the procedure.

A block west of our house on 6th Avenue (now Olsen Highway in honor of ex-governor Floyd Olsen), the Rockler family owned a small, elegant fur shop. Nortie, the son, hurt both of his legs in a toboggan accident at about ten years of age and limped badly on both legs. He probably had some permanent damage and disability.

In that same house on 6th avenue, my Aunt Betty married my Uncle Elmer. The ceremony took place under a special canopy set up for the occasion in the living room. Even today, I thought my memory of many of the details was accurate until I recently saw photographs which convinced me that my recall wasn't that great. Some of the things and objects of that period I remember were: men straw hats with narrow brims, pearl gray suede spats with black shoes, double breasted men suits with matching vests of the same cloth. Could be that vests were to look more elegant, to keep warm or probably both. Men, when dressed up, always wore a tie.

We had two neighborhood movie theaters, the Homewood on Plymouth Avenue costing ten cents and the Glenwood on Glenwood Avenue which cost a nickel and later went up to ten cents.

My allowance was ten cents a week and eventually increased to a quarter. If I needed more, my parents were generous. My friend, Hersh Berkus, convinced me to sneak into the Homewood theater with him through the side exit but I was never comfortable doing this and didn't try it again. Reminds me of the time when he stole a cap in Swatez department store and finally convinced me to do the same. When I wandered in the house wearing the cap, my grandfather asked where I acquired this new cap. I think I said I found it or some other lie, but when he looked me in the eye and asked me again, I told him the story. He didn't scold me. Instead, he took me by the hand back to the store and had me apologize and tell the owner what I had done. That was a first and last time.

We kids did lots of playing and hiking as there were many places to go, a favorite was Theodore Wirth (Glenwood) Park. As most kids, we did some crazy and stupid things. I found my dad's .32 caliber revolver and some shells in the side pocket of his car's front door on the driver's side. I took some cartridges and with a friend went across the alley into an empty lot. We put the cartridges on a flat rock and began exploding a few of them by hitting them with another rock, listening to the bullets whizzing through the tall weeds. We also placed nails and pennies that ended up flat on the streetcar tracks. We also put 12 gauge shotgun cartridges on the tracks. It was scary hearing the explosion and the pellets hitting the sides of the streetcar and seeing the alarmed passengers. We didn't do that more than twice. A little too scary and risky. I often wonder why so many of us were not injured or killed by some of the idiocies we committed.

In the winter I would go down in our basement and melt lead in the old coal burning furnace, plate coins with mercury from broken thermometers and sneak wine from a barrel of kosher wine my grandparents made and kept to celebrate the Jewish holidays. I sometimes wonder if any of those activities, aside from the wine, may have been a predisposing factor contributing to my developing asthma years later.

Plymouth Avenue was the main street and commercial center of the north side Jewish neighborhood. I recall Stillman's grocery, Strimling Pharmacy, Abe's delicatessen and Malcoff's delicatessen. One of the strange things that I wasn't aware of until traveling to other cities that had Jewish delicatessens, was the fact that all the Minneapolis Jewish delicatessens always served the corned beef and pastrami sandwiches cold, whereas in the rest of the cities I visited they were always served hot.

I attended Harrison grade school until we moved. The student body at Harrison was composed primarily of Scandinavians and a smattering of Jewish and a few negro students.

I was embarrassed if my mother walked past the school and stopped outside the high wire fence to talk to me. It made me feel like the little insecure boy that I was.

Ralph Wright was a black bully who constantly harassed everyone until he pushed my friend Morris, "Moishe" Londer too far. Moishe challenged Ralph to meet after school in the alley. Naturally the word spread like wildfire and most of the student body gathered to witness what everyone thought would be the slaughter of poor Moishe. The fight ended with Ralph badly beaten. After that fight, many other students took their revenge, fought and beat Ralph, he was no longer a menace or threat.

Moishe Londer was strong and helped his dad who was a junk dealer. His older brother, Label was drafted in the army and was soon discharged with mental problems. I imagine it was sort of a battle fatigue although he never left the states or was in combat.

White haired Willis, a Finnlander in our sixth grade class, was taller and probably a year older than the other students. He wore bib overalls and definitely looked odd and out of place in that environment. He was a holy terror. One unforgettable day he chased the lady teacher around the room with a chair leg that he just had broken off one of the classroom chairs. The authorities must have removed him from the school as I never saw again after that incident.

Our teacher was having our class tell what our fathers did for a living. When my turn came, I said that my father went around selling rags, soap and matches. Actually he was a traveling salesman for a company that dealt in wholesale textiles and among themselves they would slangingly refer to their products as rags. I only knew that in his suitcases I'd see matches and soaps samples from the various hotels.

My friend Jesse Goldberg lived in Los Angeles but spent time and vacations with his mother when visiting his grandparents who lived across the alley from us. He was of medium height, very athletic and well built. I was going to say handsome but actually he was pretty with long light brown wavy hair and long eyelashes. He was a gymnast from an early age and an excellent handbalancer. I was only beginning to work out at that time and maybe even before I started. In any case, I was envious, still skinny and not very tall. Unlike me, he seemed very confident and more worldly than I. Our neighborhood was on the edge of the black neighborhood so it was not uncommon to have blacks among us. Jews and blacks got along quite well with little or no major disturbances that I was aware of at the time.

Walking down the street, two blacks were coming toward us. We were about 15 and they were a few years older and larger than us. I don't remember exactly what anti-Semitic remark they made as they passed us, only that Jess beat him up and they both took off running. I was immobilized and just stood there. Jess never seemed to be afraid of anything or anyone. When Jill and I lived in Redondo Beach, I finally located and went to visit Jess (his Mexican wife is deceased) at his house on Motor Avenue in Los Angeles. I figure we must have been between forty and fifty years of age at the time and we hadn't seen one another since we were fifteen. As I recall he has five children, I believe all or mostly sons. Since he fathered early they were all adults. Jess and his children were all avid motorcycle riders. I know he's fractured about every bone there is to fracture. Jess's family owned thriving furniture stores in Southern California and Nevada.

I joined the Boy Scouts at thirteen and left the program three years later as a Life Scout, just below the top award of Eagle Scout. I believe it was first troop 95 and then troupe 66. I don't recall many of the activities nor camps that I went to, except Camp Wawatasso, on an island in Lake Minnetonka. I do recall taking my exam for my merit badge in astronomy, pointing in the direction that I memorized when asked to identify stars and constellations but really couldn't pinpoint or locate them. Not an honorable achievement.

There was a lovely young blonde maiden on the island. I was envious of the other boys that would talk to her, something I didn't have the courage to do. I think her last name was Bacon.

Most of us kids made our own slingshots from a forked branch, rubber bands cut from inner tubes, which in those days were actually rubber, and leather from the tongue of a shoe in which to hold the missile. These slingshots were the cause of some dead squirrels, many broken windows in the neighborhood along with a few spankings. My mother had a black belt in the drawer under the gas range, which, to my good luck (and good behavior), was rarely used.

While riding my bike home from Lincoln Junior High School one April afternoon, I could feel the hot spring sun beating down on the back of my neck. When I arrived at the house I could barely make it up the few steps to the house and upstairs to my room. I felt weak, nauseated and sick. I was ill for a few days and since then I don't tolerate heat. I feel ill if I spend any time in hot water, such as Jacuzzis, saunas or steam rooms.

Although I have spent most of my life in the sun and the beach getting tan without a problem, during the past few years if I feel radiant heat from the sun, fire, etc., I began to get that same sick feeling. Consequently, if I stay out of the sun unless there is a cool breeze and away from radiant heat from fires and other sources, I don't notice the heat. Lately I have been biking and walking on the beach or doing all my physical activity where there is usually a cool breeze.

The Minneapolis 1940 Aquatennial was a ten day affair. My main interest was visiting the Sioux Indian village set up on the parade grounds. I always had, and still have, an interest in the plains Indians, especially the Sioux (Lakota). There was a complete village with many teepees, horses, chunks of beef on drying racks in the sun. I became acquainted with an old Sioux chieftain, One Bull, who was adapted as a baby by Sitting Bull, both who were in the battle of Custer's last stand at the Battle of the Little Bighorn. I spent every day, four to five hours each day for the duration of the festival, mostly with chief One Bull and his wife in or around their tepee. He was eighty seven, an old wizened warrior. I didn't encounter anyone that could speak more than a few words in English, although it appeared that they understood more than they could speak. We tried to communicate with their sign language with very limited success, due to the fact that I didn't know sign language.

It was obvious that One Bull was fascinated with my Swiss jack-knife with its various applications such as screwdriver, awl, saw blades, bottle and can opener, all in one. I let him handle it and when he handed it back to me, I motioned to him to keep it. Giving a friend something of yours is a cultural trait of Indians. The next thing that happened left me flabbergasted and speechless when he placed his indescribably beautiful magnificent chief's beaded eagle feather headdress on my head. It almost reached the floor. I was bewildered, instinctively believing that this was his offering to me in friendship. I knew that I couldn't accept such a treasured personal item even though I would have loved to have kept it but didn't want to offend him. How to ease myself out of this delicate situation? I looked at his tomahawk and smiled and he understood. When I returned his headdress he smiled in acknowledgment and gently pressed the tomahawk into my hand and with his right hand over his heart, then he reached out and put it on my heart. I was one happy, emotional little thirteen year old boy.

I almost felt part of their family. We would share food together and I forced myself to eat many of the things that I didn't want to eat, dried beef that hung in the sun for days with flies all over it, grasshoppers, etc,. They also spent much time trying to teach me their language. They were a noble people. I shall always treasure and remember that emotional experience. My friends and fellow scouts couldn't understand why I spent all my time at the Indian village.

My first trip west was with my dad when I was in my early teens. We stopped in Mandan, North Dakota. I was in awe of the Indians posing in full regalia at the train depot. I still have a photo of them which I purchased. The Mandan was the more peaceful tribe of the Sioux Nation.

I was exited about making a long bow in the woodworking class while attending Lincoln Jr. High School in Minneapolis. I don't recall if I used lemon or yew wood but do recall shaving the upper part too much resulting in excessive flexibility in that part of the bow. We also made our own arrows.

When all was finished, I took my archery equipment home and was anxious to try it out. I stood in our back yard with my two younger brothers standing nearby awaiting the results of my handicraft as I set up a target. Stepping back about 20 paces, I notched my arrow drawing the bowstring to my chin, sighted the target and let fly. The arrow flew off at a 20 degree tangent and penetrated a rain pipe on the side of the house about 10 feet away from the target I was aiming for.

My cousin Tom, a physician in Minnesota, married a beautiful Pawnee Indian girl who was raised by the Lakota (Sioux). She is very intelligent and involved in an organization dealing with young foreign students in the US. In their living room there is a life size painting of her dressed in a fringed deerskin Lakota dress. She was one beautiful Indian maiden.

My uncle Paul's wife Sari was a dark beautiful exotic lady. One day on Plymouth Avenue she passed in her car and I called out, "Auntie Sari". She replied, saying don't call me aunt in public, just Sari.

My introduction to the new marvel of television was at Paul and Sari's house where the family would gather for the evening in front of the small black and white screen to watch the weekly one hour movie sponsored by Gross-Kronick's dry cleaners. At commercial time we would all rush to the fridge for snacks.

Plymouth Avenue, Sixth Avenue and Glenwood Avenues, listed in order of their importance, were the major North Minneapolis commercial thoroughfares of the north side (primarily Jewish section) during the years I lived there from 1927 to 1950. They remained under those conditions for a few years more. The original population in the Plymouth Avenue neighborhood was eventually populated by blacks which resulted in its burning and destruction during the riots in mid July of 1967. I understand that most of the edifices and businesses that were there no longer exist. I don't believe the changes on 6th or Glenwood Avenues were nearly as radical.

Chapter III
Rites of Passage –Teen years

My parents bought our first house at 826 Elwood Avenue North around about 1939 or 1940, a duplex on a corner lot across the street from the Emanual Cohen Jewish Community Center. On the other end of our property, about 100 yards away, was Irving Park, the size of a square block, with two tennis courts, a sand box, some benches and a water pump. The park was on Irving Avenue but the real name was Elwood Park. A few friends and I found some condoms, which we enjoyed filling with water from the pump in the park. Going through items in the attic, I came across a woman's diaphragm but had no inkling of what it was. We occupied the upstairs and rented the downstairs to the Nudells. I recall that one of their young sons was playing with a gun and accidentally shot himself and died. At the Emanuel Cohen Center there was a frozen hockey pond in the winter where we used to play hockey with broomsticks.

The Leamington Hotel in Minneapolis had its famous, delicious Henry VIII hamburger for thirty five cents consisting of more than a half pound of prime beef and a thick slice of sweet Bermuda onion. The Mung Hing Chinese restaurant served all the chow mein you could eat for fifty cents and Bridgeman's 35 cent banana split was a special treat.

Armistice Day, November 11, 1940, presently called Veteran's Day, an early winter snowstorm hit the Great Plains of the upper mid west, east of the Rocky Mountains with a record snow fall in some areas of up to 22 inches, with drifts that were considerably higher. In the Twin Cities there was no transportation in city streets for a week. I was upset because the milk deliveries ceased. My father was on the road on the way home from his route from Montana, North Dakota to Minneapolis. This area bore the brunt of the storm with many casualties of travelers freezing to death in their vehicles. We anxiously listened non stop to the radio news.

Our worries ended when our father came safely home. This was one of the worst blizzards in US history.

I was ten and decided I wanted a dog. After some pleading and begging someone in the house brought me a puppy. Things were going well until I discovered that my grandparents were giving the dog milk with coffee. I was upset because I was told that coffee stopped ones growth and I wanted my dog to be big. I don't recall how long I had that dog nor what became of him.

My next dog was a six month old black pup. We would throw him out of the second story window into the eight feet of snow drifted against the wall. After some time he would find his way to the back door. We repeated this many times and the dog loved playing in the deep snow.

We had a four foot wall on the side of the alley which was now buried completely and level with the additional two feet of snow on top. My youngest brother was playing in the deep snow when he inadvertently stepped off the alley wall suddenly sinking another few feet. We had quite a time getting him out. In spite of the inconveniences, we boys enjoyed those rare experiences.

While lying in bed for a few hours during the day, listening to a football game with my dog sleeping at the foot of my bed, there was a noise and the dog woke suddenly but couldn't get up immediately. I could see he was frightened so I quickly reached for him trying to help him up. Looking panic stricken, he bit me. I was aware of rabies and frightened myself for quite a while after looking up the symptoms and the horrible results that follow without immediate treatment. There wasn't any problem but I worried for some time. It's sometimes difficult not to be a hypochondriac.

Room 208 was my home room at Lincoln Junior High where Ms. Bollinger was our home room teacher. Our class had an outdoor picnic at Theodore Wirth Park. I was paired with an ugly skinny dishwater blond Finnish girl, Martha Maki (I was no bargain either). About five years later, I saw this same girl/woman walk past with her girl friend on 6th Avenue and Dupont when I was in the park with a buddy. She was gorgeous, stunning and the most well endowed woman you could imagine, a real knockout. Unfortunately, I was too timid to speak to any girls until I was eighteen.

Big Williams and Little Williams were the nicknames the students gave for the two female teachers in junior high school with the same last name. I recall Big Williams habit of rapping a male student on the breastbone with two knuckles of her right hand for punishment.

A few years later, after I began doing gymnastics and bodybuilding, I was on another trip with my father. We were in Hot Springs, South Dakota in the heart of the Black Hills. There was a park in town with a fairly steep cement stairway of 33 steps which I walked to the bottom in a handstand. People gathered on the upper deck watching me and applauding.

Two of my aunts and uncles had homes on Lake Minnetonka which is about 15 to 20 miles west of Minneapolis. The lake is composed of numerous connected bays, narrows, and islands with a total shore line of 120 miles. I was a very excited 15 year old when we spend the night at my Aunt Sari and Uncle Paul's house on the lake before leaving for a three week trip with my dad to Montana. Early the next morning before the others were awake I went to the dock and took the row boat out on the lake. When they couldn't find me and saw that the boat was missing they finally, with binoculars, noticed that I was very far out. When I saw them frantically waving from the dock I knew I was in trouble. My dad was upset and said that he'd send me home instead of going with him to Montana. My world had ended. It was a great relief when my dad relented and we were on our way.

The scenery through the Dakotas is flat until nearing the Missouri River when undulating hills give way to the impressive Bad Lands of North Dakota, the Black Hills of South Dakota and the flat lands of eastern Montana. I was excited seeing my first real mountain appearing in the distance west of Livingston, Montana. In Glendive, in the eastern part of the state, I finally convinced my father to buy me a second hand .22 caliber, single shot Winchester rifle from the hotel's bellboy. I was always interested in guns and through the years became fairly proficient and knowledgeable about firearms.

After much pleading I convinced my dad to let me off to roam the countryside while he spent the day with his customers in town and then pick me up when he finished in the late afternoon. In those days much of the land in those areas wasn't fenced so it was real open country. It was glorious having whole days by myself, shooting everything I saw. I shot rattlesnakes, lizards, gophers, jackrabbits, hawks, eagles and almost anything that moved. After a while I was remorseful and limited my shooting to only varmints and targets such as cans and bottles. I liked putting up milk cartons filled with water and seeing them explode when hit with a .22 caliber long rifle hollow point bullet.

Days later near the Great Divide between Butte and Helena my dad let me off with my rifle. I became lost and was worried. This was wild, deserted wilderness. I knew that I wasn't too far away and after an hour of aimless wandering I finally heard the honking of a car horn and eventually located our car. On that same trip we stopped to try my new fly rod at a small mountain stream. I caught a small eight inch trout and before I landed it, suddenly I saw a frog. I hurriedly asked my dad to hold the rod while I picked up my .22 rile and shot the frog and then took the rod from my dad to land the tiny trout, which we released.

My dad almost always returned from his trips to Montana with holes in his pockets from the wear and tear of the heavy silver dollars that were in vogue in that state in lieu of paper bills.

There were times in the summer when the temperature reached the high nineties and often a few degrees over 100 Fahrenheit aside from the high humidity and not more than a degree or two cooler at night. One record breaking year the temperature soared to 108 degrees and remained in the hundreds for five days. I removed the screens from my bedroom windows hoping it would let in a breeze but the only things that came in were mosquitoes. I soon put the screens back on again.

— — — — — —

I borrowed my Dad's 1937 maroon Hudson Terraplane and with four friends loaded it with supplies and left for the north shore of Lake Superior to cool off. Most of us had headaches from the heat but as we neared Duluth, "The Coolerator City", it began cooling off and our headaches disappeared. Going up the north shore past Two Harbors it was actually chilly by comparison and we had to dress warmer. We put up our pup tent, put the bottled sodas in the lake which is always very cold and the food in some small trees so the animals wouldn't get it, mainly the numerous black bears. Some of the local boys told us that they would stand on the top of the hill of the local dump and shoot at the bears with their .22 rifles. Possibly few were killed, but many were probably wounded and suffered. The urge to feel having such power over other creatures seems to bring out the insensitivity and cruelty in some humans.

Unless the snowfall was more than two feet deep and/or the temperature fell to below 20 degrees below zero, we walked the half mile to grade school and junior high and the mile and a half to high school. There were about three or four students from wealthy families living within a few blocks from where we lived who had cars and drove to school. The rest of us peasants walked. I don't recall if there was food for sale in school, in any case most of my friends and I carried our own bag lunches.

When my mother was a girl, her father would take her in his horse drawn milk wagon from their farm in Hopkins to the Parade Grounds in Minneapolis from where she would walk to North High school, the two miles each way winter, spring and fall, rain, cold, or snow. There was rarely a day she was late for school. The principal gave orders that, under the circumstances, any tardiness would be excused. I believe she told me she was never absent or late.

My mother was very active and healthy until a few months before her death from a massive stroke preceded by TIAs (transitory ischemic attacks) months before her death just before her 92nd birthday.

The bane of many of us Jewish children was being obliged to attend Hebrew school for a few hours daily after our regular schooling. As Jewish custom, I had my Bar Mitzvah (rite of passage) in 1940 at our local synagogue. I really looked forward to and enjoyed the many nice gifts that followed. I do recall my parents sending me up to the attic to enjoy the many presents while the adults partied below. Most of us dreaded the long hours of memorizing in Hebrew and the long recital we had to give in front of everyone at the synagogue at our Bar Mitzvahs. Luckily many of the parents, mine included, gave us the option of not continuing with Hebrew school after our Bar Mitzvahs. The modern Hebrew language has differences from the old, which was then classified as a dead language.

My Hebrew school was the Talmud Torah, eight blocks from our house on 8th Avenue and Fremont in north Minneapolis. The two teachers I remember were Mr Turchik and Mr Semach. I personally didn't learn very much, partly due to the teaching but mostly to my lack of motivation as this was a situation almost forced upon us. My brother Yale continued after his Bar Mitzvah. He was always more motivated and disciplined than I.

During my pre teens and early teens friends and I often would walk to the outskirts of the city and into the extensive surrounding parkland areas with many ponds, lakes, streams and woods. One pond in particular we called Goldfish Pond but I believe the proper name is Birch Pond. We would visit it in the early spring when the ice was melting so we could catch many dormant goldfish by hand and carry them a mile or more home in a bucket of water. Sonny "Popeye" Schwartz and his sister Rae were with us. His nickname was due to one of his eyes being slightly crossed. She was walking in front of us and I couldn't help notice as she undulated sexily along. She was a sexy looking and well endowed girl for her fifteen years. Usually by the time we arrived home few of the goldfish survived. Until our mid-teen years we also played most sports, baseball, football in summer and hockey and skiing in winter. I did continue with my favorite winter sport, downhill skiing, which was practically in my back yard just across the street and across the creek about six blocks from our house on Xerxes.

In my teens, my father would take me fishing when the men in the Pink Supply Company went on their annual fishing trips. The ones I distinctly remember were to Lake Mille Lacs in northern Minnesota, famous for wall-eyed pike (actually a member of the perch family and not a true pike). Lake Mille Lacs is a large, shallow water, sandy bottom body of water that can get wild if the weather is bad, and one normally fishes out of sight of land. In Minnesota and when in season, there is nothing as good eating as wall-eyed pike.

With my Dad and his two brothers, Mart and Paul, we went fishing in Woman's Lake in northern Minnesota. Mart was an avid muskie fisherman with a large heavy tackle box full of lures. I believe that record muskies weigh more than sixty pounds. My dad and Paul enjoy fishing but they're not addicts. Mart had an inboard motor boat and a canoe. My Uncle Paul, carrying a case of beer, stepped from the dock onto the gunwale of the canoe, overturning the canoe ending up with both him and the beer in the water. My dad would laze on the stern with the ever present cigar in his mouth and a straw hat, and as often happened, my dad was the only one who caught any fish the first day. Marty could never get over the fact that my dad knew so little about fishing and this happened more than a few times. I wasn't very happy when it was time to eat and I saw that they brought along their favorite Jewish delicatessen type foods that required little or no cooking, salami, onions, herring, pumpernickel bread and beer. In my younger years this was not my idea of food which led us having to make the long boat trip to the other side of the lake, where the only little grocery store was located, to buy something I could eat.

When Mart was younger he worked on a salmon fishing boat in Alaska and later was a link trainer instructor in the US Air Force in Tonapah, Nevada, before joining the same company my dad worked for, also as a traveling salesman. After many years Mart started his own company in the same line of merchandise. My father worked for the same firm until he retired. Mart passed away from a heart attack at fifty two years of age, leaving a wife and two sons.

My first "romantic" episode was with two Swedish neighbor girls, Dorothy and Gunborg, in our pre teen years. I think it only consisted of kissing and touching. Another occasion with a buddy a few years later at night in North Commons park we were on the swings and met two girls who we walked home holding hands and kissing.

I wasn't sure where to insert this uniquely male experience, usually in teenagers or older. The painful and accidental catching of one's male organ while zipping up your pants. I'm not sure that all males have inadvertently done this but for those who have, zipping up with care becomes the rule of the day, which almost always limits this painful mishap to a one time occurrence.

December 7th 1941, Day of Infamy, I was sitting on a window ledge in the game room of the Emanual Cohen Jewish Community

Center across the street from our house on Elwood when the news came over the radio of the Japanese attack on Pearl Harbor.

Across the street from the center there was a brown brick, three story building that I believe housed young Jewish girls. Some of us guys would stand outside in front of the Center and watch one of the well endowed girls undress in one of the upstairs windows. This went on for a while and I can only imagine that she was unaware of being seen.

I had just entered North High School consisting of the 10th through the 12th grades and at the same time became interested in building up my skinny body. I almost sent away for the Charles Atlas course by mail but thought twice about spending the money. I finally got up enough courage to approach our high school gymnastic champion, George Patten. He had won the US National High School all round Gymnastic Championship. I asked George how I might build myself up. He showed me how to do push ups. I was only able to do a few but as time passed I did at least 100 push ups daily, even when I was ill and the doctor gave me medication and told me to stay in bed. I always did a few more to be sure that I didn't shortchange myself. Upon finishing doing my quota of push ups I didn't have enough strength to do another push up and had to roll over on the floor so I wouldn't have to use my arms to get up.

When I was sixteen I made a set of weights and other improvised equipment. I cast the plates of various sizes and weights of cement for a barbell and dumbbells from molds of bowls, cans, etc. I bought a solid steel bar one and a half inches in diameter for the barbell instead of the standard one inch bar. That was 70 years ago and I'm still using weights.

As I began diversifying my exercises I was inspired to join the gymnastic team. Later I will relate more about my physical training and my association with George who was instrumental in my indoctrination into the world of physical culture.

My dad jokingly referred to my working out as hard work without getting paid. That didn't excuse us from our chores such as changing the storm windows and screens twice a year, cutting the grass in the summer and shoveling snow in the winter.

Chapter IV
Xerxes & North High

I was 17, in the middle of my high school years, when our parents bought our new home at 1754 Xerxes Avenue North, situated on the northwest Minneapolis city limits. From our living room and upstairs bedrooms we had a breathtaking panoramic view to the west, overlooking Bassett's Creek and the two competitive ski jumps in the wooded hills of the extensive Theodore Wirth Park system, often referred to as Glenwood by the locals, where we skied, sometimes at night by moonlight. I often went with my friend Norman Oakvic and a few times we were accompanied by his friends from the Norwegian Consulate speaking only in Norwegian, although they were fluent in English.

There were no ski lifts. Consequently, we were accustomed to spending most of our time and energy climbing, either side-stepping or herringbone. I skied only downhill, no cross country nor jumping. During the summer my friend, Reuben Vodovoz and I would take turns climbing the steps to the top of the high ski jump taking turns carrying one another piggy back for exercise.

This was a newer and more upscale neighborhood. I attended North High School, a mile and a half walk. North High was one of the larger schools in the twin cities. I entered North High School in January of 1942. George Patten was captain of the gymnastic team, which incidentally was one of the best, if not the best high school gymnastic teams in the country and it was strange that our two coaches of the gymnastic team, Lou Burnett and Tom Kennedy, had little or no knowledge of, nor ever participated in that sport.

One of the gyms I occasionally worked out in was a small neighborhood bodybuilding gym on 19th Street and Queen Avenue in north Minneapolis, a half mile from our house. In the basement was a Russian -Turkish style steam bath where one could get lashed with oak leaf switches soaked in a wooden bucket of soap suds. My friend Margo Bobkin was the owner. His older brother Harold played Be-Bop on the piano so we called him Be-Bob Bobkin. My youngest brother Dick began working out with me and improved continually, his asthma was somewhat better as he went along. When we had bad attacks, we had to lay off exercise.

Even before we moved to the house on Xerxes Avenue we would walk a mile or two to the park area to catch frogs, turtles, crayfish, fish, fireflies, snakes etc. I loved to watch the large, multicolored dragonflies swooping and hovering wherever there was water; especially in the ponds. Further down Bassett's creek was Fruen's mill where we always could find crayfish under the rocks. Twin Lakes was another close by, out of the way, area that could only be reached on foot.

Doc Stanwood was the athletic director of the downtown Minneapolis YMCA. The weight room was small. One couldn't help notice Ralph Kraski, the ever present bodybuilder. He was of medium stature, sparse brown hair, pale complexion, in his forties. He was constantly exhibiting his extreme, grotesque upper body, ape like musculature, compared to his thin bowed legs. Most of us knew him very little and avoided him. He was more concerned with flexing his muscles for those present. I don't mention these things to degrade him. To my knowledge he posed no problems to us or to others.

Donny Karja, Paul Sylvester and I worked out on a high bar in a nearby empty lot. We filled a pit under the bar with sawdust and wood shavings to cushion our dismounts. Some days after our workouts we would jog four and a half miles to the beach at Lake Calhoun, do some gymnastics and handstands and jog home. Soon after, I became asthmatic, severely limiting my running and endurance.

At fifteen I finally bought the gun of my dreams for $17.40, a new

Remington model 512 P bolt action .22 caliber rifle with a 28 inch barrel and a tubular magazine holding 15 long rifle cartridges. It was my pride and joy. It was always polished and the barrel cleaned after each use. It was in mint condition when I sold it many years later. I don't know why I sold it, maybe I needed the cash. I went with friends a few times to hunt small game but they were not as careful and paranoid as I about gun safety and from then on I went alone. Until I was ready to shoot, I never had a cartridge in the chamber since I didn't want to only rely on the safety mechanisms on guns. Years later at police shooting ranges,with highly qualified instructors, I thought some of them were not too careful where they pointed the muzzle and some of their other handling techniques. Maybe I'm too paranoid about firearms even though I love and respect them. There is no such thing as being too careful with firearms.

For awhile I was a member of a team at the Bryant Avenue Police Station practicing target shooting with Winchester model 52, .22 caliber target rifles under the supervision of the police marksmen. I would devour the gun enthusiasts' bible, Stoeger's Gun catalog. I would amaze others with the data, ballistics, trajectories, etc, by memory, of almost all firearms, domestic and foreign from .218 caliber varmint to .600 caliber double barrel Krupp elephant rifle. In fact, my friend Howard Delman (Noodleman) had at one time owned that very same Krupp gun.

At sixteen I worked on a farm in Reading, Minnesota near Worthington in the southwest corner of the state on the South Dakota border. The owner, Milford Davis, an ex-senator, had two sections (1,240 acres). Since there was a shortage of manpower during the war, the University of Minnesota gave a two day course for boys or young men that were interested in farm work.

Two of the boys I knew. One was Martin Thingvold and the other's name I don't recall. I looked forward to this new adventure with anticipation. I don't remember what transportation brought us to

Worthington, where we were picked up and driven to the farm near Reading.

In southern Minnesota there is a large German population. Some of the cities and towns have German names. In the summer it is common to see these farmers in their bib overalls at the outdoor cafes drinking quantities of beer. They are generally large with big bellies.

It was a well equipped farm and had eight Arabian riding horses aside from the impressive working horses, Clydesdales, Percherons, Belgian Bays, etc. I was in the barn in a stall currying one of the huge work horses when he put his hind hoof on my foot. It didn't hurt but I couldn't get my foot free. Finally after trying to push the horse with no results, I saw the farmer in the yard and called him, embarrassed as I was. He smiled upon seeing my situation and gave the horse a hard knee to the ribs and the horse moved over releasing my foot. He said just give him a hard kick in the ribs if this happens again. I mentioned that I was afraid that I might hurt the horse if I kicked him really hard. He chuckled and said there is no way that it would even bother the horse.

Some of my blunders were: turning a hay rack too sharply, taking out some fence posts and turning over the loaded rack and bringing into the house the skim milk which was for the pigs and giving the cream to the pigs. The farm family was very understanding of us city kids.

Some of the other boys were acquaintances and having been there longer than I invited me to go riding on one of the Arabian horses. They saddled the horses (with English saddles, yuck). I think I might have done better with a western saddle. As soon as I mounted, the horse made a dash out of the corral jumped a ditch and a fence with me clinging to his mane. Finally we got him back to the corral and as I was about to dismount he headed into the barn where he reared and I hit my shoulder on the overhead rafters before I finally dismounted. I guess the lads thought that was a funny prank giving me the most spirited horse. I had never been on more than a carnival ride on a docile pony. Spirited horses sense who can dominate them and who can't. Had I not had to leave because of an allergic episode, I likely would have tried to learn to ride.

We had it easy. We didn't have to get up till seven thirty, the food was great and abundant and we even had homemade ice cream. I've always liked the big farm style breakfast of eggs, bacon, sausages, potatoes toast with juice and milk aside from the women bringing sandwiches, snacks and drinks twice a day when we were working in the fields.

After four or five days on the farm I became congested and had trouble breathing. The farmer gave me quinine thinking I had a cold. I noticed that I had red welts on both forearms from shocking sheaves of grain, which I didn't realize at the time, was an allergic reaction. I was sorry to have to leave as I enjoyed the experience and was also just getting chummy with one on the neighboring farm gals. I was put on the train back to Minneapolis.

My mother took me to the chief allergy specialist, Dr. Stoesser, at the University of Minnesota School of Medicine. I went through a battery of allergy skin tests. Some of the tests were positive but it seemed when I ate those foods or was exposed to these allergens, I didn't get any bad reactions. I had just begun bodybuilding exercises a short while before my farm experience and asked the doctor if I should continue doing these strenuous exercises. He said I should only do light exercise such as playing the piano or squeezing tennis balls, otherwise I could end up in a wheelchair watching the other boys through my window playing outside. I did this faithfully for two weeks until one day I said to my mother that I was going to continue doing my calisthenics and weightlifting. When necessary I was given injections of adrenalin and used an inhaler during asthmatic attracts. There were times I was ill, with bad attacks of asthma or otherwise in situations where I was unable or it was inconvenient to exercise. I was disappointed when for any reason I couldn't exercise and felt I wouldn't progress as rapidly. As the years passed the asthmatic episodes were less frequent and bodybuilding and gymnastics were my main activities and goals.

In the early years with simple asthma, even if the attacks were severe, an injection of adrenalin, epinephrine or other rescue inhalers often gave full relief and the victim's breathing would be normal. With constant use of these drugs over time the effect was diminished and other drugs were developed. My brother Dick's condition was much more severe than mine and he was given many different medications throughout his life beginning when he was a few years old. I mentioned previously that in his teens he worked out with me and he improved continually until his latter years when he began having similar problems as before. I believe with the passing years and many different forms of treatment and medications through the many years, he was eventually over medicated. He had no choice but to put himself in the hands of the medical community. Many of those drugs are no longer used as they proved harmful with adverse secondary effects. It seems a rule of thumb that when one ages the immune and other systems deteriorate and consequently give rise to the return of previous pathologies, example, post polio syndrome and chronic bronchial asthma, to name a few.

– – – – – –

In the summer months during the three years of high school I did a variety of things when not working. Much of the time I would be working out at the gym and at the beach. Our favorite beach, Lake Calhoun's Main Beach had a high bar, parallel bars, rings, sand and a plenitude of ladies. Later we would walk across the street and over the railroad tracks to the peat bogs at Lake of The Isles where we practiced tumbling. The peat bog was resilient and we could get more height and the tumbling was easier on our legs. The only other sandy beach on Lake Calhoun was Thomas Beach a mile distant on the opposite side of the lake.

I was explaining to some friends that to get enough lift to do a back flip, one had to use the upper body for lift aside from spring from the legs. I was standing in the sand and said to demonstrate and prove my point I would just use my upper body without using my legs for additional spring. It was embarrassing landing on my head and face in the sand. In later years we switched to 32nd Street beach where there was grass and a flight of stairs that we would climb and descend in a handstand. Also there were fewer people.

Some of the friends I recall who worked out with us at the beach were: George Patten, Sonny Schwartz, Norm Oakvik, Don Overbee, Ole Lee, Lee Laitz, Ray Paskoff and Ted Bryan. Ted was brought up under the Hitler Youth Movement and consequently had many problems adjusting socially. He was very haughty and a bully with people that he thought were easy to bully. He got along OK with us except for one time when he made some anti-Semitic remark in front of Ray Paskoff. Big mistake. Ray beat him up badly which is the last time I saw Ted misbehave, at least in our presence. From then on Ted was very docile and careful what he said around us. Seems strange that he hung around us as half of us were Jewish. Maybe it's because we tolerated him and considered him somewhat of a friend. Ted had a good natural physique. He still had a pronounced German accent and would brag about his arms, "aums." His girl friend was Marge "Mauge." I always wondered whatever happened to Ted and how he made out.

Left to Right: George Patten, Marshall Benjamin, Don Overbee, Sonny, "Popeye" Schwartz, Norm Oakvic, Frank Stephan and Ole Lee.   Minneapolis - circa, early 50's

Ole Lee was a special personality in our neighborhood, revered for his gymnastic and his physical prowess. He was basically self taught and self educated.

I was voted best physique when I graduated North High School in January of 1945 and the girl I had a crush on, Evelyn Bolin, who I'm sure was unaware how I felt, was voted best feminine physique. After our graduation ceremony I got up the nerve to kiss her and her response felt very mutual. I would have continued pursuing her had she not left immediately after for Hollywood to be with and work with her stepsister, Arlene Dahl, the actress.

Until university I really didn't like school, probably because of my timidness and shyness. The only social contact I had in school was with others on the gymnastic team and a few other boys. I would have loved to have had the courage and confidence to be able to have been more social and talked to some of the girls.

Aside from gymnastics I also worked out with weights. There were periods when I would work out in my basement with weights for a few hours, practice gymnastics and handbalancing a few more hours and ski at night for a few hours. We only had time to eat four big meals a day and sleep for ten to twelve hours a night. We weren't able to keep up this pace more than a few days at a time.

Unfortunately, George Patten graduated and joined the navy after my first semester. George was the national all round high school gymnastic champion in 1945. George was always very modest about his many accomplishments and non critical of others. I had won second place in the Mr. Minnesota bodybuilding contest in 1948. First place went to a professional bodybuilder from out of state working at Alan Stephan's (Mr. America 1976) gym in Minneapolis. I worked out often in Stephan's gym and was friends with Alan and his charming wife, Grace. They were both nice, good people. She had a 14 year old brother who also worked out but sadly died of some illness shortly thereafter.

My youngest brother Richard Kiefer, "Mister Colorado 1957"

From the time I was twenty I was only in Minneapolis when visiting from Denver or California. Before we moved to Denver, I made three trips from Minneapolis to Los Angeles with my dad and one of which was with my Aunt Betty. I'm reminded of an event after eating supper in a nice upscale hotel restaurant in Grand Island, Nebraska when my aunt asked the waiter to please wrap her piece of remaining chicken to take out. The waiter appeared dumbfounded as he probably had never had a like request. In those days it was not a common practice and in many societies considered poor taste. She explained to me that she considered it foolish to waste good food that one had paid for. She was very rich and generous and certainly wasn't in need. To this day, I have no qualms asking for a doggie bag, no matter where I am or with whomever I may be.

Another time we made the trip with Zelda, a middle aged relative who had to stop at every restaurant, gas station and hotel toilet along the way. We thought it humorous and joked about it during the trip and after with family. It was probably an insensitive thing to do and I'm certain that Zelda wasn't overjoyed about friends and family knowing about such a personal item

My dad and I flew from Minneapolis to Los Angeles in January of 1948. Nearing the Los Angeles metropolitan area we could see through the window a thick blanket of black smoke from the smudge pots to protect the orange groves from freezing. We were surprised upon landing, like everyone else aboard and the local residents, to see a layer of snow on the ground. A rare sight in Los Angeles except in the higher neighboring hills and mountains.

It was during this visit that I was driving my Aunt Betty's large Cadillac to Daniel's market in Beverly Hills, where many of the movie people shopped. As I was entering the parking area I suddenly saw a man exiting the store, crossing the parking lot at a rapid pace while eating an apple. I slammed on the brakes as he dove off to the side, rolling over and dropping his apple. I wasn't accustomed to driving a large, heavy car and couldn't have stopped in time. There wasn't any power steering or power brakes at the time. The man was short, slim and athletic looking. I stopped and apologized profusely and he graciously accepted my apology and went on his way. After I recovered my wits a few minutes later, my aunt asked me if I know who that was. It was Kirk Douglas.

I enjoyed the month staying at my Aunt Betty and Uncle Elmer's home with their two children Lynne and Mark at 208 South Rexford Drive in Beverly Hills. We were one block off Wilshire Boulevard where I would take the bus directly to the Santa Monica pier. I spent almost all my time at Muscle Beach on the left of the

Pier and worked out with many of the notable handbalancers, acrobats and bodybuilders. Since that time I have lived near Muscle Beach for short periods of a month or two each winter and the summer of '55 until September when I left for Spain.

My cousin Lynne introduced me to one of her girlfriends, Joyce Hartfeld, from a very wealthy Jewish family that resided on their lavish estate in an upscale Beverly Hills enclave. I visited Joyce at her at her invitation at the family mansion and was overwhelmed passing through the electronic gates, up the long driveway and being greeted at the door by the Philippine doorman who announced my arrival. The family was very congenial and seemed very comfortable with my presence. Undoubtedly more comfortable than I was in their presence during my initial visit. On the estate was a large swimming pool, tennis courts and other sport items. Joyce was an excellent swimmer and gave lessons at her pool. Her parents were good looking people along with her younger sister whom I thought was very attractive with her long black long hair, lovely figure and sensuous face. She was only in her mid teens, Joyce being a few years older and heavier. I was in my early twenties. I really wasn't as interested in seeing Joyce more that a few visits in spite of my friend Howie's urging me to continue and marry into such a wealthy family, something that never appealed to me.

— — — — — —

When it was time to return home from Los Angeles to Denver, I hitch hiked and made it home in three days. I got a ride with a gentleman and after he drove all day asked if I would drive after we stopped at a cafe for coffee. I was not a coffee drinker but had three cups of coffee with milk and sugar and proceeded to fall asleep as soon as I got behind the wheel. Needless to say we stopped for the night. He dropped me off in Las Vegas.

I caught a ride in a pickup truck with a rancher who asked if I was sure I wanted to accept a ride that would let me off on the highway in the high mountain country of Utah without the assurance of getting another ride and being stuck in that desolate area with no food, water or lodging. It was early morning on a beautiful, warm spring day, so I got in and we were off. It was a little scary on the mountain curves and his taking nips from a flask of liquor. He had to leave the main road to get to his ranch so I got off on the highway beside a rushing mountain stream with the sound of the constant banging of rocks against each other with the heavy current from the spring run off from the nearby snow covered peaks. It was a glorious feeling being alone with nature, the warm sun on my face, the fresh spring air, birds chirping, flowering foliage and the permeating smell of pine. I was hoping I could spend a few delightful hours before getting another ride. Before nightfall I did get another ride but really don't remember any details for the rest of the trip home.

— — — — — —

My mother was the economist and my dad was the generous one. When my father returned from his business trips he always emptied his pockets with a lot of change on the floor when my mother and us kids were around, We would scramble for the money. One time my mother, in her haste, inadvertently stepped on my hand.

Accompanying my father on a business trip, we were eating in a restaurant in Fargo, North Dakota. In the next booth were two young marines on furlough discussing their date for that cold winter evening. My dad overheard them and asked if they had a car. When they answered that they had no transportation, he gave them his car keys and told them to leave the keys at the hotel the next morning. That was my father.

My mother had to be careful not to let him know if there was anything she'd like because chances are that it would be there the following day.

My father enjoyed conversing with people, meeting strangers and neighbors alike, especially entertaining children with his jokes, blowing smoke rings and doing other tricks with his cigar smoking. The kids loved my dad.

Whenever my dad and his two brothers got together, mostly on week end evenings when they were all in town, there were hours of continual jokes. I loved listening although I didn't understand them all. Jokes seem to be one of the talents of salesmen. Occasionally they would mix in some Jewish humor which is different than American humor. I think Jewish humor takes a special mind-set, especially with the interjection of Jewish or Hebrew words and expressions. My mother didn't understand all the humor and went to bed. I stayed up later.

Chapter V
The Great Lakes & Other Jobs

I joined the US Coast Guard, certificate #300351, on February 14, 1945, eight days before my eighteenth birthday. During the summer vacations of 1945 and 1946 I worked on the ore ships on the Great Lakes as an ordinary seaman deckhand. Our first ship was the Daniel J. Morrell out of Duluth to Fairview, Ohio and return. Sonny Schwartz was with me on that trip. The first night suddenly there was a horrendous noise like the ship was coming apart. We jumped out of our bunks, put our life jackets on and scurried up on deck. I guess we looked foolish to the rest of the crew. Our cabin was adjoining the chain locker and the racket was the anchor chain being let out. The ore boats are all steel construction, 740 feet in length, approximately 78 feet wide and there are no watertight compartments. When an ore ship went down it sunk fast, forming a vortex or eddy that would suck down anything nearby. One wouldn't last more than a few minutes in that icy water.

We worked during the day and slept all night but we could also eat or snack on any of the four hour watches aside from our three regular meals. My mother told me before leaving home how I would miss her delicious cooking. Well, in spite of her good cooking, I didn't. The food was great aboard ship, especially the night we had sturgeon steaks, a meal I won't forget.

Our duties, when in port, were to be swung over the side on a boom in a bosun's chair to the dock below. It was quite a drop if the ship was unloaded and high on the water. The heavy steel cables were thrown to us from the deck to place the looped ends over the various stanchions along the dock in order to constantly move the ship to align the chutes with the open hatches to load the iron ore or coal. We wore steel helmets to prevent being hit by chunks of iron ore crashing down the chutes. There is always the possibility that a cable could snap like a whip and injure or sever a body. Loading coal wasn't as dangerous as the lumps were smaller and lighter. Both loading and unloading almost always was at night, the worst time, often on wet slippery docks and one had to be careful not to accidentally slip and fall between the ship and the dock and be crushed as the ship would move up to a few feet back and forth from the dock during the loading and unloading procedures. There have been injuries and fatalities due to these dangers. Once loaded or unloaded we were hoisted back aboard to batten down the hatches. On the return voyage we usually were laden with coal with relatively the same loading and unloading procedures as the ore. The iron ore was open-pit mined from the ranges of northern Minnesota, the large Mesabi range and the lesser Vermilion, Gunflint and Cuyuga ranges.

At sea we were usually swabbing the decks, chipping paint or painting during the day. On Lake Superior only, the drinking water was pumped to us directly with no filtering as it was clean and with a distinct iron taste. I always liked that water. I doubt if water is still used untreated with the years of pollution throughout the Great Lakes.

It was interesting going through the "Soo" locks at Sault Saint Marie and passing through the Saint Claire River between Detroit and Windsor in Canada. One August night it was too hot to sleep in our cabin and a number of us took our mattresses out on deck to sleep. During the night we passed through the channel and upon awakening in the morning found ourselves covered with soot, having passed through that heavily industrial area. It took a lot of washing, scrubbing and bleaching to get rid of the soot.

Approaching the locks one of the older deck hands told me to get the key for the locks from the captain. I just ignored the order as I knew it was a prank. Off duty some of the seamen would gather in groups. The more seasoned men liked to tease us newcomers. I was sitting in one of the groups when one of the men was showing off his knot tying skills and bet that he could tie any seaman's knot faster than anyone there. I happened to specialize in tying knots and hitches as a boy scout. I guess they were amazed how fast I could tie any of the knots. The most common and useful was the bowline, which I could whip through in a matter of a few seconds. I think the challenger was embarrassed and avoided me for the next few days.

The following year I went with my friend Howard Noodleman (later changed to Delman) aboard the Harvey H. Brown from Aloise, Wisconsin to Fairport, Ohio, and on the return docking in Gary, Indiana, where we terminated our employment. The food and the conditions were not nearly as good as the last ship. There was an unfortunate experience as three of us deckhands were painting below in a forward hold when one of the fellows about our age fell from a high overhead beam to the steel deck below and hit his head. A large deep gash ran across the side of his head. He was taken off, unconscious, by helicopter. We were never told of the outcome.

On another occasion we had problems with one of the guys. It got so bad that Howie and I grabbed him one night and held him by his feet over the water on the railing. He never bothered us again. No, we didn't let go.

We were anxious to leave and disembarked in Gary, Indiana after midnight in a deserted dock area of the waterfront and asked directions from a black policeman, the only person in sight in that deserted slum like area. He was apparently drinking and wasn't too coherent. Eventually we found our way to the bus depot in South Chicago. I met a very nice looking well dressed woman who invited me to go on the bus with her. I didn't know her destination and would have gone but didn't feel right about leaving Howie, a good friend, alone since I came with him and thought it only right we stay and go home together.

I had a questionable happening, I got a metal sliver in the sole of my left foot on the ship. I never had it taken out and after awhile it didn't bother me. One night while in bed thirty or forty years later a small encapsulated cyst came out in the plantar fascia of my right foot with a shiny piece of metal. Is it possible that it traveled through my body all those years or could it have been my error and it was the same foot?

I had a girl friend, Arlene Bovey, who I had met at my hangout at the beach at Lake Calhoun in Minneapolis. We were never sexually intimate. I wish that I had saved the letters she wrote when I was aboard ship, primarily for the exquisite penmanship that was equal to commercial calligraphy. I was really taken with her but she was very Catholic and was interested in a permanent relationship -- marriage. She was a marvelous, beautiful person, both physically and personally.

My first job was a paper route as most kids had at one time or another. Many black families lived in the area and collections were not always easy. At one house a black man came to the door almost nude leaving the door ajar and while he went to get some change to pay me I caught a glimpse of a naked white woman lying on a sofa.

During the 1940's, the University of Minnesota football team, the Golden Gophers, were champions of the Big Ten Conference under the coach Bernie Bierman. A few of my childhood pals would go to the games outside of the stadium to sell football souvenirs. Many of them fared very well. At their urging, I tried my hand in this new endeavor. I was too timid to approach people and was a dismal failure and never tried that again.

I have labored in various construction jobs and worked on the section gang of two railroads, The Milwaukee Road and the Minneapolis, Northfield and Southern of Jesse James fame. The work was hard, ten hours a day in the hot sun with a pick and shovel, non stop. The only rest was when we would take turns at holding the spike. There were two spikers, one on each side, with their long handled spike hammers to set the spike. You held the spike with one hand, arm outstretched perfectly still, looking away hoping they didn't miss and hit your hand. In all the time I worked on the section gangs I never saw them miss. Amazingly, after a hard long day's labor after supper I would workout with my weights at home. One can't say enough about youth and motivation. I thought physical labor would be a healthy way to make a living and build myself up physically but rapidly came to the conclusion that there were better and easier ways.

I posed in a jock strap at the Walker Art Center near the parade grounds in Minneapolis. Twenty minutes of posing and a five minute rest for one and a half hours at $1.25 per hour. Not bad change for an eighteen year old in the mid 1940s. I always thought how ugly men's jock straps were and frankly would have rather posed in the nude.

I worked as a traveling salesman in Minnesota for New York Notions Company of Chicago when I was about nineteen or twenty. I first went to the Chicago office to indoctrinate myself with the products and the first trip I took on the road was with Sid who was to show me the ropes. Sid was in his early forties, fat and roly-poly and of good humor. On one occasion in a restaurant in a small town, without telling Sid, I went to the kitchen and mentioned to the cook that he was Duncan Hines, the famous food critic. Word seemed to get around to the waitresses and Sid was surprised at the service of being waited on hand and foot.

I really wasn't a good salesman and never liked the idea of asking or trying to convince people of anything. I spoke to my dad about the problem. He said being a successful salesman was mostly a matter of being friendly, honest and trying to do the best for the client.

I recall one of the trips with him to a large department store, Pred's in Bismark, North Dakota. Many of the clients my father serviced would tell my dad to write up the order for whatever my dad thought they needed.

The company I was working for came to Market Week at the Radisson Hotel in Minneapolis where many companies exhibited their products. It was always interesting with lots of free food and drink. Also many of the companies brought with them or hired local beautiful women to entertain clients (and probably themselves). I believe some of the women may have been employees of the company in some capacity.

I was in Bemidji, in northern Minnesota on business during the winter of 1947 or 1948. The temperature (before wind chill factor existed) for two days was 51 and 52 degrees below zero. I was advised to cover my face and take very shallow breaths if I had to go out. I didn't leave the hotel as breathing outside there was a danger of frostbitten lungs. The occasional cracking sound of pine trees splitting open was heard during the night. I couldn't believe that my '47 Plymouth, parked outside started the next morning.

On another business trip I made during winter there was a sudden snowstorm with zero visibility and a snowed-in highway. There were occasional brief let ups with unlimited visibility but cars were snow bound. You could see the town of Drayton, North Dakota that appeared to be about a mile away. I realized it was much further and knew better than to try and walk through the deep, drifting snow especially when it would undoubtedly resume snowing off and on. Too many have perished walking in circles when one can't fix points of reference for orientation. I had to spend the night in the car without using the heater as the car was almost covered with snow and had to wait till morning when the snow plows opened the road. My car was a very light gray color and the driver of the snow plow said he almost crashed into me but saw my antenna and realized there was an automobile under the drift. As a precaution in winter, we carried blankets, food, water and extra warm clothing and boots.

A few times I helped George Patten and his Dad moving pianos and refrigerators down two or three flights of spiral stone stairways in various old churches. His dad was sixty two at the time and still quite strong. I also helped carry twenty seven pound bundles of roofing up a ladder two stories to roof a house. Minnesota roofs are very steep due to the heavy snows. I wanted to impress the others by carrying three bundles on my shoulder up the two stories instead of one or two bundles up the ladder, but only a few times. It was too tiring and enough showing off trying to impress the others. One had to be careful going up the ladder and in order to keep your balance you had to use one hand to grab the next rung for each step up and the other hand to stabilize the bundles carried on your shoulder.

My friend, Herman "Sonny" Schwartz, an excellent gymnast and a grade behind me practiced hand-to-hand balancing with me after our gymnastic practice in high school. Sonny was a natural top mounter and I was the bottom man. Our initiation to show business happened when we looked in the phone book for an agent and came across the largest ad for a Glyde Snyder Productions, who booked many of the top entertainers in the Twin Cities, surrounding areas and some neighboring states. He consented to see us audition at the 32nd Street beach at Lake Calhoun where we usually worked out with the rest of our gymnastic friends.

We performed our routine on a small table about 32" high, 30" in width by 48" in length in white bikinis that we made from a bed sheet. We struggled through our eight minute non stop routine except for a short break when my bikini almost fell off. There were many people at the beach watching. Later we wore white elastic bikinis and gymnastic slippers for all performances. Glyde choose The Manley Brothers as the professional name for our duo. I would have chosen a name that included my partner. We received a call from Glyde, our agent, that we had a show the following week.

Our first show was a convention in St. Paul, Minnesota with an audience consisting of a few hundred retired railroad employees. We told Glyde, our agent, that we weren't ready and had never completed our new routines. He said that it was booked and we would be there. Back stage before going on we were very nervous. Sonny had vomited but when it was our turn, on we went. For the first time we completed our performance without any errors or mishaps. I'm sure that the audience was aware that we were shaking throughout the performance, nevertheless the audience was appreciative of our valiant effort and applauded loudly. I don't know whether it was for the quality of our performance or for our valiant effort, hopefully for both.

Following that we worked at many conventions, night clubs and other events. During much of the time Sonny had a job and I was a student at the University of Minnesota. It was great making good money in a short time. The most intense engagements we worked were the Gay 90's Night Club and Alvin Burlesque Theater, both in Minneapolis and within three blocks of one another. During the week we did two shows a night at the night club and four at the theater and on week ends we did an additional performance each night at both venues which was six each day during the week and eight per day on the week end. Fortunately it was only for one week. The money was very good but it was physically draining. It wasn't only the physical strength and energy of the performance but the preparations of setting up our table and transporting our equipment from one place to the other with little time in between.

Most of the equipment and props for my three different acts over the years, the Manley Brothers, Manley and Jyl and Manley, my single act, were improvised or devised by me. Basically they were simple for most of the props and items I wanted and needed but I couldn't find any designs or patterns. The tables used for The Manley Brothers and Manley & Jyl were very similar, all our tables had chromed legs.

There was a short hiatus in my professional handbalancing, show business career when eventually Sonny, my balancing partner, married his girl friend Joyce and relocated for reasons of employment to Los Angeles. After he was there a short time he phoned me and asked if I would drive out his '36 Buick. I put an ad in the paper to find someone to share the ride and expenses. I received a call from a gentleman and I naively agreed without any additional information or meeting him. When he appeared I was sorry that I accepted so readily. His unshaven appearance was that of a down and out ex-boxer or ex-con, but the worst of all scenarios was that he was a vehement born-again Christian. Otherwise he was no problem. The worst thing of the long three days and nights was having to listen to him and his Bible. I hope in future situations I will have sense enough to get more information and meet the person before making any decisions or commitments.

In 1948 when George Patten returned from the Navy we both met at Cooke Hall, the gym of the University of Minnesota and began rehearsing basically the same routines that Sonny and I performed. Glyde, our previous agent, offered us a contract. He agreed to contract us on the condition that we would practice for a few weeks with a professional ex-handbalancer who would coach us. He was an old handbalancer but I don't recall if he really showed us many new things except a some risly foot routines where the understander or bottom man, lying on his back, balances the top mounter on his feet and the top mounter can do any variety of moves. We worked continually with Glyde and at times with another agent, Pete "Petey" Peterson, while we were students at the university. Petey didn't have as much work, elegant shows or clientele but was an easy going pleasurable gentleman, the opposite of Glyde Snyder. Glyde often swore and could be quite insulting. With our troupe of about a dozen performers, mostly girls, in a restaurant in one of the rural towns, he looked around before we were seated and in a loud voice said "let's get out of this green bucket of slop." You just want to slink away with your head down with embarrassment.

The musical accompaniment for the Manley Brothers for both acts, one with Sonny Schwartz and the routines with George Patten was a medley of waltzes including Waltz of The Flowers from the Nutcracker Suite by Tchaikovsky and culminating our major effort was the waltz, My Hero.

Chapter VI
University of Minnesota

I entered the University of Minnesota in the spring of 1945. Tuition cost was $25 per quarter and about the same amount for books.

After two years majoring in physical education, I didn't feel that was the profession for me. I suddenly developed a whim to play piano. I purchased a piano and was taking lessons at home with a teacher. I practiced quite a bit, mostly with songs that I liked from Irving Berlin. The teacher always accused me of not practicing. In short, I was terrible and was convinced I had no musical talent.

I asked to transfer to the department of music. The dean of the music department asked what musical experience I had, to which I replied, "none." He said that I didn't have the requirements or the musical background and they couldn't accept my application. After a few petitions he agreed that if I could pass the Seashore Musical Aptitude Test they would consider accepting me on a trial basis. I did exceptionally well on everything except timbre (tone quality) so was able to began my studies. I did well with theory and harmony. It was not difficult learning theory of intervals, chords, notes, etc. as they are all based on mathematics but when it came to the practical aspect of identifying notes and chords by ear or singing I was completely lost. So after a quarter or two in the music department my possibility and dream of being a pianist vanished. I continued my studies mainly in the field of physiology and the physical sciences.

I received my draft notice and reported to Fort Snelling for a physical examination for induction into the armed forces during one of the most critical times of World War II during the Battle of the Bulge in early 1945, just after my 18th birthday. I remember waiting in a room with eight others. I was in great shape physically and very tan having just returned from a few months at Santa Monica's Muscle Beach. All the others were pale, out of shape, in their mid twenties and previously classified as 4Fs in the draft (unfit for military service). They jokingly said goodbye and wished me luck in the army saying they have been examined a few times before, were rejected and would be classified as 4Fs permanently. One of the doctors asked me why my nose was stuffed up and I mentioned that I was asthmatic. He told his orderly to get my doctor on the phone. I was rejected and all the other eight rejects in the room were inducted into the army. Dr. Siperstein, our family doctor, stated that I had allergies, hay fever, sinusitis and asthma. The military wasn't looking forward to paying more service related or aggravated disability pensions.

Doctor Ralph Piper was director of the Physical Education department and his assistant Sheldon Beise, a well known ex-football star, was assistant director. Beise told us all in a group that there were two ways to get an "A" in his classes. This strange narcissistic system of grading consisted of the following two requirements: be academically good, perform well and pass all the exams, the other way was to be able to duplicate one of his feats of strength, feats that he claimed to have performed in his heyday consisting of lifting a heavy weight of one hundred pounds overhead with one hand, lifting his heavy oak office chair off the ground with one hand and performing a standing back flip. I duplicated all three which got me the grades promised but I think he was a little embarrassed that one of the freshman students could perform all three. I certainly wasn't good in any of the major sports I wonder how many other students were able to do all three of Beise's physical feats? I should have asked him at the time.

I would assist in the class of gymnastics, rope climbing, etc. The football players that take these classes usually have difficulty in many of the activities requiring upper body strength due to their weight and heavy trunks and legs. They probably weren't happy with me grading them on rope climbs, chin ups and other similar activities. They evened the score with me in football fundamentals, they really banged me around. I had to have my left knee taped and wired for the practice sessions and it has bothered me ever since..

The University of Minnesota had a cafeteria but many of us still took bag lunches some or most of the time unless we bought the thirty eight cent special. My buddy Howie was invariably in line ahead of me and would wolf down his meal before I sat down a minute later. Sometimes we would take advantage of White Castle hamburgers when they were having a special of four for 24 cents and would take them to Brown's drugstore on the corner and have a fifteen cent malted milk. The metal canister was filled to the rim and was too thick to drink through a straw.

On cold winter days when Howie and I would walk to classes the three or four blocks between campus buildings, I almost always had trouble breathing with my asthmatic condition and always re-member Howie would jokingly say, "You can breathe. Open your mouth." If I was huffing and puffing for any reason he would repeat that, even to this day. The heavy odor of linseed oil in the morning going to the university when crossing the Mississippi River on the streetcar almost always exacerbated my asthma.

Howie was infatuated with Miss Riddle, our anatomy professor, mainly due to her muscular, well defined calves. We were both majoring in Physical Education and had some classes together. Our coach McMillan in basketball fundamentals would sudden-ly shoot the ball without warning when we were in a group in a circle around him. I didn't play basketball but wasn't too clumsy but Howard was a riot. He couldn't dribble or do anything, never physically having done more than bodybuilding. We couldn't stop laughing at his antics on the court. Howard complained to Neils Thorpe, our swimming coach, that it was difficult to swim with me in the life saving techniques as I wasn't buoyant. The coach said that with little body fat one may not be able to float.

One of the professors, Ed Haislett, started a voluntary club consisting of doing 100 push ups, 100 sit ups and 100 squats on a daily basis. I don't think I continued too long as it was too much work and boring. Howard has always surprised me with his endurance.

I had a date with Babs Copeland, a snazzy looking copper headed coed and asked Howie as a favor, if he would tell her that I would be about ten minutes late. Instead he told her that I couldn't make it and that I had asked him to take her out in my place. He always said "Everything was fair in love and war," which never bothered me and something I always understood and accepted about him. It was embarrassing at times with Howie when we would speak to women as he would stare at them from a foot away, almost face to face, through his thick lenses due to his poor eyesight.

Years before, soon after Howie and I met in the mid '40s when we were 17 years of age, another one of our fantasies was ignited when we came across an article in a magazine offering as a prize for entering a contest for an expedition to the Mountains of the Moon in Africa to accompany Cmdr. Attilio Ghatti, a famous Italian explorer, another day dream we didn't follow through with.

I weighed 190 and George 155, which is heavy for a top-mounter. Sonny weighed 125 to 130. At times Sonny and I would have our differences but working and working out with George was a pleasure. We never had any problems getting along. He was never critical but knew how to resolve any problems by always asking me what I thought and if I had any ideas. That way we were both equally involved in arriving at any solution. George is the one person I know whose advice and ideas I would always welcome.

I think George and I performed off and on for three or four years, during much of that time we both were students at the University of Minnesota. It was a marvelous feeling being young, single and making good money doing what you loved doing. During the summer vacations we performed at many fairs throughout the Midwest, Minnesota, the Dakotas, Wisconsin, Iowa and Montana.

George bought a new '48 Chevrolet sedan that we traveled in for our shows.

A few of the following memories stand out. In Cooperstown, North Dakota there was a sudden hail storm with hail the size of golf balls and everyone at the fair had to run for cover. The show was postponed until later and there was a lot of damage in the town including George's windscreen and roof on the car that had deep dents throughout, in spite of the metal chassis in those years being stronger than in today's automobiles.

During the Korean War, I received another draft notice to report to Fort Snelling the following morning for military service. We rushed back after our tour of fairs in Montana. This entailed driving the 600 plus miles all night. Usually my hay fever/asthma is bad during that season in farm country. Combined with little sleep and drinking milk my symptoms should have been severe with much congestion. I purposely drank milk that morning at my aunt Florence's house where I spent a sleepless night before having to report. I almost always wheezed to some degree even when feeling well but when I was examined there were absolutely no symptoms of my asthma and they gave me a clean bill of health. I mentioned to the doctor that I was rejected before because of my asthma. He said this time I was accepted.

When the time came to report to the railroad station for transportation to Fort Leonard Wood, Missouri for basic training, I bid goodbye to friends and family. While talking to a group of other inductees at the train station one fellow asked me if that wasn't my name over the loudspeaker to report to the duty officer. I was shocked when the officer told me I could go home because my record indicated that I was asthmatic. I asked if I had to sign some sort of release and the reply was "No, just go home." This was my second rejection, the first in March of '45 and this one three years later. I was in a trance but overjoyed at the same time about not having to serve in the army. I had recently lost my younger brother Yale in the first Marine division, who was fatally wounded in the invasion of Inchon, Korea, three weeks after his 21st birthday.

I went directly to my aunt and uncle, Paul and Sari's house and realized immediately that they were all at the synagogue at their son Mike's Bar Mitzvah. I walked over and as soon as I entered there was a look of shock on everyone's face as I had said goodbye that same morning I was supposed to be off to the army.

The fairs in Montana (I forget the towns) turned out better than we expected and as a bonus at one of the towns we met two beautiful girls from a local ranch who were there with their horses. We spent quite a bit of our time with them riding double. One of the advantages of being in show business was the easy access to women. It was often necessary for us and the females to change in the same room. When working with Glyde's group, there were young girl dancers in the chorus line. Glyde kept a sharp eye on his girls and his beautiful showgirl wife, Ardelle.

Sonny was a natural as a top mounter but sometimes would jump off if he felt he were going to fall but George hung on in spite of everything. George told me from the beginning, no way was he going to abort and it would be up to me to carry on. At an outdoor show at a summer fair, in a high hand-to-hand stand on our table near the edge of the six foot high stage with a bright sun in my eyes, I lost my point of reference and orientation and started to walk backwards and had to step off the table. Miraculously I still held George in the high-handstand position. We finished our routine and I'm certain that no one in the audience was aware of what took place. Later, rehearsing in the gym George asked me if I thought I could step off the table backward by myself. I replied. "Of course I can," I tried but was unable to manage. No telling what strength and determination a person is capable of under dire circumstances. Another incident with George lying in a pike position on my feet and the sun in my eyes, we swayed to one side and George ended up momentarily balancing only on my one foot. I was sure we'd have to abort but we regained the balance without mishap.

George and I discontinued performing after I moved to Denver. He came to visit me and we toyed with the idea of calling an agent and doing a few shows. I was reluctant as there was a lapse of maybe a year, more or less, but George was always more confident than I. I thought we did a show or two in Denver but when I asked George about it he said we didn't so I must have been wrong. Later, after I contacted Maravene, my old sweetheart after sixty years, she recalled that we did a few shows there, in fact that's where she and I met.

Lee Laitz would sometimes drive me to the beach or we would double date in his 1932 Plymouth with the front bench seat hinged so it made into a bed which proved to be interesting making the interior what he intended it to be. After tumbling at the sawdust pile at the mill, on the way home, we always stopped at the A&W root beer drive-in for a root beer float.

Often I was short of cash. One evening I went downtown just to walk around. I only had two tokens for the streetcar and only one left to get home. I was waiting on Hennepin Avenue and Seventh Street at the streetcar stop when I noticed this gorgeous redhead in red high-heeled shoes, a green above-the-knee skirt and bare legged. I approached and began conversing with her when her streetcar arrived. With my last token I boarded. It was midnight and was headed in the opposite direction from my return home but it was well worth it. I walked her home where she entered quietly as not to wake her husband and children and later took her family's car and drove me home as the streetcars didn't run after 1 am. I recall wearing a tight white tee shirt, slacks and my huaraches. I think I must have been twenty at that time. This was during the Second World War and there was a shortage of young men and many lonesome Minnesota women.

My uncle Mart had a canoe at the boat racks at Lake Calhoun to which I had access and used very often. Actually I don't remember anyone else ever using it. Those were very economical and very romantic evenings and nights taking my dates canoeing. Often we would go from Lake Calhoun under the bridge through the channel to Lake of the Isles, through another channel to Cedar Lake and sometimes through yet another channel and under the bridge into Brownie Lake which is as far as one can go in that direction. The only drawback was the mosquitoes when they were out, making it miserable, especially since one had to keep one's clothes on. I had one memorable episode on a date with this red headed lady who I just recently met. We were in the middle of Lake Calhoun, both lying nude in the canoe when suddenly this intense beam of light suddenly appeared above us. We were terrified, knowing it had to be the police and we would be in big trouble. With a sigh of relief we realized it was only the streetlight overhead. We had unknowingly drifted ashore.

Along the short walk from the 32nd Street beach to the bathhouse at Lake Calhoun, I was walking with one of my workout buddies in our bikinis and noticed two ladies walking toward us. When we approached, the tall woman and I stood transfixed, staring at one another without speaking. It seemed like a long time but I think it was only a matter of seconds. I think both she and I knew instantly that an intimate connection would ensue.

The following morning as I was ready to leave her apartment, she was upset that I was leaving before anymore intimate activity. I told her I'm sorry but needed my energy to work out at the beach. I noticed a wedding ring and engagement ring on the dresser, which she said belonged to her sister and brother in law who had the apartment next door. I'm certain they were hers. I never contacted her again.

Vicente Carrasco was very talented, very artistic and well mannered gay Cuban. We became close friends once we established the the fact there would only be friendship between us, nothing more. It remained that way throughout our relationship. Most of my friends and family adored him.

He had a photography studio on Hennepin and 7th Street in the heart of downtown Minneapolis. His clientele consisted of many well known personalities.

I have never seen such a fantastic Latin dancer of rumba, mambo, etc. When he was on the dance floor, everyone cleared the floor and stood transfixed in awe. He could dance with a beginner and make her look like a queen and a good dancer. He exuded joy when dancing and when he was among people.

One of the favorite local clubs for Latin dancing on the outskirts of Minneapolis was The Point. One night a local professional dance team, the Le Vays, was present. They have always admired his dancing and approached him to ask for private lessons. He politely declined in spite of their generous offers, replying that he only helped friends and never charged anyone. I was aware that they tried to persuade him a few times but without success.

Vicente could also dance Spanish classical and flamenco with castanets. His Cuban friend, Rene Ochoa was performing with the Dorothy Lewis Ice Follies. Ms. Lewis asked Vicente to join the troupe but he wasn't interested.

Chapter VII
Denver

My youngest brother Dick had very severe asthma ever since he was a year or two old. My mother took him to various parts of the country to see if he felt better in a different climate. They tried Arizona, California and Colorado where we eventually moved in 1950 and bought a home in East Denver at 1445 Monroe St. Sometime after 1954 we moved to 1230 Ivy Street, a few miles east of our house on Monroe Street.

My dad usually relaxed under a large catalpa tree in the patio in his shorts smoking his cigars, usually "White Owls," (about 15 per day, but he said he didn't inhale!!!). He rarely had a cigar out of his mouth, even if swimming or taking a shower. I recall seeing a photograph of him in the Great Salt Lake sitting in the water in his shorts wearing his straw hat and a cigar in his mouth. He was a great joker. One morning my mother came running into the house excited, shouting that the catalpa tree had fruit, apples and oranges. Earlier my dad had tied the fruit to the tree.

Our Mother, in her later years was secretary to Rabbi Samuel Edelman for 17 years and also a volunteer and prominent in Jewish organizations. She was the recipient of many awards for her charity work. She was the interpreter for the Yiddish speakers, being fluent in the various dialects of Yiddish. She spoke, read and wrote Russian until leaving the Ukraine at seven or eight years of age.

Anne Kiefer

Anne Kiefer has been an integral member of BMH for the past forty years. Born in Russia, she came to the United States in 1908. She moved to Minneapolis where she met and married the late James Kiefer, to whom she was married for over fifty years.

In Minneapolis, Anne was the President of the Ladies Auxiliary of the Talmud Torah. She was the dietitian for the Stay-at-Home camp of the Jewish Community Center for three summers and was also involved in the "Children's Home" and the "Old Home." Anne was also a devoted member of Beth El synagogue.

In 1949, Anne and her family moved to Denver. She began working in the Hebrew school office and, in 1951, Anne became the secretary to Rabbi Samuel Adelman. She retired in 1967 and found a new interest in the BMH Women's League. A dedicated and vital member of the sisterhood, she was voted "Woman of the Year" in 1972. She was Chairwoman of the baking committee for the Purim Carnival from 1968 to 1985. In 1986, Anne was honored by the Jewish Community Center when they named her "Woman of Valor" for her commitment to Judaism.

Anne continues to be active at BMH as well as in the community. Presently, she is the Chairwoman of Volunteers at the synagogue. She is also the Vice President of the SAGE group at BMH. Anne also gives a great deal of time to the JCC's Woman's Forum and she is a member of the National Jewish Hospital's Woman's Auxiliary.

Throughout her years as a member of BMH and of the Denver Jewish Community, Anne Kiefer's accomplishments and her devotion to her religion are certainly worthy of the title "Woman of Valor."

Our first winters in Denver had many sunny and mild days. One windless December day my brother Dick and I sat in the sun in our back yard in our bathing suits with snow covering the ground and the temperature around 0 degrees Fahrenheit. We were actually hot from the sun's radiation and even got some color. Frequently we would go to play tennis at City Park, about four blocks from our house on Monroe Street. On the 17th of March we were playing tennis. It was about 60 degrees at noon, sunny and warm, at 3 pm it was 34 degrees and snowing heavily, not unusual for mountainous areas. When the trees are in leaf and there is a heavy wet snow many branches break under the load.

Both my brother Dick and I were avid skiers. Denver was an ideal location. Some of the local areas we skied were Loveland and Berthoud Passes and our favorite, Arapahoe Basin, one of the highest ski areas in the world at 13,050 feet elevation, for late season and powder snow. Montezuma Bowl on the backside of A-Basin is a wide open bowl prized for its deep powder skiing. Most of my skiing in Colorado was during the 50's, well before the advent of snowboarding. Many proficient skiers liked A-Basin for its lack of other amenities and entertainment, just basic skiing. It was one of the smaller areas with mostly advanced skiers, consequently there were rarely crowds or lift lines.

Dick's friend Carl Garver was an excellent skier and a member of the ski patrol. Both he and Dick were better skiers than I. Dick's wife Sharon is also a skier.

Occasionally I went to White Sands beach in southeast Denver. It was a small artificial lake with a beach of trucked-in sand. Denver had many nice parks, City Park being the closest and probably the largest, having tennis courts and a small lake, Phipps Museum of Natural History and Phipps Auditorium which often presented interesting programs, Cheesman park with its extensive lawn and the Greek style pavilion with colonnades.

City park was about a square mile in size. I always enjoyed Phipps Museum of Natural History. One of the presentations was with a famous bounty hunter of jaguars in the jungles of the Matto Grosso in Brazil. His name was Sasha Seimel, El Tigrero (the tiger man). He used only a spear with which he stalked the jaguars in the tall grass and when the animal made the final charge he impaled the spear in the animal's neck. To prevent the animal from sliding down the spear and clawing him, the spear had a large metal stop or block where the iron blade joined the wooden shaft. As the cat would leap, he anchored the butt of the staff on the ground to be able to absorb the impact of a beast that can weigh up to 350 pounds. I was very impressed with the skill and danger involved. His accounts can still be checked on You Tube on the internet.

Dick and I were sunbathing in our bathing suits on the hill adjacent to Red Rocks Amphitheater on a warm winter day and were pleasantly surprised to look up slope to see a group of antelope staring at us just fifty feet away. In a matter of seconds they bounded away.

The Red Rocks amphitheater is a natural bowl near Golden, Colorado, ten miles west of Denver. It's the site of many entertainment productions. One of my favorite presentations was that of the Peruvian singer Yma Sumac and her husband guitarist Moises Vivianco. I had the pleasure of speaking with both of them in Spanish after their performance.

My brother Dick and I, along with others, posed professionally in G-strings individually and at times with a partner for bodybuilding photos in Red Rocks for Don Whitman of the Western Photography Guild. Red Rocks was a great natural background for photographers. I had an idea who might buy those types of photos. A few may be artists but I doubt if the majority were artists. I was flattered when I noticed in the local newspaper that one of the large bodybuilding gyms in Denver had been using my photo for their advertising.

We often worked out in our basement where I had weights and other equipment. My brother Dick's health and strength slowly improved. We both went to various gyms and the YMCA, aside from doing exercises in the park. Interestingly enough, the Denver YMCA had a group of amateur trapeze participants. I was tempted to join as a catcher but never did.

Till now, I've made little mention of my younger brother Yale. He joined the Marine Corps a year before we moved to Denver and was stationed at Camp Pendleton, near Oceanside. After basic training he was sent over to Korea and was killed hitting the beaches at Inchon, Korea on January 23, 1951, three weeks after his twenty first birthday. I remember the tragic, fateful morning when the doorbell rang and the telegram arrived. Sad as it was to lose a child, our parents never came apart in front of us. As difficult as it was, they went on with life.

We kids were spared much of the understandable agony of parents who have lost a child and have grieved and became embittered for most of their lives. My parents were close friends of a couple whose thirteen year old beautiful daughter was run over and killed. For years afterward it was painful and embarrassing being with them as they constantly brought it up and wept.

PRIVATE FIRST CLASS

YALE SHELDON KIEFER

MARINE CORPS

For service as set forth in the following:

CITATION:

The President of the United States of America takes pride in presenting the Silver Star (Posthumously) to Private First Class Yale Sheldon Kiefer (MCSN: 1089515) United States Marine Corps, for conspicuous gallantry and intrepidity while serving as a Platoon Runner of Company A, First Battalion, Seventh Marines, FIRST Marine Division (Reinforced), in action against enemy aggressor forces in Korea from 18 to 23 January 1951. With his company pinned down by enemy fire from a heavily fortified entrenchment while conducting a patrol mission near Chisa-dong on 23 January, Private First Class Kiefer promptly charged forward through a hail of hostile machine gun and small arms fire to an open area approximately twenty-five yards to the front of his platoon. After observing the strength and disposition of the enemy, he directed accurate and effective fire against the emplacement, remaining in his exposed position and continuing his bold efforts until he was mortally wounded. His daring initiative, aggressive determination and courageous devotion to duty throughout this period of intensive action served to inspire others to heroic endeavor in destroying the hostile force and in facilitating the completion of his company's assigned mission, thereby reflecting the highest credit upon Private First Class Kiefer and the United States Naval Service. He gallantly gave his life for his country.

Included is the citation for Yale that I just discovered on the internet after sixty one years. I did have a conversation with Sherman Richter, a highly decorated retired Marine sergeant that was from our neighborhood in Minneapolis who was being evacuated in the same helicopter as Yale. He said that although Yale had a head wound, he was surprised that he didn't survive. Sherm enlisted right after December 11th, 1941 Day of Infamy when the Japanese attacked Pearl Harbor practically destroying our Pacific fleet and he fought through the countless battles through the duration of the Second World War in the Pacific theater including Viet Nam and Korea.

Another marine mentioned that in boot camp Yale did all the physical training so well that the drill sergeant made him do extra hard exercises, one was running a few miles around the track at night with bucket of wet sand in each hand. I remember Yale telling me on furlough from boot camp that he never minded doing those extra chores. Even if they were hard and often disagreeable, he felt they forced him to be a better man, in better physical and mental shape and to have the discipline to keep from breaking your spirit, otherwise it could have a very negative effect. For whatever reason, maybe envy, his drill sergeant had it in for Yale and they fought it out in the ring. Another marine told me that Yale left the sergeant pretty beaten up. Yale was a very peaceful and respectful person but if pushed too much he wasn't to be fooled with. One friendly confrontation with my friend Ray Paskoff, an ex-marine a few years older than Yale, neither would give in and Ray was as tough as they come. Both were stubborn in that respect. My brother Dick and I are much more easy going. I don't remember either of us getting into fights

I am the oldest, the only one left except possibly for our younger brother Dick, who can remember many of Yale's characteristics and who he was. At that age we three brothers were six foot one an a half inches tall and weighed about one hundred and eighty to one hundred ninety pounds. Yale was the more serious and ambitious He always won awards as the top student, president of his class and received the American Legion award for citizenship. He was also active on the various sport teams in school, worked out with weights and on the gymnastic team. He also worked after school delivering papers and on week ends stuffing papers at the plant downtown. I must admit, I was a spoiled first-born Jewish boy and didn't do more than required. Yale, without being asked, would volunteer to help wash walls, mop floors or whatever he felt he could do. Whatever he took on he finished. My son Yale had the same character as my brother Yale. My mother was in awe, noting also both were left handed and both had a birthmark in the same area on the inside of the left forearm. A coincidence?

I remember that our friends Sandy and Howie Delman, who lived in the foothills of La Cañada, invited all of us, including my mother who was visiting, for a Christmas dinner. While we talked and celebrated a few hours before sitting down to eat, my son Yale would go in the other room with an armful of text books to study until time to eat.. There were times I asked Yale if he'd like to join me in certain recreational activities and often he would decline in order to study.

Our immediate, extended family and many friends and acquaintances mourned his death and sent their condolences. He is buried alongside our parents at Mount Nebo, a Jewish cemetery in East Denver where Dick and I have driven and stopped to pay our respects. Both Dick and I have the same philosophical outlook about burials, having subscribed ourselves to Science Care, an organization that arranges upon death, dedicating our bodies for anatomical studies in various medical schools and universities, which we consider a useful purpose. We miss Yale and often think about him. Fortunately we do have some photos and would very much like to do a brief biography which I intend, with Dick's help, to incorporate into Yale's military write up on the internet which mentions his citation of the Silver Star.

Our parents were also friends with a married English couple. We thought that their heavy English accent was more pronounced than when they lived in England. I imagine that is likely if they wished to flaunt their English accent.

— — — — — —

I was getting embarrassed living with my parents and not working. I applied for a job as a taxicab driver. I hardly knew the city so had to rely on maps and the passengers. I really wasn't concerned as much about making a lot of money but took advantage of my idle time to park in a sunny spot and study my Spanish books. The company was beginning to install radio communication and when they told me to bring in my cab for installation, I told them they could install the others first, I could wait. The worst experience I had with that job was driving an elderly lady when the rear wheel come off and we were stopped, blocking traffic in the middle of one of the busiest intersections in the city at 17th and Glenarm during rush hour. I'm sure it wasn't as long as it seemed that we were stopped before the relief cab arrived. In a way that job was interesting as far as meeting people and getting to know the city better.

About the time I was driving the taxicab, I met the son of one of my mother's Mahjong playing friends, Ben Kaufman. It was at his house visiting and for the first time that I ate fried brains but the interesting part of my visit was while waiting for him to change clothes for rehearsal with the Denver Symphony (he played French horn), I started reading a small pocket book of his, Learning Spanish Through Stick Drawings. In the forty five minutes I waited I got through half the book, which I borrowed and never returned. I was unaware at the time that this book would be a turning point in my life.

Two blocks from our house the corner drug store had a lovely Mexican-American girl, María Gallegos, eighteen years old whom I went with for a year and practiced my Spanish. Actually I learned more from speaking with her parents who were more fluent. I met many girls and women during those years. Our house on Monroe Street had a partially furnished basement with its own entrance with narrow windows a few feet above ground permitting natural light to enter and was more finished and furnished than the basements in the Midwest which were completely underground. This furnished me a private setting most of the time.

Over a period of a year or two I would periodically go the small, old theater, Mexico, next door to El Paso del Norte cantina to help in my quest to learn Spanish. I never saw another gringo in the theater. It was very disappointing that after two years of intensive study that I could understand so little of the dialog.

One film I shall always remember was Tizoc or also known by another title, Amor Indio, with Pedro Infante and María Felix, two of the super stars of Mexican films of the era. The film was in technicolor, a rarity at the time.

Tizoc, Pedro Infante, was a Mexican-Indian peasant and María Feliz, a beautiful Mexican lady. Tizoc was enamored with María and they fell in love. It ended tragically with their being killed by a prejudiced mob of their peers.

El Paso del Norte was a Mexican restaurant on Larimer Street and 21st Avenue in Denver. I had to be cautious as the food was highly spiced with various chiles. The clientele was basically Mexican laborers who usually took mouthfuls of dried chile along with each bite of the highly seasoned fare that was served. Chiles are the one spice I don't tolerate well. Horseradish and garlic are fine. Also I have never liked curry, but prefer the natural taste of most food. Denver, like much of the southwest and southern California, abounds with Mexican restaurants.

Many evenings and nights I would go to Mexican bars and restaurants in a four block area on Larimer Street. Another locale for the braceros and generally lower class Mexicans in the area was the night club Acapulco on 20th and Larimer Street. There was a Latin trio of musicians with a blind piano player. In the air over the dance floor there was a pall of acrid smelling smoke, which I didn't realize until I was told, was marijuana. This area was populated wholly by this element, rarely seeing a non Latino. I have seen brawls, knifings and a few shootings with some severely wounded combatants, including two people dying and one person dead. The police only ventured into this area when summoned, and in numbers. Even my Spanish speaking friends after one visit would never accompany me there again.

I became friends with one called "El Grande." His real name was Alberto Aguilar. He was fairly tall and well built and always well dressed and very polite. He was also called "el matón." It is rumored that he had killed some official in Mexico. He frequently went back and forth between the two countries. He was respected and feared by the local Latino population. Seeing that he was my friend, no one bothered me.

I distinctly remember a Mexican woman patron who was often present at the bar. She was beautiful with copper red hair, tall and a great figure in a tight white dress that accentuated her lovely figure. I went out with her one night only to find out that she had eleven children and was thirty one years old. I can't vouch for what she told me. Normally I didn't normally flirt with the Latina women in that neighborhood, it was too risky, for many reasons; but in this case the temptation was too good to pass up.

Many of the people on the dance floor were drunk or high either smoking marijuana or simply breathing the heavy pall of marijuana smoke hanging in a cloud over the dance floor, my first and only experience with marijuana.

Most of the Mexicans were friendly and invited you to drink liquor. So a group of us would be sitting at a table and everyone would treat to a round of drinks. After each person bought a round many were quite inebriated and often things got out of hand and serious fights would break out. It was a great offense refusing to drink with one's companions. I ordered soft drinks so as not to offend but many of them looked down upon someone who couldn't keep up with the rounds of hard liquor. For an excuse I tried to explain that I don't drink hard liquor as it exacerbates my asthma. This type of invitational, social group drinking is accepted and practiced in many cultures around the world.

— — — — — —

While still performing my single handbalancing act in Denver, I had a performance at Five Points, a juncture of five streets, in an all black nightclub in a black neighborhood. I was intrigued watching individuals dancing alone among the partnered couples. I think this is commonplace in some cultures where there is no stigma to dancing alone expressing ones feelings and spirituality.

I wasn't much of a dancer but at times enjoyed the dancing at the Acapulco although I preferred socializing mainly at friend's get togethers and parties. At the Mexican venues the dancing consisted of ranchera music, corridas, valses and boleros. At the Latin parties they also danced porro and bambuco colombiano, mambo, vals venezolano and a few other dances of that period. At these Latin parties put on by friends there wasn't as much pressure to drink strong drinks. At the bars, beer and hard liquor predominated. At the parties wine, beer and sodas were consumed.

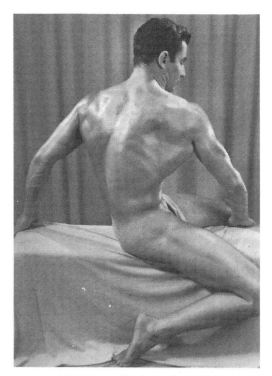

Denver, Colorado 1952

Red Rocks, Colorado 1952

Chapter VIII
Physical Therapy

Another friend of my mother, Helen Levy, had a son, Herbert Levy, who was the chief physical therapist at Colorado General Hospital and president of the local physical therapy chapter. They all tried to convince me to get into physical therapy school. I knew that I could never have entered the physical therapy program had it not been for the influence of Herb Levy, Doctor Dinken and Doctor Gersten. I consented and through their influence I was accepted. Our class consisted of eight students including myself, a total of four girls and four boys. The administrative director was Dorothy Hoog, clinical supervisor, Adelaide Doing, administrative head of the Physical Medicine Department, physiatrists Harold Dinken, MD and research director Gerry Gersten, MD. I believe we had one of the finest physical therapy schools and departments in the country. A few of the student's names I can recall in our class of '52 were: Jim Clinkenbeard, Joe Luckman, both from Montana; Woody Hatton from Kentucky, Paul Hughes and a girl Beverly, etc.

There was much studying and lab work involved during the concentrated year course with the last quarter of internship at three different hospitals, one of which was Fitzsimmon's Army Hospital. I was probably the only one ever to graduate without ever having been on the University of Colorado campus.

There was only one national registry organization that I was aware of at the time. We all passed our examination for membership in the National Registry of Physical Therapy. I stayed on as a staff physical therapist at Colorado General Hospital, the medical center affiliated with the University of Colorado for seven months until I left for Mexico on a three month scholarship from Denver University.

During the two days of the Jewish high holidays I, like most Jews, didn't go to work. Doctors Gersten and Dinken were also absent. After the holidays Doctor Dinken admonished me for being absent those two days. I guess it slipped his mind so I reminded him that I was Jewish and he soon realized his error.

Fortunately for me, our department had a doctor that just arrived from Mexico City, Dr. Luis Spamer Conde, specializing in Physical Medicine. We instantly became buddies and best friends, both socially and professionally. We double dated, partied and were together constantly. Naturally we spoke Spanish exclusively, for which he always said that his English would have improved faster had we spoken in English. Luis and I were well known for always flirting with the ladies and I think our department wasn't too happy with our dubious reputation.

I was interested in skin diving. As with most asthmatics, holding one's breath is a problem, consequently I would occasionally time myself. Luis had been a member of the Mexican national swim team and had competed in the Pan American Games. His specialty was the butterfly, the most physically taxing of the competitive swim styles. There were large Hubbard hydrotherapy tanks used for treating polio patients in our physical therapy department. We were discussing breath holding, Luis, myself and two other physiatrists were present to check our times. Luis and I changed into our swim trunks. I got in first, took some deep breaths to hyperventilate, floating face down in the water. I held my breath a minute and a half. On Luis's first attempt, we clocked him at three and a half minutes which amazed us all. At first we thought we must have erred on our timing, so we repeated the test. On his second attempt we were all astounded when he did four and a quarter minutes.

In the early 50's I was at a friend's house in his basement making a surfboard type craft of my design to use as a spearfishing and free diving platform. We mixed two cans of a liquid to make a rigid foam for flotation. I took one whiff of the fumes that were emitted and was unable to breathe. I was in a panic and barely made it up a few steps to the phone to call my brother Dick a few miles away to bring a rescue inhaler as quickly as he could. I prayed that he would be home. I could barely gasp out the message. I was certain my time had come. Fortunately he was home and must have broken the speed limit to arrive as soon as he did. I believe that saved my life. Normally I always carry my rescue inhaler with me but at the time I wasn't having any serious breathing problems and didn't have it with me. A lesson learned.

My first earthquake experience occurred in Denver and there was talk that a possible contributing factor was the extensive underground excavations at the Rocky Mountain Arsenal not far from the city. It seemed comparable to the temblors I've experienced here in California. One of the largest I experienced was the 1994 Northridge earthquake in the valley.

Back in Denver I met and became friends with Manuel Rodríguez who lived on Birch Street and played classical guitar and Mexican songs. I am sorry that I didn't get to spend more time with him and concentrate on learning more. I still have the scores of sheet music he wrote for me.

When I returned to Denver in for one month after my first stint in Spain, I had never had an opportunity to see the movie The Ten Commandments, a movie in which I had a small role. I found out it was showing at a small movie theater in Golden, Colorado just outside of Denver. Years before Maravene had given me an old German Zeiss Ikon 35 mm camera. I asked some professional photographers if the photos would come out under those conditions and was assured that it wouldn't work. I had nothing to lose but a roll of color film and primarily I wanted to see the movie. I chose an aisle seat in order to have a direct view of the screen. I was amazed and pleased that all 36 exposures came out beautifully clear. I still have most of the color slides. My friend Penny Hankin recently gave me a DVD of The Ten Commandments for my birthday which also contained the original version filmed many years before. I have taken and may take other photos of clips from the film on my television screen now that I have that option.

Just a few blocks from our house was the Bluebird Theater that always had double feature showings. I was interested primarily in seeing the western movie, the other being Lilies of the Field with Sidney Poitier. I really was not interested in the latter which turned out to be a marvelous film.

All the time I lived in Denver there were many lovely ladies available and I knew many lovely Latinas. I was the only non Latin, honorary member of our Latin soccer team with my Latin friends. Aside from the games we had many parties.

Ana Rossell and Me

Ana Rossell was president of the Pan American Club in Denver when I became a member in the mid '50's. The club was a social club open to all who had an interest in Hispanic language and culture. We had many professional members, doctors, lawyers along with students from Latin America and other distant lands.

Summer outdoor parties were most often held at the lavish homes of many of the affluent members. I never noticed any class distinction at any of our functions. We had many interesting guests, speakers and always Latin music for dancing. Often our talented members would perform or at times a group of mariachis. When Ana's term as president expired,without her dedication and efficiency, the club slowly disintegrated.

Ana was an artisan in pre-Columbian Incan weaving, which she did with her looms at home. They had four children, a boy and three girls. The family was very cultured and educated and involved in Denver society. Ana occasionally traveled to other countries where she demonstrated her expertise and instructed weaving.

Women's clothes have never been much of an interest to me but I was very impressed with dresses that Ana had woven and was amazed at the beautiful designs and particularly one red and black dress that looked very Spanish. Later when I was married to Jill I would have liked to have bought it for her. It was priced at $1,500, so I didn't mention anything to Ana about buying.

Years later, Ana arrived at the Burbank airport for a visit. It was a sight to behold when she walked down the ramp. A beautiful dark woman in a beautiful tailored beige suit, bedecked with gold earrings, necklace and numerous rings on her fingers. Everyone one stopped to stare at this exotic, curvaceous gypsy-like creature. After greeting her, I told her to please do not wear any expensive jewelry in Los Angeles.

Ana and her children and I would do things together. They children referred to me as uncle. We remain good friends and have maintained contact and been together at various times throughout the years.

Ana has been a workaholic by nature as long as I've known her. We talked many times about not working so much and she always said she will cut back, but up until the past few years she worked continually. Aside from her weaving she has worked and consulted for some of the most well known, expensive companies primarily in the US but also in Europe.

Chapter IX
Maravene

Maravene   Maravene and Me

Somewhere in the interim, when I was 24, I met the first love of my life, an exotic dancer, Maravene. George and I did a show in Denver where I met Maravene who was the headline dancer. There was instant chemistry. She was, and for me always will be, the most beautiful, exotic woman in the world. I couldn't believe I had such a desirable lover, when she could have had any man. She was six months older than I, married with two children. But that didn't pose any problem except wanting to be with her as often as we could. Actually she was divorced which I didn't know at the time as her ex-husband was always hanging around in spite of a restraining order.

Maravene was part Hawaiian and as a young girl sang and danced with a her family who had a Hawaiian band. She was five foot ten inches tall barefoot, luscious full lips, high cheekbones, long dark hair and an extraordinary full figure. She stood out like a proud, magnificent Hawaiian queen.

I could not imagine being apart from her, she would take me to all her shows and often I would stand guard at the dressing room door. Maravene was very generous and paid all the expenses and travel as I was going to school during this time. Many of the men tried to get into the dressing rooms to see the girls and often I stationed myself outside the dressing room door. Luckily I was well muscled and probably looked impressive so I didn't have any problems. I was and am a very pacific, non violent person but when it came to protecting Maravene, I did things that I didn't believe I was capable of doing. She had to change her phone number every few weeks as higher ups such as city and state officials, mayors, governors, etc. would somehow get her number. If I were there she would have me answer the phone which would often discourage their calls.

When we entered our hotel after a show in Montana, Maravene was still dressed sensuously in a knee length tight skirt, four inch stiletto heels, black fishnet hose and her long hair in a high chignon. A statuesque showgirl could very well have given another impression. To my great surprise my dad was in the lobby. I had no idea, but he was a traveling salesman and coincidences do happen. He had no idea I was going with anyone and he was very congenial when I introduced her. If he hadn't seen us, I would have attempted to leave so as not to embarrass him. Being from a rather conservative family and background I'm certain that he was disappointed but never mentioned it as far as I know. My father was very polite and always the gentleman. I doubt that he ever told my mother or anyone else. I always wondered what he thought of the situation.

I concentrated working on a single handbalancing routine so Maravene and I could be in the same show now and then. I was quite tall and muscular for a handbalancer, six feet one and a half inches, one hundred and ninety pounds. Performing solo was quite a change after working years with a partner. I felt quite alone the first few performances as there was no one to share the companionship, blame or consolation if things didn't go right.

I note that on YouTube and other venues there are many similar acts from all over the world. I was always proud of our performances but have to admit that many of the present day acrobatic and balancing acts perform on a much high technical level than the performances of our period. I am impressed with their precision and their techniques.

The equipment for my single act was the most difficult and complex as I had no experience, knowledge or means of acquiring information. The idea came from watching a Venezuelan handbalancer, Sósimo Hernández, who was performing in Curly's Bar in Minneapolis. I don't remember if I spoke to him or just remembered his routines. It was a matter of trial and error. I didn't do the machine work or the carpentry but had to purchase the material and describe what I wanted to the various craftsmen. I had an inlaid rectangular iron plate, welded to the underside of the table with the two receptacles that the pedestals fitted into, The hand grips for the pedestals were cast from bronze with ball bearings seated in the bases permitting free 360 degree rotation. The wood blocks had to be prepared so they would not slide on one another too easily. I often was envious of acts that didn't have a lot of equipment and props to haul, set up and take down. Then again I was thankful, considering there were acts that had much more equipment and difficulty in setting up than mine.

My music was a medley of rumbas starting with the song, Mamá Inez, to which I entered the stage dancing rumba on my hands in a handstand position for ten seconds before mounting my table. A brief description of my routines was, a handstand on the pedestals to the music of Ravel's Bolero, lowering myself to a half arm lever and rotating 180 degrees, repeating the same with the other arm and a few additional maneuvers, followed by a series of handstand presses, then to the rumba, El Ombú, building up the blocks, rotating from one pile to the other in a half arm lever, pressing into a handstand and lowering the two piles of five wooden blocks in each pile, one by one while maintaining a handstand position, then lowering myself down to the back of my neck on the edge of the table and a neck spring to the floor as my finale.

Maravene had an upcoming contract for The Hogan in Colorado Springs. Had I known how she got a contract for me on the same bill, I may not have accepted. I found out later that the owner, Danny Fontecchio, said no when she requested that I perform on the same bill and Maravene said that she wouldn't work if I couldn't be in the same show. He said he would sue her for breach of contract, she replied that she didn't care. Since she is in demand, he backed down and we were together. Her ex-husband Bob dropped in to see us at our motel. I imagine he knew what was going on but never mentioned anything. Maravene and I had adjoining rooms with a door in between instead of one room which we usually had when further out of town where we were not known.

Maravene would sometimes drop me off or pick me up in her Cadillac at Denver University. It was very flattering when the other students and professors saw me with this beautiful, sexy woman. Showgirl dancers seem to have a special poise and allure.

Bob, Maravene's ex-husband, was an electrician and he was an amateur boxer. We were amicable although I always felt some tension due to the situation. I think my physical appearance probably deterred him from any confrontation as I certainly didn't want any confrontation, be it physical or otherwise.

He used to travel locally with his pick up truck to different taverns and bars that had pinball machines. These were legal only for entertainment but all establishments paid off money for winning scores, the higher the score, the more money. He offered to take me with him just for standing around while he would secretly drill small minute holes in each side of the machine even though people were standing around watching the games being played. He had a small drill hidden in his sleeve and wires in each sleeve on his fingers to run up games by tripping certain mechanisms. It's amazing that people were so interested in the lights and whistles that they never noticed what he was doing. When he finished he plugged the holes with colored clay that children use and one couldn't notice anything without a careful inspection. We'd get anywhere from $50 to $100 per ten minute game and sometimes do one or two games in the same establishment and go on to another place or two and repeat the procedure. He would give me half the money. I did this a few nights but was always nervous and uneasy.

The last time I went with him was to a small town south of Colorado Springs. I did notice an old time western movie character actor, Bob Steele, sitting at the bar. I think they were getting suspicious after we collected two winning games when my friend said we'd better leave, which we quickly did. He mentioned there was nothing they could legally do if they caught us, only beat us up. That was enough to dissuade me from continuing and to end that risky endeavor.

Maravene and I broke up little by little as it was not comfortable going with a dancer with two lovely children among other things. Julanne, the girl was eight and Harold, I believe was ten. I liked the children, Julanne was outgoing and vivacious and Harold was quiet. I had an immature idea of life and couldn't grasp the realities, whereas Maravene was a mature responsible woman and mother with two young children to support. Sometimes when years pass, one realizes the lack of understanding and the reality of situations.

Under the circumstances with her domestic situation with two young children to bring up and support, her work and the fact that I had an intensive and concentrated year of study in physical therapy school and left for Spain soon afterward, our relationship withered. I had wished with all my heart that we could have worked things out but I had this intense burning desire to go to Spain. As intent as I was to go, interesting things kept presenting themselves and I kept putting off leaving.

I often thought of contacting Maravene at various times through the years when I was visiting family in Denver and regret that I never did, feeling it might not have been prudent to interfere with her life. I couldn't imagine that such a beautiful desirable woman wouldn't either be married or with someone and I didn't want to take the chance of being disappointed. I never stopped wanting her all though the many years that we had no contact. I have never forgotten her as my first lover and best friend. I thought of her often during those many, many years.

I was determined, and finally did contact Maravene after a difficult search to locate her. I wrote to her one year ago but she was in mourning, having just recently lost her husband and a step son. She married when she was seventy after remaining single all those years. She suggested waiting a full year before contacting her again, which I did. We are now corresponding. I have no romantic illusions but she was an important part of my life 64 years ago and I am interested in knowing how she fared through the years. Just received her letter with many nice photos and I shall reciprocate. When she received my letter which included copies of my two favorite photos of us taken sixty years before, she was emotionally touched and couldn't believe that I kept them that long. We have been in constant contact by phone and by mail during the past year reminiscing and talking intimately about the past with the realization that we undoubtedly may never see one another again but remain kindred spirits although I am still very tempted and feel that we still have a mutual closeness and love.

Chapter X
Peñuelas & MIT

It was my good fortune to meet Professor Marcelino Peñuelas at the University of Denver. He was from Valencia, Spain. He was fortyish, short, balding with glasses but with a sparkle in his eyes. I never liked literature or poetry but he made things so interesting that I actually took courses in Spanish literature, poetry and other related subjects in Spanish. I joined the honorary society of Romance Languages and involved myself with related affairs and activities in the Denver area. It was at this time I joined the Pan American Club with Ana Rossell as president. I was literally immersed in a Spanish speaking environment.

I went to Denver University during my lunch hour to study Spanish. When the hospital found out they offered me an extra hour for lunch to continue studying Spanish without docking my salary. I joined the Spanish club. Through the university I met other Spanish speaking students and Spanish speakers. At a meeting of the Spanish Club they were electing officers and they elected me president. I didn't run nor want any office. I tried to refuse but they insisted. I was upset but lady luck entered and a few days later I was called to Dr. Campa's office, the dean of the Spanish Department, who told me I didn't qualify for office as I wasn't enrolled at the university at the time.

In one of my classes at Denver University we were choosing topics for discussion. Someone suggested, Euthanasia. I suggested that Youth in Europe might be a more appropriate topic at the time. There was laughter at what was interpreted as humor, what in reality, was my ignorance. I didn't know the meaning of the word.

I had two good friends for years who stayed at my house in the basement for a brief period, Julio Hernández Cota from Ahome, Sinaloa, Mexico where his family was involved in agriculture and Fernando Rodríguez Montero of Monterrey México. I erroneously referred to Fernando as a Monterreylleno which was quite hilarious in Spanish instead of the correct denomination of Regiomontano. We cooked large cauldrons of Mexican refried beans now and then, which is an inexpensive and nutritious mainstay for many Mexicans and other Latinos. Many years later when in Mexico I visited them and their families. I had many Latino friends that were students at the Colorado School of Mines in Golden, Colorado. A close friend from La Paz, Bolivia, Francisco "Pasita" Ponce. I also was friends with the brothers, Duzan from Cochabamba, Bolivia, Juan Francious from Venezuela, Carmen Mitchell from Puerto Rico, Ana Rossell from Lima, Peru and others whose names escape me at the moment. There were many Latin American students from all the Latin American countries studying at Denver University, University of Colorado, School of Mines at Boulder, Colorado and Loretto Heights College for Catholic girls. Denver, like all the southwest has a large Spanish speaking population, primarily of Mexican extraction.

Bolivar was our soccer team composed almost wholly of my Latin American student friends. Since I never played soccer, I was made the honorary coach. We competed against other local teams. At one of our games we were short a player and they convinced me to play goalie. I was unable to stop any of the goal shots, even the easy ones. Very embarrassing to say the least. Win or lose we always had lively parties afterward. After one of our games I noticed two men standing nearby and couldn't help wondering what language they were speaking. I couldn't make out what they were saying, it sounded somewhat like a combination of Spanish and Italian. This was my introduction to Rioplatense Spanish.

My good friend, Francisco "Pasita (raisin)" Ponce's nickname was imposed on him by his Latin buddies. He told me this was because when he went shopping and couldn't speak English and that he didn't know what to ask for, they told him to ask for raisins. He was one of the nicer and polite ones of the group, good looking and modest. While he was attending the School of Mines, his father, a physician in Bolivia, was caught up in politics and exiled, consequently "Pasita" lost his source of financial aid and had to work to survive. He soon married a lovely Mexican-American girl, Teresa, with a child and had a difficult time supporting his growing family. Eventually he had a furniture store and a radio station and today is a very successful businessman. He is one of my favorite people. We did many things together and after sixty years of not seeing one another we got together on my last trip to Denver.

Francisco "Pacita" Ponce & Me - Denver

Professor Peñuelas asked me if I'd like a three month scholarship to Instituto Tecnológico y Estudios Superiores de Monterrey, Mexico. When I told him I wasn't even registered at the university at the time, he replied, not a problem. I did get the scholarship.

My father loaned me his Hudson Terraplane to drive to Monterrey, Mexico from Denver through Colorado Springs, Pueblo, Raton Pass, El Paso Texas crossing the international bridge into Juarez, Mexico. Just entering the Mexican zone a uniformed officer pulled me over, opened the car door and got in the passenger seat of my car. He said I didn't stop at the sign, which was a lie and that I would have to spend the night in jail. He ordered me to drive on for about six blocks and a few more blocks to a side street where he had me stop. He ordered me to open the glove compartment and trunk. He checked out the contents which were only a few clothes and books, nothing of value. Finally he waved me on through customs. Naive as I was, I told the official in the custom booth that the police officer that stopped me said I would have to spend the night in jail. He looked bewildered and waved me on through. I drove late into the night and stopped at a small run down motel. I had trouble sleeping as I had no water to drink and one doesn't dare drink anything but bottled beverages in Mexico. After midnight I finally got out of bed, dressed and found a cantina, bought a bottle of orange drink and returned to my room and finally got to sleep. Normally I wouldn't be thirsty at night but psychologically knowing that I had nothing available, I was thirsty. In the morning I continued on through the village of Paila, Coahuila which seemed to be only a stop on the road with a gas pump and a saloon. I was thirsty and entered the saloon to buy a soda. There was only the bartender and one customer, a gaunt, ragged, man with a heavy, drooping mustache, probably in his fifties, but appeared much older. He was leaning over the bar with a red bandanna around his neck, large sombrero, boots with an old long barreled revolver tucked in his waist band. He kept staring at me, his hand near his pistol with what I took to be a menacing look. I was very uncomfortable, I took my drink and left hastily out of the door into my car and on the road again. The area was high desert and passing through Torreón, Coahuila, I began the long descent into Monterrey. It was hot and humid in sharp contrast to the cooler highlands from which I had just come. The contrast in the flora was noticeable, cactus and sparse vegetation in the higher elevations gave way to palm trees and more abundant foliage in this lower elevation.

The campus of the institute was beautiful, park-like with green lawns and spacious areas with low buildings. I shared a dorm with a young Mexican lad in his late teens, Jorge Valladares. His father was the Mexican Cultural Attache in Washington, DC. Jorge was a nice, clean looking, well-bred boy who spoke fluent English. Nevertheless we conversed mostly in Spanish. Our meals at the school were a combination of American and Mexican food. Disappointingly, the bread that was served was white bread. I doubt that many Mexicans eat white loaf bread.

The classes were small and I don't remember the ethnic make up of the students. One of the professors, Sr. Cuervo, was in his thirties, tall and slender, handsome with an aquiline nose and dark complected. The Mexicans refer to this institution as their MIT (Massachusetts Institute of Technology). In spite of being a technical university our classes dealt with Mexican history, language, customs, etc. The American and Mexican versions of the history between the two countries is quite different on different sides of the border. Maybe the true facts about some of the conflicts between the two countries fall somewhere in between.

One of the most exciting pastimes on the campus was watching one of the voluptuous, long haired secretaries who would saunter sexily in her high stiletto heels, short skirt and nylon hose along the long promenade on the campus. She was a sight to behold, which she seemed well aware of. She was nicknamed by the local students, La Coca Cola, obviously for her buxom breasts, slender waist and ample hips. Most of us were quite familiar with her scheduled walks.

I became acquainted with two Mexican brothers who were employed as dishwashers in the kitchen. They played guitars and would sometimes play at parties, weddings, etc. I have always loved Latin and Mexican music and after work they would take me with them to some of their gigs. I bought a cheap guitar for ten dollars made in the town of Paracho, Michoacán, which mass produces low and medium priced guitars. The brothers would help teach me chords and songs. After their performances we went to a hamburger stand on the edge of town. As I recall, a large hamburger, always with beans and chili, cost one peso and a beer about the same, a total of two pesos or seventeen cents US.

I was invited for supper at the house of my friend Fernando Rodríguez Montero and family. A lovely typical Mexican dinner except for the delicious tamales, which initially had a sweet taste but when the chile took effect my mouth was on fire. I also went with Fernando to a well known popular restaurant in Monterrey, called La Siberia. The food was mouth watering as long as I ordered without chile.

On other occasions we would go to the main plaza on Sunday afternoons and evenings when the single women would parade around in one direction and the single men in the opposite direction with the purpose of subtle flirtation and getting acquainted. It was fun joining in, a different experience for me. There was often bitter rivalry between the locals and the Mexican-American Texans coming down to flirt with the local girls. They had money and autos which were scarce commodities with the locals and often fights broke out.

The university organized a few excursions, one of which was to Las Grutas de García (caves or caverns). I didn't feel well or for whatever reason, I didn't go. I have fond memories of my stay in spite of the fact that I didn't care for the hot, humid weather and for quite a few years afterward was plagued with intestinal discomfort and diarrhea which was diagnosed years later as amoebic dysentery and treated with antibiotics. I only drank bottled beverages but other food such as salads, were rinsed with the local tap water.

My return to Denver must have been uneventful as I have no recollection of driving two or three days covering 1,300 miles although I did stop for lunch in a small village somewhere east of the Sea of Cortez. The only eatery was in a house with two small round tables in the living room. I ordered shrimp soaked in garlic (camarrones al mojo de ajo). I mentioned to the woman that I would like lots of garlic, On the side she brought me a bowl of minced garlic.

A man was sitting at the other table and we began an interesting conversation about his experiences as a turtle fisherman.

Two other times I went to Mexico in the early '50s for short visits. I bought a yellow, older Volkswagon station wagon that needed body work. I drove to Tijuana and left my vehicle at a garage for the three days and went to Rosarito Beach, where I stayed at the old Rosarito Beach Hotel, spending most of my time on the beach.

I met two American girls who had a red, two seater sport car convertible. They suggested going to Puertonuevo for a lobster dinner. The girls took turns driving and the girl who wasn't driving would sit on my lap. It wasn't very comfortable in the small bucket seat but had it's compensations.

Another time I drove down with friends to that same town and parked in front of the restaurant. During those years there were only four restaurants in town, all specializing in lobster. I believe the whole meal, including the beer was about five dollars US aside from the the four hubcaps that were no longer on my car.

Chapter XI
Muscle Beach

During the five years I lived off and on with my parents and brothers in Denver I would go to California for a few months during the late winter and early spring. The main attraction was Muscle Beach at the Santa Monica pier. During those years Muscle Beach consisted mainly of bodybuilders, gymnasts, weightlifters, handbalancers and some adagio dancers and wrestlers. There were professionals in all the above categories but the majority were amateurs and aficionados. The first few years in California I stayed at my Aunt Betty and Uncle Elmer Sussman's house at 208 South Rexford Drive in Beverly Hills with my cousins Lynne and Mark, both younger than I. My transportation to the beach was the bus on Wilshire Boulevard that went directly to the Santa Monica pier. Later I would rent an inexpensive room near the beach.

From Denver I left for California in March with the intention of working my way to Spain as a deckhand on a foreign freighter. My aunt would let me drive her Cadillac to the ports of San Pedro, Wilmington and Long Beach in search of possible transportation to Spain but most of my days were working out with the handbalancers, gymnasts and bodybuilders.

Muscle Beach was our Camelot, a Mecca and spawning ground of dreams, aspirations and illusions. We usually had little money and lived frugally, as many did, but we were well and had a healthy life style. Everyone was friendly and helpful, we were birds of a feather. The playground director was Deforrest "Moe" Most, who lived in the Purser apartments on the beach. I remember that he had Samoa tattooed on his left shoulder. He was married to a red headed girl from St. Paul who I ran into briefly fifteen to twenty years later when an hour into one of my flights from New York to Madrid, I noticed this attractive woman with an empty seat next to her. I left my seat half way back in the plane and asked her if the seat was occupied. We struck up an immediate conversation and after two hours we discovered that we knew each other. She was the red headed, freckled faced girl with pigtails from St. Paul who came to Minneapolis and worked out with us at the beach, later she moved to Muscle Beach where she eventually married and had children with Moe. During all that time we've only seen one another in our brief bathing suits. To quote an old cliche, "Sorry, I didn't recognize you with your clothes on."

I rented a room, more like a closet, in Ocean Park, a few blocks from Muscle Beach for five dollars a week and later shared a room with my friend Howard Noodleman, a few blocks away. Aside from the horizontal bars, parallel bars, rings, weights and other exercise equipment there was a platform stage where we practiced and performed balancing, acrobatics and pyramids anywhere from three to five people high. Often Moe was the base. Other gymnasts, weightlifters and handbalancers completed the many risky stunts and pyramids. Some of the spotters for the dangerous feats were great and I never heard of any of the beach regulars really getting seriously injured. A few of the better ones were Moe, Harold Zinkin and Russ Saunders, to name a few.

Professionals Harold Zinkin and his balancing partner, Bruce Conners, helped us learn certain tricks, techniques and routines. Bert Goodrich and partner George Redpath were also professionals. Other luminaries were: Les and Pudgy Stockton, Steve Reeves, Mr. America and Mr. Universe, Vic and Armand Tanny, George Eifferman, Reg Lewis, Eric Holmbeck, Baron Leone, both professional wrestlers, Russ Sunders Canadian movie stuntman, world famous Joe Gold founder of Gold's gyms, Tony Roma, Malcolm Brenner, Hymie Schwartz, John Grimek, John Farbotnik, Johnny "Whitey" Robinson, Wayne Marlin Trio, Johnnie Collins, Relna Brewer, Gordon McRae, Jim and Kay Starkey, Dr. Don Brown, Paula Unger, Wayne Long, Glenn, "Whitey" Sundby, Dodie and Wally, Jack LaLanne, Frankie Vincent, Mickey Hargitay and wife Jane Mansfield, Chuck Pendleton (Gordon Mitchell), Arnold

Schwartzenegger, Zabo Kozewski, Terry Robinson, Pepper Gomez, Wally Abro, Beverly Jocher, Miss Muscle Beach 1952, Bob McCuin and many others that I cannot remember and others I may not have known. I felt very much a part of Muscle Beach even though I was not one of the luminaries.

Howard had a young crow, Albert Einstein, as a pet. We would take him to the beach and whenever there were people around he began crowing, shrieking and having a fit and staying away from us. The spectators thought that we must beat him and gave us dirty looks. I'm convinced Albert did this deliberately and knew exactly what he was doing, putting on an act to embarrass us in front of the onlookers. When we were alone with Albert we never had any problems and got along splendidly. We had to be careful as crows have a tendency to steal and hide shiny items.

Howie and I shared a double bed in our one room apartment in Ocean Park and were constantly fighting our way from the middle of the sagging mattress to our own side of the bed. The adjoining apartment was occupied by two New York Italian guys who would periodically invite us over for a spaghetti dinner.

Howie and I had an idea that we would gather the numerous starfish from the shallow waters off the beach, dry them on our roof, paint them with metallic paint and sell them. The apartment manager told us to get them off the roof. The neighbors were complaining about the putrid odor. They probably wouldn't have sold anyway.

I bought and old little two seater French Simca convertible which was a copy of the Italian Fiat Topolino. Howie helped me fix it as I am not knowledgeable about automobiles. Howie was very handy and could make or fix almost anything. We often had to push it to get it started but it was great fun driving for the short time I had it.

We used to get up early and make a breakfast of a pound of ground beef, some cottage cheese, after which Howie would drop me off at the studio on his way to work and pick me up in the evening.

I had an interesting experience with a lady I met. We spent three hours in her apartment and when I got up to leave, she got out of bed and I said it wasn't necessary to see me to the door. She said she was going upstairs to see Jack. I guess three hours wasn't enough for a nymphomaniac. It was enough for me. I didn't see or call her again. One night about a week later, I was sitting at home and the phone rang at 8:30. I told her I didn't want to see her and not to come over. I think she was drinking and said she was on her way. I was desperately trying to locate my room mate Howie who I previously told about this lady. I finally reached Howie at his brother's house in the Valley and he'd be home in about 45 minutes. Our apartment was located on Fountain Avenue between Santa Monica Boulevard and Hollywood Boulevard.

She arrived about 9 pm and I had to "entertain" her till Howie arrived at 10:15. I usually slept in the bedroom and Howie on the living room couch but I was glad to go to sleep on the couch so they could use the bedroom. My sleep was constantly interrupted what seemed like every few minutes when I heard her moaning and groaning. About 1:30 am I heard her say "You're not a man, you're an animal," and short while later, "Manley might be getting jealous, I better go and give him a blow job". I was dead tired and shooed her immediately back into the bedroom. I guess that was her excuse for taking a well needed break.

Howard and I left her sleeping and he was driving me to work when I had to ask him about last night as the constant moaning went on till the wee hours. We never talked much about our sexual prowess. It turned out that Howard has a continual erection with no problem and had six or seven orgasms, she evidently had countless orgasms. I was amazed and envious at Howie's sexual prowess. When we arrived home after 7 pm, she was still sleeping. Finally we got her to leave and that was the last time she called.

I was alone on a drizzly March morning, seated on a bench next to the weightlifting platform at Muscle Beach. Entering from the opposite side of the beach, Steve Reeves, just after winning the Mr. Universe contest, came over, put his foot on the bench, raised his pant leg flexing his calf. I don't think he was bragging, just his naive way of getting acquainted. We spoke now and then and he was always friendly and likable. In my opinion, aside from being handsome, he had the perfect bodybuilder's physique.

While I was working at Paramount Studios on the Ten Commandments Howie and I would often eat supper on Thursdays at a nearby Italian restaurant, all the spaghetti you can eat for fifty cents. On other nights at Rand's Ranch Wagon, a restaurant with a large dining room where, after 9 pm we could eat non-stop till midnight for $1.20. There was a wide variety including meats, seafood, etc. You could also have desert and even a breakfast before leaving, all included at that price. It was amazing the quantity of food we could eat and go to bed immediately after without any problem. Both Howie and I are big eaters, more gluttons than gourmets.

My aunt Betty once invited Howie with us to their house in Coldwater Canyon for dinner with the family. As usual Howard devoured the lavish meal in minutes. That's the last time my aunt ever invited him.

One of the blessings of Muscle Beach was the abundance of beautiful and accessible girls and women. Many would come expressly to make contact with the masculine bodies. Naturally we were very cooperative and had many great times and also some weird ones. Lots of endorphins cursing through our veins from our constant working out.

Many onlookers would come and watch and often huge crowds on holidays gathered around to see the performances of handbalancing, pyramids, adagio and more, all performed on the large platform, in front of "Silent Leo" Khoury's bar.

Mae West, sex symbol of the 30's and 40's, had a revue featuring many of the well known bodybuilders of Muscle Beach that premiered at the Stardust Hotel in Las Vegas in 1954 and lasted a few years. Years later, returning to Muscle Beach was very different. Only a few of the old crowd were seen occasionally and most of the weightlifting equipment and gymnastic bars were gone. The bodybuilders and weightlifters are now going to the new Muscle Beach located in Venice. The old Muscle Beach was on the left side (when facing the ocean) of the Santa Monica pier. For many of us who longed for the old Muscle Beach, which was a large part of our lives, it was a sad day in 1958 when it ceased to be Muscle Beach. The old Muscle Beach as many other entities in history has disappeared. Sadly, it will never return. It served for many years as a catalyst for many of us to follow the principles of health and fitness before the advantages of these types of exercises became recognized as beneficial and were more widely accepted in this country.

I understand there are still some acrobats, balancers and gymnasts who occasionally are seen at the site of the old Muscle Beach. For many years afterward on Labor Day weekends some of the old timers would gather to socialize and reminisce. As most have passed on I doubt if any of the old timers show up at our old haunts anymore.

Me, Reg Lewis (Mr. America '60, Mr. Universe '57),
Chuck Pendelton, and Joe Gold.

Muscle Beach, Santa Monica, California 1954

I had two possibilities to work my way over to Europe. The first, a Swedish ship, the S.S. Paramatta. I didn't accept the offer because they would not get to Europe for approximately seven months, first to Canada, Australia, Africa and a few other ports of call. Days later I spoke to the captain of a Greek ship scheduled to arrive in a month at Bilbao in northern Spain. I showed him my passport, my seaman's papers and my Coast Guard Certificate. He offered me transportation working as a deck hand. I was elated and had a week before they sailed so went back to the beach until it was time to depart.

I reported to the dock early that morning with my duffel bag over my shoulder. I climbed up the gang plank only to come face to face with the captain, who gave me the devastating news, he had decided that it might not be legal. I assured him all the paperwork was in order but it was his call. Needless to say, I was very disappointed. I thought that if I went back to Muscle Beach with my friends it wouldn't be as bad as going home and moping.

Chapter XII
The Ten Commandments

I pulled into the parking lot adjoining the beach and parked with no problem. Usually all the spaces were occupied. I walked to the beach and was in a state of shock to see an empty beach on a beautiful sunny day. This was unreal. This never happened at Muscle Beach. I began to work out with a little handbalancing. As I was resting, sitting on a bench, I noticed two middle aged men nearby. The rest of the beach was deserted. One was a tall, slender, freckled redhead and the other was a squat, dark complected man, with numerous bright colored rings on many of his fingers. The swarthy one came over, sat down beside me, began a conversation and while talking had his hand on my knee. They were both wore slacks and tee shirts and me in my bikini bathing suit. My first thought was these were a couple of queers or sexual deviates of some sort, not unusual in southern California, especially in these beach areas where scantily clad bodies abound. He invited me over to meet his companion. I figured there was no harm in being courteous and saying hello. He introduced himself as Buddy Brill and the dark one as Fouad Aref. During the conversation they asked if I would like to earn nineteen dollars a day for three or four days as an extra in a movie. For sure, I thought, these guys were on the make. I'm certain they saw that I was dubious so they said that if I was interested to report to Paramount Studios at nine the following morning. They gave me directions before they departed. I surely could use the money and now it began to sound more reasonable.

After a sleepless night, I went through the famous gates of Paramount Studios and was directed to go on to the set that was indicated. I was flabbergasted to see the area with fifty or more of my counterparts, the tanned male bodies from Muscle Beach milling around. Seated on his high directors chair, was the famous director Cecil B. deMille. As soon as I entered he ordered an aide to get photos of me and dress me in a guards uniform. I was paired off with Chuck Pendleton as we were both tall and of similar builds. Little did I know that Buddy Brill was the casting director and Fouad Aref was the Egyptian technical director. "O ye of little faith" but on the other hand, "beware of Greeks bearing gifts."

The film was "The Ten Commandments" starring Charleton Heston, Yul Brynner and a large cast of well known actors and actresses. The result was that Chuck Pendleton and I were given silent bit parts and took home ninety seven dollars per day for about two months until that role ended, instead of the nineteen that the extras were paid. This included our daily make up pay and since we were very tan, we received the extra pay without the uncomfortable chore of dabbing our whole body with pancake makeup. We were clad as Egyptian palace guards with a helmet, leather band across one shoulder and chest, slit skirt and sandals. After a month, almost all of the bodybuilder extras were terminated and first assistant director, Francisco "Chico" Day, asked me if I was interested in continuing but in different roles, to which I graciously agreed to in spite of a reduction in pay to sixty seven dollars per day. When the other beach boys were let go, I think one of the reasons that I was offered a chance to stay on was that I was always available on the set while many of the others roamed around and had to be called when our sequence was to be filmed. Chico, the first assistant director and I got along really well and when not shooting we spoke in Spanish. We were shooting a crowd scene with the Hebrew slaves in the mud pits making bricks, I was on a high hill overlooking the slaves. Almost all the slaves and many others were Latinos. Chico gave me orders over the loudspeaker in Spanish. Everyone cheered and applauded except DeMille who said that was enough of that, because any delay in shooting was costing five thousand dollars a minute. Chico invited me to his home for a Mexican supper with his wife and family but for some forgotten reason, it didn't happen. Chico's brother is Gilbert Roland, the well known actor. When I asked Chico about his brother, he indicated that they didn't speak to each other. I never brought up the subject again.

As I was walking across the studio lot across the street to a small supermarket, owned and operated by an Armenian family, to eat lunch at the small food bar in the corner of the store where the owner's wife prepared Armenian style food for the customers, I saw this striking blond in the lot and said hello. She seemed very receptive and after a few minutes, I asked her if we could see each other that night. She said I could come over at eight. While writing down her address I asked her name. She gave me a look of disbelief and walked off without a word. I asked a man standing nearby if he knew whom I was talking with. He said that was Zsa Zsa Gabor the Hungarian born actress. I can only assume she was offended that I had no idea of who she was. I never was a movie buff and was only aware of the identity of a few of the older popular stars.

A constant source of problems for the directors were the female movie struck extras constantly trying to place themselves in front of the camera, which invariably entailed repeating the shot. The filming was a very interesting and exciting experience. Aside from the glamour of Hollywood, the technical aspect of filming an epic of this magnitude is impressive. Some of the scenes and the background were filmed on location in Egypt with Yul Brynner but mostly at Paramount Studios in Hollywood. I feel privileged to have had even a minor role in what was the most colossal epic of that era.

The Ten Commandments - Hollywood 1955

me, Charlton Heston and Chuck Pendelton

Yul Brynner, me, Henry Wilcoxen and Charlton Heston

me and Charlton Heston

Twelve of us "musclemen" practiced for days carrying a heavy litter over rough terrain. I had trouble with pain in my left knee when negotiating a turn. On particular turns I bore an inappropriate amount of the weight and complained that we should be getting extra pay for hazardous work. The producers rejected my demand and having given them what amounted to an ultimatum, I decided not to give in and foolishly resigned before the picture was completed in another few weeks. Later, after we corresponded, I was forgiven and had an offer for a studio contract for a year at Paramount which consisted of five days a week for four hours in the morning of classes in various skills such horseback, pistols, swords, etc. or whatever the directors might call for. The pay would be two hundred dollars a week unless we were filming which would be a base pay of three hundred a week plus overtime and make up. It was very tempting but I was yearning to go to Spain and it seemed every time I had planned to go something else would turn up. I finally made my decision to leave for Spain.

I was still interested in studying guitar and was envious when the famous Brazilian classical guitarist, Laurendo Almeida, would go to Debra Paget's dressing room to give her private lessons.

I couldn't picture Edward G. Robinson in a biblical role. To me he was type cast as New York or Chicago hood.

I liked Charleton Heston. He was courteous to all. He wasn't very agile, rather clumsy in his fight scene with Vincent Price. I didn't think he was as powerful an actor as Yul Brynner. Yul would often ignore some of us non important ones when we would say hello. He always carried himself with aplomb and with an aloofness as if he owned the world. He was impressive for a man of small stature.

Although I was in many scenes throughout the film my prominent scenes were, as one of the two Egyptian guards bringing Moses in chains before the Pharaoh, banishing Moses into the desert and one of the corner bearers of the litter for the Golden Calf idol, aside from many of the crowd scenes.

It occurred to me that every time the film is shown and has continued to be televised from its inception every Easter, that I have been
seen and will continue being seen by millions of people throughout the world whenever it is shown. It was filmed in 1955 and
released the following year.

Chapter XIII
Spain

Although I studied Spanish and associated with many Spaniards and others in the US in preparation for my new adventure, being in Spain was not exactly what I had imagined or fantasized what it would be and for the first six months I was disappointed and let down. If I hadn't told everyone that I would be away for a few years, I would have been tempted to return to the states the next day except for the embarrassment of having to face my friends and family.

My parents and some of my family and friends expressed their opinions, usually negative, regarding my plans to live in Spain, especially the second time with Jill and the children. More than one person couldn't understand how I could give up a good physical therapy practice and risk not being able to make a living in Spain.

My parents rarely forbade or discouraged anything I wanted to do, even things they weren't in favor of. I know they were concerned that their oldest son and their only grandchildren would be leaving, living halfway across the globe. No one knew how long it might be before we might see each other. My parents were in their mid 60's at the time.

In Denver, the years previous to my leaving for Spain the first time, I met and conversed with groups and individuals including a Spanish Folklore Dance company from the Canary Islands that was performing in Denver and anyone who could give me information on the subject. I was friendly and spoke at length with one of the main female dancers. I spent time conversing with a group of Spanish Air Force aviators training near Denver and of course my friend and professor Marcelino Peñuelas. One of the main topics of conversation was the lifestyle, conditions and anything else that I could learn about their country.

In spite of my thorough inquiries and speaking with Spanish visitors about cost of living, etc. before leaving for Spain, I found it more expensive than I assumed, to live the lifestyle I desired. I was under the impression from all the information I had that one could live well, like a king, on about a dollar a day according to most of the Spaniards I spoke with. I am sure it would have been a meager living. Nevertheless it was very cheap compared to the US, so I can't complain.

September 1955. I spent three days in Manhattan staying with Vicente Carrasco's Cuban lady friend, Lily de la Nuez. Lily was absolutely gorgeous but unfortunately there were no romantic moments even though we shared the same bed. She took me to a Cuban restaurant, " El Liborio", for supper in Manhattan where she had her apartment. I was hesitant to make any romantic overtures for fear of offending a friend of my dear friend Vicente. I'm afraid it was an opportunity lost. I am certain that if this opportunity had occurred a decade or two later the result might have been much different.

I sailed to Spain aboard the Italian Line's now defunct "Saturnia," third class in a eight bunk cabin shared with five Puerto Rican ex G I's on the way to Madrid to study medicine under the GI bill. We departed from New York, stopping in Lisbon and disembarking in Barcelona. The voyage cost $178 aside from the air fare from Denver to New York.

Many first class passengers socialized with us as they said it was too boring in their class and we were not allowed in first class. Most of my shipmates were Puerto Ricans and a few other Latinos. They all wanted to go ashore in Lisbon to tour the bordellos. I had no interest and don't recall if I went ashore or stayed aboard. We went to Madrid, where I and three of the Puerto Ricans stayed in a pension at Guzmán el Bueno, 86, in the neighborhood of Argüelles not far from the University of Madrid. The nickname the locals gave the neighborhood was the three Ps, Puerto Ricans, Panamanians and prostitutes (Portorriqueños, Panameños y putas).

Doña Concepcion, "Conchi" and her daughter managed the pension. Full pension, including meals was seventy pesetas, less than two dollars per day. One of my shipboard companions, César, entered my room while I was out and borrowed one of my ties without asking, possibly a cultural trait. From then on I locked my room. Some of them didn't think twice about borrowing things without permission,

I had a bad case of the flu. Conchi made me a large glass of cognac with milk, sugar and who knows what else. I was never a great believer in home remedies, especially if they contained alcohol but didn't want to hurt her feelings and the fact was that I felt so bad I was willing to try anything. She said it would make me sleep and I'd feel better in the morning. It tasted terrible but I managed to force it all down and spent the rest of the night sweating and not sleeping. I didn't feel good for a few days but I slowly recovered.

My pensión was close to the barracks of General Franco's Moorish Guard. Periodically we would see them parading on their beautiful horses with hooves painted in gold and festooned with colorful trappings. The riders were attired in their colorful Moorish uniforms. I am truly sorry that I didn't take any photos of this extravagant spectacle. When Morocco gained independence, the Moorish Guard was disbanded.

When I first arrived in Spain, I was determined to learn to ride horses. I bought a book by an Argentine horseman. I went to a small stable on the outskirts of Madrid asking if I could learn to bridle, saddle and curry the horse before and after riding him. My roommate Earle went riding with me. They had English saddles instead of the Andalusian saddles similar to our comfortable western saddles. The first time we had no problems as the horses were plugs, not spirited animals. The second time I asked for more spirited horses. This time was much different. The animals know when you're nervous and react by trying to give the rider a bad time. It may be by suddenly side stepping to throw you off or some other equine antics. Earle's mount's cinch was probably loose as his saddle spun hanging around the horses belly with Earle on the ground. We were going along a wide path, one side was open countryside and the other side a steep incline. I had no worries, it only seemed natural that a smart animal would keep going straight or with a tendency toward the open country. I guessed wrong. I tried to direct him away from the incline but he started climbing the hill, probably because the stable was in that direction. We neared the top, the horse clawing his way up on his front knees. We reached the top, one shaken jockey and a bleeding horse. They say the best thing to do to conquer your fear is to try again. Either you dominate or the horse will. This coward knows better and admits he doesn't get along with horses.

— — — — — —

In the summer of '57 or '58 at Stella, a swimming pool restaurant in the section called Ciudad Lineal, I saw a group of tall, beautiful girls whom I assumed were not Spanish. They belonged to an English modern ballet, the Bluebell Girls, named for their director, chaperon and owner, Ms. "Bluebell" Leibovici and her husband. Most of their troupes were composed of tall English girls but there were a few Scandinavian and German girls in a few of their troupes. Aside from the Leibovicis being English (actually she was born in Ireland and her husband in Romania), they preferred English girls, claiming English girls were more dependable and more disciplined. The Bluebells were and probably still are one of the most successful and sought after of the show dance ballets. They are booked in the most elegant clubs and theaters such as the Lido in Paris, the Mikado in Tokyo, the Stardust in Las Vegas, etc.

I picked Jill Rossiter, the most beautiful and the best dancer with the best legs. Mrs. Leibovici was always worried about losing her girls especially the better performers when they fell in love and eventually would leave. I had the idea of doing some sort of act with Jill combining her dancing talents with my balancing and lifting. She had to finish her commitment to finish their present tour. While I was working I took advantage of traveling to where they were performing to spend time with her. While they toured in Spain it was a simple matter going to where they were but I couldn't go as often when they were outside the country. I did go to Florence and Torino for a week. In Torino I would go to Sestierre during the day for skiing while the troupe rehearsed. Eventually Jill finished her contract and returned to Madrid where we began to train and rehearse at the gym Moscardó.

Jill was from a poor family in Taunton, Somerset, England. When she was fourteen she worked at a factory sewing buttons on men's shirts. She took ballet lessons at a young age by helping teach and work at the studio in lieu of paying for her lessons. When the owner became ill she asked Jill to take over the teaching of ballroom dances. Jill spent some years either dancing or studying with the Sadler Wells, the Royal English Ballet, before joining the Bluebell Girls. Jill never had a chance to finish school. She was self conscious at her lack of vocabulary and correct grammar but made up by having good common sense which is often more important then academic learning.

When I went to Taunton to visit her and her mother, I stayed in their caravan on the property about a hundred feet from the house. When I would go to the house their flock of geese would attack me. They are as bad and more aggressive than most dogs and serve as deterrents to strangers.

— — — — — —

I joined Gimnasio Moscardó, Calle Pilar de Zaragoza 93 so I could workout at bodybuilding. This gym was affiliated with a political movement of which I never quite understood but kept from getting involved or asking questions involving Spanish politics, unless they were close friends, in which case they seemed very open. Later I did find out that General José Moscardó was with Generalísmo Franco Baamonde's National Party. I get the feeling that Spaniards and maybe other nationalities have a habit of never agreeing with one another and even if they both have the same viewpoint they'll find points to argue or disagree on.

José Luis Torres was the instructor and in charge of the gym. He had been a trainer for the Spanish Olympic Team. A close friend of José was Luis Bosqued, originally from Zaragoza. There were about a half dozen regular bodybuilders. The only other person I can remember was Tomás Maldonado. After the gym we often went to a nearby restaurant, Hermanos Ordás at Diego de León, 63, in the section Salamanca of Madrid. We all became fast friends and reunited about 50 years later.

A handbalancing duo from Argentina was working in Madrid and happened to rehearse in our gym. I would balance with them primarily with the top mounter Dino of Dino y Elvis. Across the grounds of the gym and pool complex on the top floor of an adjoining building was the dance studio of one of Spain's most famous flamenco dancers, Antonio Gades. His specialty was the Farruca. We could see the silhouettes of the dancers through the translucent windows of the studio.

This was a neighborhood restaurant owned and run by two brothers from the province of Asturias in the north of the country and specialized in that regions gastronomy. An example of a meal we would usually order consisted of an appetizer, salad, meat, bread and wine, all in ample amounts for 30 pesetas or the equivalent of 75 cents US. When in season, a huge bowl of strawberries (the tasty, small berries) with fresh whipped cream was an extra 20 pesetas or 50 cents US. I stopped in for a meal after a 17 year absence and was flattered when the brothers immediately recognized me by name.

Both the gym and restaurant were near Avenida de Las Américas on the way to the airport. Los Rascacielos was a nickname for a group of buildings on the corner of Avenida de Las Américas and Francisco Silvela. These "skyscrapers" were approximately 6-8 stories high.

Another famous restaurant was the Edelweiss with German cuisine, a restaurant with large portions and comparable in price to Hermanos Ordás. I often ordered the Bismarck Garni, raw ground beef with a raw egg on top. There were two other German restaurants within a few blocks, all close to the American Express Office and the courthouse. The waiters there also all recognized me after the many years of my absence. Many of the waiters in the Eidelweiss had been there for more than 30 years.

It was somewhat of a culture shock eating what the average Spaniard ate compared to what I was accustomed. The quality of the food and the cooking in most poor households left a lot to be desired but good Spanish cuisine is outstanding once one understands and develops a taste for what they may consider to be exotic foods. Many uninformed people believe the fallacy that Spanish food is similar to that of Mexico and other Latin countries. After the corrida (bull fight) it's a treat eating a steak of the bulls that were killed that some of the good restaurants serve. Garlic and olive oil are essentials in Spanish cooking. Except for some Basque dishes with hot chilies, most food is not highly seasoned or spicy as is Latin America. The first time I went out to a restaurant for lunch I finished off with a carafe of sangria. I felt light headed as I wobbled across the street, my first experience with sangria. Many years later when my parents visited us in Spain we had sangria with our meal and my mother who doesn't drink or like alcoholic beverages was warned so she just ate the remaining fruit. She was feeling really giddy after finishing the alcohol soaked fruit, not realizing the it had absorbed the alcohol.

One cannot be in any part of Spain without coming in contact with the then dreaded and feared Guardia Civil in their green uniforms, black belts, boots and black patent leather tricornered hats. They had almost unlimited authority and were known for the violent punishment and death they dealt out to the unlucky prisoners. They were definitely not to be challenged except later by the Basque ETA separatist movement. There was an instance of some tourists driving down a highway who came across two Guardia Civil standing in the middle of the road with their hands up signaling the car to stop. They didn't stop but continued on. The Guardia machined gunned the vehicle killing the occupants. They enforce the law. During Franco's reign crime was at a minimum. One felt very safe from the criminal element, women could walk down the darkest street in the worst part of town safely. Men might stop and flirt by complimenting or flattering them but didn't touch them. They were aware of the cases of men accused of rape in the custody of the Guardia Civil. If ever released they were not physically capable of committing the same offense twice. Later, as the government became more lenient and permissive, crime increased.

The first time I applied for a Spanish driving license I failed the driving exam. I asked to see the results of my test but they refused my request. I'm convinced that I did well but I believe they automatically failed one on the first attempt or so I've been told. The second time I passed. In the '50's some of the middle-aged and older Spaniards were able to afford small automobiles. They were seldom good drivers, lacking the skill and confidence acquired when starting at a young age. Most wealthy Spaniards had large vehicles or limousines with chauffeurs. I'm glad that I don't have to drive anymore in any of the congested large cities in Spain, Europe or Latin America. It's just too dynamic, undisciplined and nerve wracking.

Often Spanish unarmed soldiers roamed the streets and one felt sorry to see their poor uniforms and know that a private only made fifty centimes, the equivalent of two and a half cents per day. Life must have been miserable unless they had family or someone to send them money. With that kind of money it wasn't easy to treat anyone or pick up any girls.

One of the main thoroughfares in Madrid is from the Plaza Cibeles, where the main post office is located, up the Calle Alcalá and José Antonio (the Gran Vía) to Plaza España. These streets are lined with shops, cafes, restaurants and bars. Many cafes have sidewalk tables, where it is customary to sit have a drink and watch the multitudes pass by especially on Sundays and holidays. We naive young Americans would walk this route back and forth to observe the local beauties, not realizing that we couldn't see as many walking for miles as we could if we followed the local custom of sitting at a sidewalk table and ordering a drink or a bite to eat, sitting for hours while watching the passing parade. A great summer refreshing, non alcoholic favorite drink of mine, found only in Spain is horchata de chufa. Looks like milk, made with tiger nuts, cinnamon and sugar and served cold. In Latin America, the horchatas are made of rice instead of tiger nut, a big difference.

La Puerta del Sol, a few blocks from the Gran Vía, is the geographical center of the country, all mileposts began from there at kilometer zero. Madrid reminds me of Buenos Aires, being a vibrant entertaining nocturnal metropolis with almost any activity, sports, art, culture and anything else one might desire.

A typical picnic in the countryside Madrid style in the early '50's, consisted of a small four passenger automobile with a folding table, folding chairs and baggage on the roof. The men in dark suits, white shirt and tie, polished shoes and the women in long dresses and hats - - a vignette of yesteryear.

I frequented many of the swimming pools during the summer months where I would sun bathe, socialize and work out if I could find some apparatus for chins and dips or someone to handbalance with. Last but not least, it was a great place to meet women. I liked the idea that Spanish men wore bikini-type swim suits, the only type I ever wore and continue wearing to this day. As time wore on some men went to the boxer type as used in the states. Some of the better swimming pools were the elegant Villa Rosa and Stella both in Ciudad Lineal on the outskirts of Madrid and Parque de Oeste at the other end of the city.

It was at Stella where I met Joaquín Blume. I chatted and did some handbalancing with Joaquín in 1957. In 1959 I received the tragic news that Joaquín, his wife and the Spanish gymnastic team perished in an air disaster over the mountains of Cuenca. Joaquín had won the Spanish gymnastic championship for ten consecutive years, competed in the '56 Olympic summer games in Helsinki, won the European all round gymnastic championship in '57 and was favored in the '60 Olympics which were canceled when Spain boycotted the games in protest against the Russian's brutal repression during the Hungarian Revolution. Gymnastic venues and clubs throughout Spain carry his name.

I just found out via Google on the internet that Gimnasio Moscardó is now called Residencia Blume.

I met Claude Escarmant, who was also a handbalancer from Tours, France, at the swimming pool at Parque del Oeste in Madrid. He had an act called Les Marthy with his partner Jean. I enjoyed doing some handbalancing with such a fantastic handbalancer. When I acquired property in Formentera, Claude came to visit us and later bought property and settled in Ibiza where he eventually formed a successful physical therapy rehabilitation clinic. He married Anamari from Barcelona and they have a lovely daughter Karina, who took over their clinic when Claude passed away. Claude had a very healthy life style and I was surprised to hear that he died, even though he was over eighty years old.

The Villa Rosa was probably the most elegant nightclub in the outskirts of Madrid. Xavier Cugat, his orchestra and vocalist Abby Lane were performing during the evening and nightly shows. I happened to see the gorgeous Abby Lane near the drinking fountain on the grounds near the pool one afternoon. I spoke to her for a brief moment when she suddenly turned as he appeared and said that Cugat follows her every moment and is very jealous.

– – – – – –

I drove alone to Málaga and on to Torremolinos. On the way I stopped in Granada at the Alcázar in the Alhambra and was especially impressed with the gardens of the Generalife where every June the Spanish classical music festival was held. The once primitive dwellings in the caves of Sacromonte near Albaicín hill in the old Arabic quarter where the gypsies live, lavish on the inside while still picturesque and original on the outside. A disconcerting sight was their bristling television antennas protruding from the roofs of the caves. From Granada I drove south to Motril on the coast and on to my destination, Torremolinos. My first lodging there was a small white shack on the beach with a thatched roof occupied by an old man, Antonio. Many of our meals consisted of "chanquete" the typical regional Malagueñan dish of tiny, almost transparent fish about an inch long, deep fried in a mass accompanied with bread and white wine. We would wait on the shore in the early morning to buy the chanquete and other fish when the fishermen hauled in the nets. When I visited the following year I was told that Antonio had passed away.

The few edifices I can recall in Torremolinos, an Englishwoman's house, one small restaurant and the house on the beach. I don't believe there were other homes that had rooms to let except for that large older house on the beach. I'm talking of the mid '50s. The town has now become a metropolis of large white hotels that line the beaches.

I later met the English woman from whom I rented a room upstairs in her old. large two story castle like house a few blocks from the ocean. She was a nice looking middle aged woman who amazed me that she could negotiate the narrow steep stairs without falling when she would come home nights drunk.

My second visit I rented a room in the other older house on the beach. The owners were an older Jewish Sephardic couple. I doubt if their neighbors were aware they were Jewish. At that time there was still a subdued form of antisemitism in Spain and most Jews kept a low profile. I wasn't aware of the fact myself until later. One day another thin wiry older Sephardic Jew appeared when I was on the beach in front of the house. He mentioned that he was from Palestine traveling around the Mediterranean countries soliciting money for the cause. He said he was called Moishe the "tiger." When I mentioned that I was Jewish he told me to come down to the living room at seven. All the shades were drawn and the four of us were seated in the subdued light of a few candles. They were speaking in Ladino which is a mixture mainly of archaic Spanish with some Turkish, Hebrew and possibly other Mediterranean languages. I had no trouble understanding most of the conversation. After that, the couple that owned the house and spoke to me before in Castilian, later spoke to me in Ladino when no strangers were present. Ladino is what Sephardic Jews speak. I would often hear a Swiss radio station that broadcast in Ladino.

While strolling on the beach I met a tall young girl and her dog Lobo. She was from Santander in northern Spain. It was romantic walking arm in arm along the beach in the evenings. I don't recall ever seeing anyone on the beach during the seasons I spent in Torremolinos. They always seemed deserted in March, too early for most Spaniards. We did engage in romantic play in bed but her dog wanted to participate and was all over us. She was a virgin when we met and a virgin when we parted.

Unfortunately many of the activities cost money, so under the circumstances I was looking for a way to make a few pesetas. Through my friends at the gym, I was able to get work as a stunt man for the movie Alexander the Great. I worked ten days jumping off walls of the Castle in Manzanares in the Guadarrama Mountains with brief clothing and sandals on to the hard cold ground without any preparation. Real stunt specialists would go through a lot of preparations preparing the hard ground and special footwear for landing on hard surfaces but the movie industry in Spain was still in its infancy We earned 300 pesetas, the equivalent of $8 per day, which for Spain in those times was considered a considerable amount. Due to the adverse conditions under which we worked I didn't continue. Most of us ended up with aches, pains and sniffles.

— — — — — —

I was in the lobby of the Castellana Hilton Hotel on the Avenida del Generalísimo in Madrid when I saw John Derek the actor with a beautiful lady. When he was standing alone I went to introduce myself having worked with him on The Ten Commandments but never met him. He was very cordial and when his companion returned he introduced me to her, Ursula Andress. I happened to be in another restaurant about six months later where John was eating and we had a short visit. The last time our paths crossed was in the Mexican restaurant, El Cielito Lindo in Madrid. We chatted and he invited me to his hotel, La Torre de Madrid, a new hotel in the Plaza de España two blocks from US Military Mission offices in Edificio España. We talked for four hours. I asked him why he was no longer acting or directing any films. He told me that when you antagonize the Hollywood film moguls, that can signal the end your career.

In my opinion he was the handsomest of all the Hollywood actors. He was congenial and I enjoyed his company. He was probably glad to chat with a countryman in English. He later married Bo Derek and recently passed away. (I'm not sure if that had anything to do with his demise).

It was not unusual to see the beautiful Ava Gardner in The Castellana Hilton Hotel. The few times I saw her there it was obvious that she had been drinking. Not being a drinker I can't tell if a person has been drinking unless they're tipsy and unsteady on their feet.

— — — — — —

It wasn't too long after I began working in Madrid that Chico Day, the director and Buddy Brill the casting director contacted me in Madrid. They were filming "The Pride and the Passion" with Cary Grant and Sofia Loren nearby. They offered me a contract to do the stunt work for Cary Grant. The stunts, as a gymnast, would not have been difficult for me. Had there been dangerous stunts, that would have required a professional stuntman. I told them I would think about it. If I hadn't liked the relative permanency of my present employment, I would have gladly accepted. Later they introduced me to the unit manager Ivan Volkman, who offered me a job as his personal translator, which I also turned down for the same reason.

I invited Chico and Buddy for lunch at my apartment and we also went out to a restaurant one evening. They said to keep in touch and let them know when I returned to the states. I didn't get in touch when I finally did return as I was 53 years old and married with children. Working in the movies, were it possible, didn't seem like a good option. I had no illusions about a career in the motion picture industry.

— — — — — —

Barcelona used Castilian, the legal language of the country even though it is in the province of Cataluña where the native language is Catalan. There has always been resentment in not being able to have Catalan as their official language and eventually they succeeded and have now reverted back to their original Catalan names. I believe the schools in Cataluña can now teach in Catalan legally. A few decades ago many of the original Catalan names and places were in Castilian,

I enjoyed going to the verbenas and the zarzuelas in Spain. Verbenas are held in open public areas where families gather with the children and usually bring food to eat during the performances and enjoy and revel in listening to the music and the dancing. The zarzuela is more upscale with popular music and operetta, normally performed in a theater or a building. They both can be outdoors and verbena performances may be on the ground if no stage is available. The verbena is more family oriented and social, whereas the zarzuela is more a formal paid performance.

In most of the cinemas and theaters in Spain in the 50's there was no ventilation or air conditioning to counteract the warm stale musty atmosphere. It got pretty smelly and raunchy in the hot summer nights. It was alleviated somewhat by employees with a hand spray guns roaming about up and down the aisles spraying perfume. Eventually most of the cinemas installed air conditioning and the other modern conveniences.

Another uncomfortable situation for me as an asthmatic was people smoking in close proximity. It seemed as if every male and many females smoked mostly cigarettes of the black local tobacco. When I was working in Vallecas, the subways in the early morning were overcrowded with workers who reeked of cigarettes and garlic. Sometimes I could barely keep from gagging.

The smoking ban in Spain progressed slowly. It began with small non smoking areas or sections slowly progressing to a relatively complete ban in many public places. At the beginning of the ban on aircraft I do recall the the local flights with rows of seats separated by the single aisle in the center permitted smoking only on designated side of the aisle which really was not too effective (everyone knows that smoke drifts directly to the non smoker).

On the larger international flights eventually all smoking was banned. To get around that, people would walk down the aisles holding their lit cigarettes down low along their side so as not to be observed and also smoked in the toilets before they had smoke sensors and alarms. Worse was when the flight employees would gather in their curtained off service compartments with palls of heavy smoke pouring out between the openings. Those problems for the most part have been resolved.

An embarrassing episode on the flight from Madrid to the US. I was seated in a non smoking section and the man in the seat in back of me was a chain smoker. I was hesitant and finally asked him if he would mind not smoking as this was in a non smoking section, or so I thought. He was very courteous and ceased for a while. Being a smoker I imagine it was difficult for him and later he began smoking again but to a lesser degree. When the flight attendant passed I explained my situation and asked if there was another non smoking seat available or to mention to him that it was a non smoking area and to stop smoking. She informed me, to my misfortune, that I was seated in the last non smoking row.

On a transatlantic flight from New York to Madrid I sat next to three Basque sheepherders who were working temporarily in the western states. We were unable to converse as they spoke no English or Spanish, only Basque.

There were two important Spanish movies made in Madrid, El Último Cuple in 1957 followed by La Violetera in 1958, both musical and in color. The starring role in each featured Sarita Montiel, a Spanish actress and singer born in La Mancha. Previously she had played in many Spanish and Latin American films but none brought her the great success that these two roles in the highest money making Spanish films of the time. The producer and musical director was Juan de Orduña.

I saw both movies twice when they were released. I rarely see the same film twice but I enjoyed them immensely. I loved the plot and also the scenes and ambiance of old Madrid.

Two Spanish singers that I like and who were popular at that time were Rocio Durcal and Isabel Pantoja for their cuplé style typical of old Madrid. Although Julio Iglesias sang very romantic ballads I find him too soft, almost effeminate in his mannerisms. Most of the older male singers of Spanish and Argentine traditional music, flamenco and tango as examples, exhibited virility and often a roughness in both their voices and mannerisms although the boleros are softer and more romantic.

El rastro (flea market) in Madrid on Sundays was always interesting and surprising. Many have found actual treasures for very little money. As the years pass those who know the merchandise and the value have made real bargains more difficult to find. It compromises an immense area with much diversity.

In Madrid, as in many places worldwide, some of the most tolerable weather occurs in spring and fall, the fall weather is usually more dependable. Summer in Madrid can be hot and winter cold with freezing and snow. Summer nights may be warm but the 2000 foot plus elevation gives some relief from the heat and the humidity.

During my last three or four visits to Spain I have made it a point to spend a few days in Madrid my favorite city. In my early years in Spain there were pensiones but they seem to be disappearing. I stayed in hostels, my last few visits in Hostel Prado a few doors from Plaza Santa Ana. I looked forward to going to a tango dance if possible and time sitting in the plaza enjoying the weather, people and activities. Children were playing, dogs running around and waiters carrying trays of food to people eating in the cafes and those eating on the benches placed throughout the plaza. This is where and when I began seriously thinking about writing my autobiography.

— — — — — —

In the late 60's, Basil Young, my ex-wife Jill's brother-in-law, flew from England to Denver to see if we could arrange a business deal for his antique business. I had returned to Denver from Spain for a brief time to accompany him in this venture. Basil is married to Jill's sister Joy. They lived outside of Taunton, Somerset and bought antiques for resale. Jill, I and the children have visited them many times and they in turn have stayed with us on Formentera more than a few times. Jill and David our youngest son stayed for prolonged periods in England where David attended the local schools. He was only six or seven at the time and when he returned with Jill to Formentera, I was dismayed at his English accent (to you Anglophiles - - sorry about that), but to my pleasant surprise he soon regained his American accent.

Traveling by train from London to Taunton I went to the dining car to eat supper. All tables were occupied and the Maitre D asked a very formal looking well dressed gentleman reading a newspaper if he minded if I was seated opposite him. He turned with somewhat of a haughty superior glance and without any word, we knew that I wasn't welcome and wouldn't be sitting there.

Basil had asked us to see if there were any local contacts in the Los Angeles area that were interested in the importation of containers of antiques from England. I don't remember the details but Jill arranged a meeting with Guild drugs, a large volume dealer of antiques in California. Jill and I were invited for supper at Guild's house and arranged a contract. I distinctly remember that we were embarrassed at how badly our host treated and spoke to his wife who was waiting on us as would a servant and not seated with us at the table. For quite a few years Basil and Joy shipped two large forty foot containers to Guild on a monthly basis.

Understanding English as spoken in Great Britain was difficult for me especially traveling outside of London and the more distant provinces. They had little trouble understanding me and I realize as a generalization the English understand Americans much better than we Americans understand the English. I'm certain the influence of American movies is a factor.

Driving with Bas was scary and more so on the curved one lane English country roads bordered by high thick hedges on both sides of the road. He always had powerful autos. I recall riding in his Jaguar at high speeds on winding roads with little visibility of the road ahead. I was concerned about our safety.

The entrance door to their house was adjoining the road with no sidewalk barriers or any space between the house and the roadway. When you stepped out of the door you were on the road. There wasn't heavy traffic but you never knew when cars or trucks would speed by. Our children were just tots during our visits and we told them not to go out of the door without us. Seems that everyone in England can't wait to get where they're going and even if there is nothing special, they still drive fast. The elderly are usually slower drivers but not always.

Bas and Joy had a sizable property. With their house there were two large barns for storing antiques. Most of the area was farm-land. During one of our visits on a neighbor's farm one of the hired local boys was electrocuted. Most of the food was homegrown lo-cally and very fresh. Their home was good size with fireplaces in the living room and the bedrooms. I really am not impressed with everything being so green, even the moss on the telephone poles and other structures. Guess I'm spoiled with a Mediterranean, Cal-ifornian type climate.

Chapter XIV
US. Military Mission in Spain

My mother's friend's son was an attorney employed by the US
Military Mission in Madrid and I was to contact him when I arrived in Spain with the hope that he might put in a good word for
me applying for work with the US Military Mission. A maid answered my phone call with "dígame" which was rather shocking
to me being accustomed to the Latin American "bueno" or "allo"
instead of the brusk, imperative command of "diga" or "dígame."
I later recalled speaking to the attorney, it was friendly but non-
productive.

During those years the US was building bases and other military
installations in Spain with the main offices in Edificio España in
Madrid. I finally landed a job with the US Navy OICC (Officer
In Charge of Construction) as a local hire in contrast to personnel
contracted from the states. Sid Watson was in charge of the mail
department and second in command was Chuck Gorospe from Hawaii. I met Earle Teitler from Long Island, who worked with me
and we ended up friends and shared an apartment. There were two
or three others in our mail department. The difference between local and stateside hires was the salary and privileges. I was working
in the post office five days per week but we did courier runs to the
various bases and facilities, anywhere from one to three days per
week. The purpose was the delivering of US mail and official US
government documents. Aside from our salary and overtime we
received $10 a day per Diem while traveling. I recall all or most of
our sites and bases that made courier runs were: Getafe airbase
until the base at Torrejón was operable (both in the outskirts of
Madrid), Sanjurjo in Zaragoza (airbase), El Ferrol del Caudillo in
Galicia (submarine base), Puch Mayor, Mallorca (radar), La Ai-
tana, Alicante (radar), Rota, Cádiz (naval), Morón de la Frontera
(airbase) and Cartagena (naval).

Some of the stops I enjoyed, especially during our many courier runs, were: Alicante and eating a Dehesa yogurt, in Murcia at my friend Pedro Rosique's bar, wines in Valdepeñas, the Moorish cathedral La Mezquita in Córdoba and numerous other interesting, charming and beautiful places.

I tried to always stop at the gym in Zaragoza and work out with the others whenever we stopped or passed through. I had a better physique then most of the Spanish bodybuilders and physical culturists as this was relatively new in Spain and more so away from the large cities.

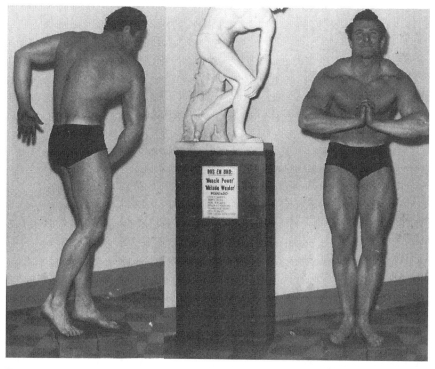

Zaragoza, Spain 1960

On one of my courier runs to Galicia I managed to stay in the same hotel as the Bluebell Girls. At night I would serenade Jill via our hotel windows playing my guitar and singing one of my favorite Mexican songs, La Malagueña Salerosa. I really don't know if Jill paid much attention but years later she told me that one of the other girls, Sally Southam, was enamored with me but I had absolutely no interest in her.

All vehicles were US Navy with Spanish drivers. Most were carryall type. Against regulations I did take Jill, my future wife, on one or two courier trips. I did get to know most of Spain making these runs continuously for about six years. The US components of the base building program in Spain also included the primary contractor Brown-Raymond-Walsh, AESB (American Engineers Spanish Bases). Our photo ID cards were official US Air Force IDs with captions in Spanish.

I was able to arrange the trips, within strict limits, to spend some unauthorized time at various beaches and do other personal errands. Fortunately, all the drivers were friendly and we managed to mutually take advantage of our situation from time to time. Although it was against the rules we frequently bought items for our Spanish co-workers from the AFEX, PX and Ship Stores if a US naval vessel was in port especially the aircraft carriers. At times the ship stores were anxious to restock and to liquidate whatever merchandise they had on board. They could care less if we bought items for the chauffeurs or other non military personnel. They had Rolex watches for $60 and the prices of all the merchandise were unbelievably cheap.

American citizens employed by the Military Mission had privileges for using US military economats and many facilities worldwide. We had an AFEX in Madrid, located on the north end of the city on Paseo de la Castellana, one of the widest of the main thoroughfares in Madrid.

The courier run from Madrid to El Ferrol would begin at 7 am and we wouldn't arrive till evening. It was difficult for me to sleep even though I had an air mattress and could stretch out in the back of the vehicle. A co-worker who also shared the runs, Bill, a Puerto

Rican from New York, would fall asleep immediately in the front passenger seat, sink to the floor and not wake up for the thirteen hour duration of the trip. I'm always envious of anyone that can sleep under any conditions at any time. I found about Bill's uncanny ability from the driver. The runs to the radar sites were in the mountains and occasionally we couldn't complete the trip due to up to three feet of snow. Another of our interesting runs was from Madrid to Puch Mayor in the mountains of Mallorca. We embarked from Barcelona with our vehicle on one of the Spanish Compañía Transmediterránea ships for the 10 hour night sea voyage to Palma. We would mingle with the other passengers and would have some very interesting and exciting times. Many of the passengers were foreign women and we had first class cabins.

A Mallorcan product of renown is the Ensaimada, a large pastry. Most visitors, foreign and Spanish alike bring them back for gifts. On the courier run to El Ferrol we usually stopped in Cacabelos to buy meats to bring home and also in Betanzos to dine on their delicious omelets. Those were the days that almost everything was made from scratch. Nevertheless that may be changing. Some of the Galician seafood delicacies are percebes (goose barnacles), centollos (spider crabs) and vieiras (scallops). Their special preparation as in most Spanish cuisine is what makes the difference. I noticed that the large crabs were served with the carapace (top) removed and a raw egg was stirred into the entrails before eating.

I was thirsty and anxious to try the bottle of fresh milk I bought direct from a small dairy in El Ferrol. I'm sure it was good quality and had lots of cream but I was disappointed when I went to my room to drink, I found hairs and it was full of lumps. Very unappetizing, I poured it down the drain.

I was surprised seeing wooden shoes, "Suecos," worn by rural people, especially notable in the northwestern part of the country. The weather is usually cool and rainy, the area being situated on the Atlantic Ocean to the east and the Cantabrian Sea (Bay of

Biscay) to the north. This area is known for it's bad storms. I understand that wooden shoes are worn in many areas of the world. I had always associated wooden shoes with the Netherlands and Scandinavia.

When working in the fields which are often damp, wet or muddy this can be an advantage over leather which doesn't hold up well when exposed to constant dampness, whereas wood was inexpensive and easily carved and when discarded is used as fire wood. Some wearers paint and adorn their wooden shoes but in the countryside when working in the fields, I noticed most shoes were raw, unfinished natural wood. Another consideration for wood versus leather is the ever present cattle dung in the fields.

My driver and I took off for a little recreation on a spring courier run to El Ferrol without recording it in our official log. We went to one of the beautiful rías of Galicia. Rías are coastal inlets from the ocean that mix with rivers and streams of fresh water and may extend for many miles inland.

It was an unseasonably warm sunny day. We were alone on a quiet deserted white sand beach nestled among the pines except for the chirping birds and ground squirrels. I was practicing handstands in the sand when suddenly my left knee locked. That was the first time it ever locked although that knee was always slightly weaker then my right knee. It was a painful few minutes and it took another few minutes to manipulate the leg to release the block. For the rest of the day the knee was unstable and I couldn't bear weight on that leg. I hobbled around till we returned to Madrid. I lied to my superiors that I slipped on the wet ramp at the motor pool. The insurance covered all the medical expenses and my pay for the two weeks I was out.

Before the surgery I spoke to four orthopedic surgeons. The main question I asked was, what do we do after the operation? Three said that I rest in bed for a week or two. The fourth, 26 year old

Doctor Martín, just recently graduated in orthopedic surgery, said, "we start physical therapy immediately following surgery." Those were the right words.

The nurses in most of the Spanish hospitals were nuns as the hospitals were religion based Catholic institutions. Under sedation I was wheeled to the operating room on a gurney. The next thing I remembered was being back in my hospital bed and my doctor smiling. He asked me if I had any idea of why he was smiling. I shook my head and he told me it was hilarious and that under sedation I was unconsciously uttering many sexual slurs and the nurses were blushing and desperately trying to look unperturbed.

Every morning a priest came to visit the patients. On the second day he mentioned something about religion and I mentioned that I was Jewish. He tried to hide his shock and mumbled a few words. He asked if it was alright if he continued his daily visits to me and I assured him that would be fine. The uncomfortable part was that every time before leaving, he would repeat three times, "sea Cristiano, sea Cristiano, sea Cristiano," meaning, "be a Christian, be a Christian, be a Christian."

The day of my discharge the priest asked me to accompany him to greet his superior. We entered this dimly lit hospital room with numerous candles and religious icons. In the bed, surrounded with black robed priests, was the pallid shriveled old priest dying of cancer. With a trembling hand he grasped my hand, looked into my eyes and repeated the same phrase three times, "sea Cristiano, sea Cristiano, sea Cristiano." I was relieved to leave the room and the hospital. They did take excellent care of me and treated me well.

I continued exercising at home with an iron boot and weights that I had. Within ten days I was doing knee extensions on the operated leg with seventy five pounds and going to work on crutches. As a physical therapist these activities presented no problems.

After ten days Doctor Martín wanted me to bear weight on my leg, I was using crutches and I said I'd rather not as yet. A few days later he asked me again. I said I'd rather not but I followed his orders and, as I assumed according to my professional experience, the knee swelled. I had to have it aspirated a few times and eventually it improved so I could function normally.

On my first courier run after my surgery, still non-weight bearing on that leg and ambulating with crutches, I had to go to the toilet in a rural restaurant. Except for the more elegant establishments the toilets in many rural and poorer areas consisted of a "plato Turco"or Turkish plate consisting of a nine inch hole in the floor forcing one to squat in order to defecate. Not many would have been able to do a one legged squat and up again balancing on crutches. For the "coup de grâce " - - - torn pieces of newspaper on a hook sufficed for toilet tissue as we know it.

Unlike the other couriers who ate and stayed by themselves I always shared a room and ate with the driver in the special section of the restaurants reserved for chauffeurs and truckers. We were charged half of the regular price for the same fare. My total daily expenses during the courier runs were about a dollar a day. I was able to save and send most of my earnings to my bank back home in the states.

— — — — — —

I went to a gun store in Madrid and talked to a salesman about possibly buying a .22 caliber revolver. Most are fabricated in the Basque cities in northern Spain. They are replicas of Smith & Wesson models and of excellent quality. I was interested in a revolver with a six inch barrel. The salesman mentioned that .22 caliber ammunition was in short supply. When I said that's not a problem he said maybe we could make a trade. I ended up with a pistol with a hand carved checkered walnut grip for one carton of 500, 22 long rifle cartridges which cost me five dollars at the AFEX. Since I was in the US Military Mission it was easy to get a permit to carry arms and a permit to hunt. Handguns and rifles are not permitted in Spain except for law enforcement and military personnel. A few times I would shoot from the vehicle window on our courier runs but never managed to hit anything. I was more accustomed to a rifle.

I was friendly with a Major Bean and his wife, son and daughter. He was in charge of the APO (army post office) in Madrid. His children were a few years younger than I, both were tall and slender. I traveled with them on various trips in their vehicle. As Mormons, I believe they were comfortable in my company. I never smoked, drank or used profane language and was fluent in Spanish and served as a companion and interpreter.

I knew it was prohibited to send arms or ammunition via the postal service. I happened to mention to Major Bean that I might try to take my revolver with me to the states. I was surprised when he said that he would mail it for me. I knew this was against regulations and I would imagine against his principles but he made special arrangements to do me this favor.

When my position with the OICC was phased out I applied a few times for employment with BRW but was turned down until Howard Keller, the assistant manager, finally told me to lie about my previous work history and put down something that appeared to be a normal work history. That worked and I ended up with a job in the warehouse in Vallecas, the poorest and roughest part of town with a large gypsy population. Some of the gypsy girls were very beautiful and exotic looking in spite of appearing dirty and ragged. The "gitanos" were always an interest of mine. I disliked working in an enclosed warehouse and craved being out of doors. After a little discord with my bosses they let me transfer to their post office which was similar to the one I worked in before with the OICC. There were probably a hundred or more American and Spanish employees in the Madrid offices alone that were employed by the US Military Mission. I have no idea how many in total were contracted in the country.

The civilian phase of the US Military Mission in Spain was phasing out. Many civilian employees were being terminated. The majority would have liked to have stayed employed in the program. I spoke to a friend of mine, Bob Guggenheimer, an American acquaintance, local hire, working at the airbase Sanjurjo in Zaragoza, who was able to stay on after most of the civilian personnel were phased out. I happened to ask him how he managed that. He replied that he was careful not to teach others how to perform many of the duties and procedures, making him indispensable in running the operation. Sounds logical to me

Mr. Keller, my boss, called me in to tell me that I wouldn't be paid for overtime for the courier runs. I said that was acceptable but I'd like a letter stating that I would not be held responsible for the US mail or documents after my regular hours. He found that he couldn't enforce that which made all of us couriers happy. I had top secret clearance when employed by the OICC and Mr. Keller was upset when they wouldn't give him clearance in spite of being my boss. They said it was a very costly and involved procedure to give a top secret clearance to a civilian and it wasn't necessary for him since I was responsible when these items were in my possession. Many of my co-workers were envious as only three members of the operating committee and myself were the only civilians on the published list of clearance for top secret. I wish I would have kept a copy as I was the only local hire on the list of four in all of the US Military Mission in Spain. It was just a coincidence that I happened to be cleared for top secret and I loved it.

— — — — — —

It was not uncommon during the 50's and early 60's to see bands of colorful gypsy caravans on the roads and highways. They were nomadic, taking their livestock, other animals and belongings with them. I wanted to take photos but they were belligerent about having their photos taken. Something about taking their souls, as far as I could make out. Respectfully I only would take photos from a distance with a telephoto lens or far enough so they wouldn't know or wouldn't be offended. I became friendly with a gypsy elevator operator in Edificio España who would teach me words in "caló," a dialect of the gypsies and also used by the hoodlums, gangsters and other low elements of Spanish society. When I come across Spanish gypsies in many parts of the world they are surprised that I know a little of their dialect and they usually engage me in conversation.

One could already see the beginnings of cultural changes occurring. Many of the young people, including the gypsies living in cities, had transistor radios and frequently listened to stateside-style music.

Earle and I rented a fully furnished luxurious penthouse apartment with three bedrooms and a full terrace facing two sides, one to the west facing El Retiro park and the other facing south. Originally the rent was the equivalent of $100 monthly, but after threatening to take the landlord to court for charging more than the official rent ceiling, our rent was reduced to $50 per month. Many rentals were more than the legal ceiling, a common practice. Fortunately we didn't have to take legal action which would have been a nightmare in the Spanish courts and even more so for a foreigner. The Philippine ambassador and the Philippine cultural attache and their families also resided in our same apartment complex at Menéndez y Pelayo, 71 in the neighborhood called "barrio del Niño Jesus" (the Christ child), an apt locale for two Jewish boys. At the time we were living in that neighborhood it was the last populated section of Madrid and to the east was countryside. Years later the urban development extended as far as the eye could see.

We hired a full time, live in maid, Manola from Córdoba, for $10 per month, full board and room included. Her room looked like a chapel, filled with religious icons. She was 45 years old but appeared to be much older with her graying black hair in a severe bun. She rarely smiled and talked little. Our normal mealtimes were from two to three for lunch and eleven to midnight for supper. She referred to Earle as "el hueso", "the bone", which isn't very flattering, signifying a dry demanding personality. He insisted on changing his socks and underwear twice daily and having everything pressed including his socks. Not my style. Often we had female guests for dinner. When I first brought Jill to dinner, Manola refused to serve her. I can only assume she might have been jealous as Jill was certainly more ladylike and better dressed than most of our lady friends. I was irritated as I was more serious about Jill than the many others. Manola never before refused to serve anyone. Possibly there were other reasons that I was unaware of.

— — — — — —

I shopped around for a flamenco guitar, something I had wanted for a long time and purchased an instrument made by José Ramírez in Madrid. His flamenco guitars were sought by the best flamenco guitarists if they could afford the 4.000 pesetas ($100). His guitars now sell for thousands of dollars. I also looked at another luthier in Madrid whose name will remain unmentioned, also well known for his flamenco guitars. I was rather insulted when I specifically requested a flamenco guitar and he took out one with fancy inlaid mother of pearl definitely something no true flamenco guitarist would be want to be seen with. I received a discount on the second guitar I bought from Ramírez because the guitar had a wedge of dark mahogany along the center of the bottom instead of the standard white spruce. I liked it for it's deeper sound, somewhere between the lower, deep classical and the higher pitched flamenco tones.

I frequently would stop and browse in La Unión Española, a large music store on Carrera San Jerónimo. They had an extensive collection and display of guitars, sheet music, instruments, recordings and other related products. I believe this is the largest and most complete music store in Spain.

A few months later I met Manuel "Manny" López, an American born Puerto Rican who was an aficionado of flamenco taking flamenco guitar lessons from Fernando Martín. Fernando lived in Vallecas in an old run down house with his wife and little boy. I had been taking lessons from another teacher but made little progress until Manny would come over and practice with me. I was just playing notes until Manny told me, you have to know the many various flamenco rhythms. We spent days doing "palmas" and "pitos," clapping out the beats to the various rhythms. That made the difference. We both ended up taking lessons from Fernando and accompanying him around town and to some of his performances at "tablaos" (flamenco shows). I was introduced to a small, relatively unknown guitar maker in Vallecas, Anselmo Solar. We often spent time in his small shop playing and watching him make guitars. It's a great learning experience sitting in and playing with other guitarists. Fernando always wanted to make guitars. I offered him a room to work in, in my apartment and to finance him until I recouped my initial investment. He eventually was able to make and sell a few but soon tired of putting in so much time. I doubt if I received any of the money but felt compensated by all the time studying with him.

Many of the special woods, fret wire and mechanical tuner keys were very expensive and difficult to find in Spain. When I was skiing in Garmisch-Partenkirchen I bought these materials from Brüder Fuchs, a company located in Mittenwald, Bavaria, a firm that specialized in wood for musical instruments. The owner was very pleasant and hospitable showing me around his facility widely known for quality musical woods. As I had an official US Air Force ID card I had special privileges in being able to bring these items into Spain avoiding the costly custom fees and shipping. I would at times send these materials through the APO (Army Postal System) to myself. This was a big favor and saving for my friend Anselmo. When he offered to reimburse me I made a deal to have him make me a guitar instead. I still have that guitar even though I rarely take it out of the case. I remember very little and won't put in the countless years necessary to play well. My son David used to practice with it and to my surprise learned to play. For the past twenty years he has performed playing blues, although he sings and plays harmonica along with the guitar.

When I went to the US military R and R (rest and recreation) headquarters in Garmisch Partenkirchen, I showed my US Air Force ID card to the person in charge for a military rate for a room. Since my ID was in Spanish, he called over a young Mallorquin man working there to see what my equivalent rank would be. He and I spoke in Spanish and after chatting awhile he winked at me and lied to the officer in charge that my rank was that of a major which entitled me to a lavish suite overlooking the Zugspitze.

— — — — — —

During my first years in Madrid I met Ted Hansen who was employed at the American Embassy motor pool. We frequently went skiing at Navacerrada in the Guadarrama mountains fifty kilometers north of Madrid. At that time there were only two inns at the summit on top of the pass, Venta Arias and Pasadoiro. There was only one rope tow or a T-bar, consequently we did a lot of climbing. Off season in the spring when all the facilities were closed we would climb and ski on small patches of corn snow in our bathing suits. On those occasions we had the pleasure of being the only souls skiing on the mountain. On one of my first ski jaunts there I went to Cercedilla, a small village in the foothills, that had an old cog railway up the mountain to the ski area. On one trip on the cog railway I met a Mexican fellow, Pedro Varela, with whom I skied and talked with the whole day. We planned to see each other again but never did.

Ted and I drove to El Alberche, a river in the mountains north of Madrid. We swam in the nude as there was no one else visible. Ted took lots of 35 mm colored slides. As I was walking out of the water he took a photo of me. I made the mistake of showing it to my mother many years later. To my chagrin she destroyed it. I really regret that I ever showed it to her. I really was quite proud of my physical attributes at thirty years of age.

My first ski trip two years after arriving in Spain was to St. Anton in the Austrian Tyrol. I rented a room in the home of Toni Spiss, a famous Austrian downhill Olympic skier of a previous decade. One wall of his bedroom was covered with countless medals, trophies, and published articles.

Years later, my wife Jill and I would ski at Navacerrada near Madrid. When we were performing in Barcelona we drove to La Molina north of Barcelona near the French border. The road entering the ski area was icy and our station wagon slid over an embankment, both front wheels over the edge. We cautiously got out of the vehicle fearing it would go down the steep bank. We managed to get assistance towing the car back onto the road. I skied for a month each year for three years in Italy, France, Austria and Switzerland. Usually I would go in the spring when it was warmer with more sunshine. Often I would ski and sun bathe in my bathing suit.

One of my favorite areas was Obergurgl in the Austrian Tyrol. It is one of the highest ski resorts in Europe. I stayed in Pension Jennewien. I distinctly recall a plaque on the office wall giving thanks to the United States Marshall Plan.

I went on a glacier tour with a group of eight and a guide. We climbed using seal skins on our skis. One of the strong Austrian girls asked me to carry her knapsack along with my own. Being asthmatic and in the thin, cold air at an altitude of 12,000 feet I stupidly accepted not wanting to seem unchivalrous. I should have refused but I was young and naive. She was in much better physical condition than I. It was an exciting trek but the climbing was agony waiting for the short five minute rest periods. From the top, in the distance, we could see the Italian Dolomites.

Costs for skiing in Austria and most of Europe were very reasonable in the late fifties. All day lift tickets were two dollars and two sessions of two hours per session of group lessons each day were the same price.

In the states the downhill style was to turn with shoulder into or in the same direction as the turn. Austria adopted the reverse shoulder style with the shoulder going in the opposite direction of the turn, later the states followed suit. Still later the style in the US reverted to a more neutral style, shoulders perpendicular to the downhill direction. I continued with the reverse shoulder technique with skis and knees together which I thought was classier and more graceful looking. If I wasn't a great skier at least I could try and look good. The ski instructors in the states would tell me to ski with more distance between the skis for a wider and more stable base. This may now be universal but I kept to the style I liked with skis close together. Social life in the European ski lodges was friendly, carefree and lively. Skiing seems to draw people from everywhere and every walk of life.

I was stopped by two plain clothed policemen in Italy who evidently mistook me for a wanted suspect. One wanted to take me to police headquarters but they checked my passport and decided I wasn't the one they were looking for.

Another favorite place was Cervinia in Italy across from the Monte Rosa plateau from Zermatt, in Switzerland. I will always remember the day I was standing on one of the slopes observing in awe, seven different avalanches falling simultaneously down the various slopes of the surrounding mountainous bowl.

Jill and I were performing nightly in a casino in Valle San Vincent, a half hours drive down a mountain road, returning after midnight to the resort in Cervinia where we were staying. In spite of getting to bed about two am, Jill would get up to take her ski lessons at seven am, I would get up later. At breakfast at a nearby table sat an Italian family. The father, mother and little boy. They were all very portly, nevertheless the boy's parents constantly kept pleading with their son, "mangia Fabbio, mangia."

Skiing at Courmayour in the Italian Alps there is an aerial cable car that goes over the top of the Alps to the French ski resort of Chamonix. I was entering the lodge after a long arduous day's skiing. Jill was sitting in the lounge surrounded by a group of young Italian soldiers. There was music playing from a phonograph, a popular song of the day, "Cuando, Cuando, Cuando," popularized by the young Italian singer Johnny Renis. I thought one of the soldiers was lip syncing the song and I said to Jill, "he sounds just like Johnny Renis." She replied, "The man you see standing there singing is Johnny Renis".

Passing through St. Moritz, Switzerland we stopped at the Kulm hotel. We noted a billboard of the nightly show in the hotel lounge and asked what time the floor show went on. The desk clerk mentioned that one of the main acts was unable to perform. I asked to speak to whomever was in change of the entertainment. I told him that we could perform on the spur of the moment that night and he readily agreed. There was no time to rehearse our complicated music with the band so we used our tape recorder. It is much easier with live music as our routine is cued and we have to follow the cues, whereas musicians are somewhat able to follow and adjust to the performers and vice versa.

I was at the airport in Zurich returning from a solo trip skiing in the Alps when I spotted this gorgeous voluptuous woman. She was very congenial and after chatting a few minutes she gave me her phone number in Barcelona. Forgetting whether I phoned her later or invited her on the spot to visit me for a few weeks, I sent her a ten dollar round trip plane ticket when I returned to Madrid.

I was lustily looking forward to her arrival. After two days I realized I was no longer interested in her company, we only had one thing in common. It was very exciting but that can wear off fast with the realization that for the most part Spanish women were normally either very promiscuous or the other extreme especially on the first date. I finally came up with a solution. I secretly spoke to Nieto the doorman and concierge, asking him to go to the telegraph office and send me an urgent telegram that I wrote and handed to him. It was supposedly from my mother stating that she was arriving the following morning, a week earlier than originally planned. Within a few hours the telegram was delivered and I was relieved as my lady companion stepped into a taxi on her way to the airport. I hope that was a lesson for me. "Be careful what you wish for."

On the train returning to Spain from skiing in Italy along the French Riviera I was conversing with two older women sitting with me in our four person compartment. One woman was French and the other Spanish. It was getting late and they asked me if I had a couchette (four bed compartment). I wasn't sure what that was until they explained. I said no I had planned to sleep sitting in our compartment. They said it would be very uncomfortable sitting up the whole night. They called the ticket collector over and requested a couchette for me. He said that they were all occupied. The ladies commented that there was an unoccupied bed in their compartment. The ticket collector said they are not permitted to put passengers of opposite sex in the same compartment. The women cajoled and insisted. Finally he consented. The two ladies were in the two lower beds and I was in an upper, opposite a young Belgian Lady. There was only less than two feet separating the beds. When the two ladies fell asleep, with the lights out my companion and I spent a good part of the night fondling one another. With the space separating us there wasn't much more we could do.

Carmen Frediani was Italian. She was a dark complected, shapely and stunning. She and her two brothers, an acrobatic trio, were performers. We were good friends and we spent time on the large balcony in my Madrid apartment. We were together various times when we happened to be in the same city. I don't remember if I even met her brothers. I believe she kept our friendship a secret. With two Italian brothers it was undoubtedly a wise thing to do.

Being an American had many advantages at that time in Spain. I was always treated very well, then and now although I don't think we Americans in general are that well thought of in many countries these days.

I met Gerson Markowitt who was also working with BRW in Spain. We became good friends and I invited him to visit us in Formentera. He eventually bought a parcel of land adjoining my land with plans to build but this never worked out due to the difficulties with the local codes and laws, especially for foreigners. Also my good friends Henry and Helen Hunter bought land adjoining my property. This also didn't work out well for them. Claude and Anamari also bought land adjoining our property and since Anamari is Spanish they didn't have any problems.

I would encounter Mark at some of our bases on my courier runs. Mark was a professor in English back in the states and became an ex-patriot living a large part of his life in Spain and Europe. After many years living voluntarily outside of the US, many ex-pats never seem to return.

In Cartagena a few of us went to the many bodegas or wine bars to sample some of the numerous local wines which in those days of the '60s cost less than a few cents US per glass. In town there was a restaurant called Denver. Naturally I was curious and asked the proprietor if he was ever in Denver or had any association with that city. He said that he saw the name in a western movie and he liked the name.

In the showcase window of another restaurant in the same city there was a huge lobster on display, probably cooked and almost two foot in length. I was intrigued and stopped to look whenever I passed. Having two large claws it was not the California spiny type lobster which lack these claws.

— — — — — —

I was now able to afford a new Citroen 2 CV from the French factory for $715 which I picked up in Irún on the Spanish-French border. Earle, who worked with me at the OICC had a Volkswagen Beetle. Earle and I were driving around in Madrid when suddenly my car chugged to a stop. In a new vehicle I always carefully check the levels. We pushed it to a garage a few blocks away. The attendant checked the engine and said we were completely out of oil - - it was dry. I frequently checked the oil level but evidently mistook the trace of oil I could see at the normal level mark which evidently was not a true indication. It was a weekend and most garages and auto agencies were closed. I asked for two quarts of oil, the full capacity. The mechanic said I'd need a new motor or extensive motor repair work. As I was pouring in the oil the attendant said it wouldn't do any good and it wouldn't go. Miraculously the engine came to life and we drove off. I didn't need any repair and never had any problem for the many years I drove it, except for a mild pinging at a speed between 80 and 90 kilometers per hour.

In my car, Earle and I entered a narrow dirt road with stone walls on both sides. After a half kilometer there were about six to eight steps we had to traverse to continue on. It was too narrow to turn around and too far to back out so we drove down the steps. The suspension of the Citroen two cylinder is amazing. I have had three vehicles of the same model during the 20 years I lived in Spain. I wanted to bring one back to California but since '67 or '68 they were illegal to import to the US as they didn't meet American specifications. I have seen a few older models in the Los Angeles area brought in before the ban. There are kits for this model advertised here in the states for five to six thousand dollars plus the cost of assembly, which is expensive. Their top speed is about 55 to 60 miles per hour, which eliminates the possibility of freeway driving. They get about 60 miles to the gallon and you could probably run them on kerosene. I really miss not having one.

We dated two Puerto Rican girls from New York who were also contracted and worked with the US Military Mission in the same building as us. We drove to the picturesque village of Calpe, known for its monolith island, the Peñón de Ifach, where we spent a few days in a small quaint inn. The scenery was beautiful as it is in many areas of the Spanish Mediterranean coast. Little did I know that many years later I would be a spearfishing with some of my Spanish diving buddies in this very place. Spearfishing in Spain prohibits the use of auxiliary air, only free diving but unfortunately, as with most laws, it is often broken, primarily by foreigners. The extensive coastline is very difficult to patrol.

I met a voluptuous Spanish lady, Amparo, at the pool. She invited me to her apartment for dinner. The main course was a Madrid specialty, Callos a la Madrileña (tripe) which is one of the few Spanish dishes I do not like. I had an acquaintance, Luis Bar Boo originally from Vigo. He was enamored with Amparo so I gladly introduced them. He deserted his wife and children for her. I was sorry he ran out on his family for a promiscuous woman. They quarreled constantly as long as I knew them. Immediately after Amparo I met and dated a lovely girl part Spanish and part Filipino. I cannot remember her name. I didn't seem to stay very long with any one woman.

Sailing from one of the Spanish Mediterranean ports on a Spanish Transmediterránea ship to either Mallorca or Menorca. I couldn't help noticing walking up the gangplank ahead of me was a young blond Australian athletically endowed girl in a mini skirt and tight tee shirt dragging her suitcase in one arm up the gangplank and a small pup cradled in the other arm. All the male eyes on the dock and on the deck seemed to be focused on her. I immediately offered to take her suitcase and was rewarded with an alluring smile.

This was a ten hour overnight crossing and we were traveling deck class which means she would have to sleep in a deck chair and keep an eye on her dog through the night. I spoke to the purser to inquire what cabins might be available. The only one left was a first class cabin which I took for one thousand pesetas, about $16. I invited her to share the cabin and to use the bunk and I would sleep on some blankets on the floor. It was an eventful night. My comment on what a first class cabin was on that company's ships at that time - - - painted steel walls, floor and ceiling and a six by eight foot room with a narrow bunk bed.

I should have been more selective of the ladies I met at the swimming pools and other public places during my first years in Madrid. At the time I didn't know that many of the non escorted or unchaperoned women were either very promiscuous or prostitutes. This has changed with time. The former very often had venereal diseases. Professional prostitutes were legal and examined periodically to control venereal diseases.

Prostitution was prevalent as in many other poor countries. A typical tale of why many women were economically forced into the oldest profession was, in many cases, due to having had an illegitimate child and being disowned and unsupported by the family. I believe and hope that situation has improved through the years.

Chapter XV
Jill, Logi & Barragán

My first introduction to spearfishing and diving was in Madrid with an American acquaintance from Florida who showed me how to make a spear gun. It was a modified Hawaiian sling using a piece of wood with a hole lengthwise for the spear and surgical rubber tubing for the propellant with a homemade triggering device. We also practiced holding our breath. I managed to do three minutes, thirteen seconds lying in bed after hyperventilating. I reached a point after about two and a half minutes when it seemed effortless and I didn't need to breathe, when my friend said I was looking pale and I better breathe. Aside from feeling giddy, I was fine.

My free diving equipment consisted of fins, mask. snorkel, knife, wet suit with weight belt and Nemrod "fragata" spear gun with 20 meters of nylon line attached to a float. The float carried extra spears, the fish stringer and other paraphernalia. The spear gun functioned by compressed air in a duraluminum closed chamber barrel containing a double O-ring embolus. A detachable air pump was used to pressurize the system. The gun was five feet in length and the spear thirty inches long. For deep dives extra weights can be added to the rear of the gun to facilitate a more rapid descent and in the event the diver has to surface rapidly the gun can be left and retrieved to the surface by the line on the float. This type of compressed air gun was used by most serious spearfishermen in Spain. In later years many have gone back to the original rubber band propelling guns.

Free diving spearfishing has its fatalities. A common one called shallow water blackout invariably results in drowning. A technique of hyperventilating before each dive diminishes the carbon dioxide in the lungs enabling the diver to hold his breath for an extended period but at the same time it diminishes the automatic reflex to continue breathing when starved for oxygen. Free divers have been advised not to continue the practice of hyperventilating in order to prevent drowning.

I personally knew two German young men on Formentera, both experienced divers that drowned a few months apart while spearfishing. The usual scenario is having difficultly bringing a large fish to the surface and thinking one can endure a little longer or basically trying to hold one's breath too long. There is no warning, no graying out period. When the blackout occurs, a breath is involuntarily taken and drowning ensues. One advantage free divers have over divers using auxiliary air or gases is that free divers do not get the bends "Caisson Disease."
I just read, according to Google, hyperventilating has little or no effect of increasing the amount of oxygen in the blood with little or no effect in breath holding. I'm not sure I'm convinced of this latest information.

Years later on a free diving fishing trip with the Long Beach Neptunes to Santa Cruz Island in the Channel Islands off the southern California coast, about twenty members in our chartered boat were primarily after large black sea bass (grouper). Toward the end of the day we noticed that one of the divers hadn't returned to the boat. He was a 46 year old gentleman who had brought along his 20 year old son, on leave from the navy, as a spectator. He was found on the bottom in forty feet of water with a 60 pound grouper hooked on his line holed up in a cave. As soon as the other divers retrieved his body the captain radioed the Coast Guard who dispatched a helicopter for aid but when they arrived it was too late as he was already dead when found. It was a sad trip home for all with the grieving son aboard. Three grouper were taken, one, 270, 120 and a 90 pounder. None by me.

— — — — — —

I had two very close buddies, Eulogio, "Logi" Fernández Salinero and Antonio Barragán who owned the only shop specializing in diving equipment in Barcelona. We were members of APS (Asociación de Pesca Submarina) in Barcelona as were many of the divers including other Spanish clubs of world class competitors from the Spanish Leventine coast and Balearic islands.

We three, Logi, Barragán and myself, in my Peugeot station wagon, drove and dove every day for a month from the French border to Almería covering more than four fifths of the Spanish Mediterranean coast (over 1,000 miles). While fishing off Cabo de Gata near Aguilas in the province of Almería, we came across two local boys who took us diving with them. They had a photo of a giant ray they speared that must have been six feet in diameter. We were amazed that they could find fish, including groupers, in five to six feet of water, where in most places that have been exposed to spear fishermen one had to dive very deep to find grouper. Evidently the area was still a virgin fishing ground that hadn't yet been exploited by divers. In waters that are frequently fished by divers the fish seem to know how to stay just out of spearing range.

A day or two later, near Almería, we went out in a boat with an old local fisherman. I saw and speared my first shark, six feet in length. It probably was similar to a sand shark as it had no large incisor type teeth and posed no threat to humans. I noticed this large yellow eye following my every movement but due to the murky water it was awhile before I could make out the distinctive shape of a shark.

Shark - Cabo Gata, Almería, Spain

After a month of constant diving, I arrived home exhausted and drawn. I had lost five pounds in spite of the hearty meals. Naturally we ate much of what we caught but sold most of the fish to restaurants. Even though this is illegal most of the spear fishermen did this and some made a living solely from this. I didn't accept any of the money.

Whenever I was on the island my normal weight being between 185 to 190 would invariably drop from ten to fifteen pounds. I can only attribute this to changing from a more sedentary to a more active life style and the absence of junk foods.

Getting out of the water on a dive along the Costa Brava on the northeastern coast of Spain, we clambered on to the rocky shore to rest on a series of steps leading to a large estate. The groundsman came to see who we were and said he was sure that his Catalan landlord, Xavier Cugat the Cuban band leader, wouldn't mind. I would have looked forward to meeting Cugat but he wasn't in the country at the time.

A safe practice when diving in the open ocean is being able to visually locate at least one of your diving companions. More than not this rarely happened and I get uneasy being alone far from land.

Free chest X-rays were being offered, Logi, Jill and I had chest X-rays taken. Logi was a smoker, Jill smoked a few cigarettes daily and I was a non smoker, never having smoked. The doctor said they were fine but my lungs looked congested and I should quit smoking. With my chronic asthmatic condition this finding is not unexpected and a good radiologist can usually tell the difference.

Logi, Barragan, Rafal and I climbed down the 600 foot steep cliffs at La Mola on Formentera near the lighthouse to dive. I speared a reich, similar to a white sea bass. I was very excited spearing this three foot long specimen rarely seen in these waters. It was a difficult and precarious climb to the top carrying our catch and equipment. We were all exhausted and went to Rafal's bar/restaurante in San Francisco Xavier to eat and relax.

— — — — — —

Logi and his wife María Teresa lived with her family a short distance from their small dairy shop on Conde de Asalto in the Barrio Chino in Barcelona near the port and a few blocks from our hotel . Jill and I visited them often. Maritere had a gorgeous, exotic looking younger sister who eventually married her nondescript, skinny beau. Love is blind, but that's love.

The Barrio Chino name reverted back to El Raval in an attempt to erase its infamous nickname. In latter years some improvements and were made. It was a seedy neighborhood in old Barcelona, the worst neighborhood in Spain, with a terrible reputation for drugs, prostitution, petty crime and unsavory characters. Nevertheless Jill never had any problem even late at night alone in that neighborhood. Men might compliment or say uncomplimentary things but seldom harass or touch a women knowing the severe penalties imposed by the authorities.

I must say that Jill was very patient, many times accompanying me and helping me in and out of my wetsuit that I used when the water was cold. She would wait alone on the shore until I came out. Diving in Palma de Mallorca, I left her at the beach where she met a group of showgirls and went water skiing. That was her first time water skiing. When I returned she was all excited and wanted me to try. I'd never done that and didn't want to make a fool of myself in front of everyone but with Jill's pleading I complied. Luckily the bay was very calm and the pilot was very good handling the boat. Surprisingly I did very well and was able to maneuver without falling. As a snow skier much of my life I was aware of the adjustments to be made for water skiing. I'm not sure if Jill was pleased or disappointed that I did so well - - maybe both.

One of my endeavors living on the island was writing a book about spearfishing and the classification of the different fish and other marine fauna along the Spanish Mediterranean coast. I would have liked to have finished and I kept my notes for years but eventually discarded them. The common names of almost all the fish varied according to the dialect in the area and I was undecided whether to use only the Castilian or also list the local names but it became too complicated and I lost interest.

— — — — — —

We met Inesita and Bob, her husband at an old building in Madrid at Amor de Dios, 4 where many flamenco dancers rehearsed. At the entrance the man who made the arrangements for the various rooms or studios had a pronounced limp. Jill and I rehearsed our act and a flamenco number, alegrias de baile, which we intended to include outside of Spain but never did. I accompanied on the guitar and Jill danced.

I was very attracted to Inesita but she was married and I was with Jill even though we were not married at the time. We had them up to our apartment to eat and went around together a few times while they were in Spain. There was a period of about twenty years that I didn't see them.

Inesita is a professional flamenco dancer soloist who has performed in many counties and movies in Hollywood with well know celebrities. She has taught and given lessons to other professional flamenco dancers.

— — — — — —

This belongs in the chapter XIV but due to the book being already formatted and ready for publication, I'm taking license to insert here.

I met two young beautiful Spanish girl-women, identical twins, in Madrid when Earle and I had our apartment. I think of them as the Majas semi-nudes (from Francisco Goyas famous paintings of La Maja Desnuda and La Maja Vestida). I refer to them as semi-nudes as they skillfully would change from their clothes into their home made bikinis which they would drape each other in by pinning pieces of cloth together in public view without exposing themselves. They were probably in their late teens or very early twenties with exquisitely formed voluptuous bodies which they constantly preened. We only visited with them a few times in our apartment and at the swimming pool, Stella. I don't really know if they had a natural or a taught technique of being able to attract and entice a suitable man for a relationship but they were adept in this area. Earle and I had our male intentions but sadly we never had any real intimacy with these luscious ladies.

Inesita

ALHAMBRA PERFORMING ARTS CENTER PRESENTS

Flamenco Alhambra 2014

"Inesita" with Guitarist Stamen Wetzel

I was living in San Pedro for ten years before I contacted them again. Later we got together now and then. I wanted to talk about flamenco but Bob would get into Greek history and other subjects that bored me but I didn't want to seem rude so I said nothing. Their garage was a converted dance studio where Inesita rehearsed daily and does to this day. She still performs occasionally, dancing in every number, accompanied by one or two guitarists and a singer. I guess she must be in her early eighties. She is very slight and still agile. She also plays classical piano and harpsichord, a very talented lady. Her mother was a concert pianist and her father an orchestra conductor, composer, violinist and archaeologist. Bob, an erudite gentleman had his own radio program dealing with classical and literary subjects, having interviewed more than ninety famous authors.

I have been at her home on many occasions and was always welcome to see her rehearse on Sundays with Stamen Wetzel, a guitarist. We have mutual friend Maruja in Madrid. Maruja has to be close to ninety but seems to get around to all the cultural and flamenco events, primarily in Madrid. Maruja is also a close friend of José Luis Torres. As of this writing I haven't seen José for eight or nine years. He's been quite ill and I haven't heard any news of his condition lately.

In Paris to our good fortune, the Lido's two musical directors agreed to compose special music for our act. There was no charge as they counted on the residuals for their profit. I believe one was René Leroux. We rehearsed with them various days. We stayed at an old hotel in Pigalle for about two or three dollars per day for two weeks. Our room was small with threadbare sheets and one small towel per week and overlooked a dirty interior atrium, permitting us to see into various rooms and for them to see into ours. On week ends many American G I's spent nights with the prostitutes that had rooms. Late one night and into the wee hours of the morning we heard the constant noisy flushing of a toilet on the floor above us. The following day I mentioned it to the Russian lady at the desk. She laughed and said that there was a ninety year old lady that lived on the floor above us. Many nights we could hear loud sex from many of the adjoining rooms through the paper thin walls. It was rather unnerving hearing that with Jill in the room as I was often tired and not in the mood.

We went to see my friend Claude Escarment and his partner Jean who were performing at the Lido with their act called The Marthys. We also had a friend, Norman Crider, from a small town in New Mexico who was a great baton twirler. He was twenty years old, gay and performed at many of the better venues including the famous Lido. Norman continually bought antiques to send back home. I imagine in later years they would be extremely valuable. He confided to us that he went to his first ballet class with women's ballet slippers that he practiced with at home. He was embarrassed when he found out in class that the male dancers didn't wear the same footwear as the ladies.

He would embarrass Jill when she would walk with him down a main boulevard in Paris and suddenly he would walk imitating a paralytic cripple. He was a nice educated young man and good company. I noticed lately that Norman was listed on Google for his notable ballet and baton twirling and was also a very successful antique dealer and expert, which didn't surprise me.

One of our favorite places to eat in Paris was a small restaurant called Haynes & Gabby at Rue Manuel 7 not far from our hotel. Leroy Hanes was a black ex GI-from Kentucky who stayed in Paris after the war with his French wife. The restaurant specialized in negro cooking from the south and was frequented by many notable black entertainers and other famous black personalities. Some of the patrons we saw while eating there were Lena Horne, Sammy Davis Jr., Ray Charles, Joe Louis, Cassius Clay and others.

We usually ordered the special, also the cheapest, with southern fried chicken that came with potatoes, vegetables and a few other items I can't recall. The price was four francs twenty centimes or exactly one dollar. They served three special piquant sauces depending on how spicy they were, Little Sister, Big Sister and Hot Mama.

Chapter XVI
Carmen & Pepe

We were contracted to be the closing act on a Spanish production called Luz al Personaje. The Stars were Pepe Blanco and Carmen Morrell. They were famous singers and movie stars in Spain during the forties and fifties. Carmen's forté was classical and Spanish ballads but she adapted beautifully with Pepe in his style of popular songs. The guitarist was Pepe Torregrosa, there was an eight girl ballet, Maestro Bernalt, his girlfriend Pili and seven or eight acts: flamenco dancers, los Rocios, comedians Los Fúnez, ventriloquist Julio Robledo, Fantasy dancers Los Thygora and possibly another number or two apart from the two stars and ourselves.

Pepe and Carmen were quite a pair, always fun except when Pepe was drinking. In downtown Valencia we were with them in their car and stopped beside a traffic cop momentarily when they prompted Jill to repeat what they said to the policeman through the window. The officer turned red and looked flabbergasted for a moment until he recognized Pepe and Carmen and realized it was a practical joke. Being with them was quite interesting, a unique, unforgettable experience.

The premiere was at Teatro Fuencarral in Madrid, May 14, 1960. The review in the ABC Madrid newspaper as follows (translated): "Special mention, well deserved, by an extraordinary, circus style number, Manley & Jyl, acrobats and antipodal balancers, who, to the sound of music, executed rhythmically, without losing any gracefulness or harmony of plasticity, dominated the most difficult routines of strength, timing and balance and, as all the cast and authors participating in the production, received much applause."

An interesting thing about Valencia at that time was that it was, and maybe still is, the only place in Spain permitted to have one of the three restaurants in the Plaza del Caudillo, Balanzat, Lauria and another restaurante whose name escapes me, alternate so that there was always one open around the clock. One of the problems that existed when I first went to Spain was not being able to eat or grocery shop when everything was closed due to their limited open hours. If you were hungry at night you stayed hungry if you didn't have access to food. Hours for breakfast were six to ten, lunch two to four and supper from eight to midnight. Now there are cafeterias and probably more options.

The first time we performed in Valencia was during their yearly major pageant of Fallas. We knew that we probably wouldn't be able to find a vacancy downtown and if we did, it would be noisy till the wee hours. We drove six kilometers south along the coast to a place called Los Corales. There were a few small rental cabins and a small restaurant. It was a warm, romantic summer night with a full moon and light breeze. For supper, that we ate sitting on our front steps, and we ate mero (grouper) for the first time. A real treat. Another time in our Valencia hotel room we had a few sleepless nights in our room adjoining the room of Rafael Farina and his wife, he a famous singer of fandangos. Both were gypsies and quarreled throughout the night.

El "Pive," was a large jovial Argentine musician working with our show's band. He and his wife would go with Jill and me on picnics at the beach near Valencia. They were older than both of us, not a good looking couple but charming, lovely people and marvelous company. They always brought their hierba mate, calabaza and bombilla (herb tea, gourd and filter straw) to sip and enough food for a nice asada, the typical Argentine grilled meats and sausages.

We sometimes traveled in the same car with Pepe, Carmen and the chauffeur but on the long hauls Jill and I drove our Peugeot station wagon. For the year that we were with them we performed in almost every capital, city, town, village and corral in the country. Often we repeated venues. Counting my other travels and the years I did courier runs, I feel that I knew Spain more than 99% of it's inhabitants.

Our cast sailed from Alcudia, Mallorca, to perform on the island of Menorca. The two venues were Majón, the capital and Ciudadela. It was a choppy sea and almost everyone was on deck seasick. Jill seems to have no problems with motion sickness and ordered a sobreasada, a spicy sausage sandwich. The waiter who was already under the weather turned green and quickly joined the others hanging over the railings. I'm always envious of those who are unaffected by motion sickness.

A scary moment, diving on the island of Menorca in shallow water, not far from shore, I heard a splashing noise and imagined being attacked by sharks or other denizens of the deep, only to see three or four pair of webbed duck's feet passing by.

Living and working in Spain gave me the advantage of attending an international physical therapy conference and an international conference of physical medicine and rehabilitation in the early sixties, the first on Montjuic and the other in Las Atarazanas, both in Barcelona. Both were very elegant, lasting three days each. I do recall, at the latter, being seated at a table with six female physiatrists. One of the entrees was lobster, which they did not care for. I gorged myself with as many as I could eat. Las Atarazanas was an impressive, castle like nave with actual different sail rigged ships and galleons of yore on display. During the dinner we were entertained by a group of "Gaiteros" from northern Spain playing their bagpipes. An Asturian waiter dispensed apple cider from a large leather botin, from which the server squirted a jet of the cider while standing on a table, filling the glasses below at a distance of five or six feet, without spilling a drop.

Montjuic is a large hill on the outskirts of Barcelona rising to approximately 600 feet in elevation and composed of a large park like area with various forms of family entertainment, an old castle along with sport and convention facilities.

We worked through much of Europe, almost always traveling in our Peugeöt 403 station wagon. In Barcelona we stayed at Residencia El Abrevadero, Calle Vila y Vilá, 79 in the neighborhood El Paralelo where many of the popular theaters and amusements were located. The small hotel and adjoining restaurant was owned and operated by members of a Catalan family. Many show people stayed there. The restaurant was known for its classic Catalan cuisine and the customers were mainly locals and their families. The owner and chef was Atenas, a large, robust man in his fifties. When Jill and I ordered shrimp they asked us why we only ate the meat of the tails, finally convincing us to try chewing and sucking the flavor from the thorax and spitting out the remaining shell fragments. From that time on we both preferred the thoraxes, where all the flavor is, more than the tails. Another Catalan specialty which I enjoyed and think about now and then is "Butifarra de Vich con monchetas blancs," which is a pork sausage with white beans.

The night desk clerk was an old gentleman with thick horned-rimmed glasses. Everyone called him the professor. He was often dozing and actually sleeping in his chair if he wasn't reading. We arrived very late one night and parked our new Peugeot station wagon directly in front of the hotel where it was clearly visible from the front desk where the professor was on duty that night. The next morning our two large wardrobe trunks and everything we used in our act was gone. I was barely able to maneuver the trunks into the limited space and imagine the thieves couldn't have removed them easily. We reported the theft to the police but it was futile. We lost all of our clothes, costumes, music, table, recorder and who knows what else was missing. It was a nightmare, devastating to say the least. I find it strange that I am unable to remember any of the details of how we ever managed to resolve the situation and carry on performing. If things weren't so cheap in Spain, I don't know how we could have managed to replace our loss.

– – – – – –

Marilda and Manna were a middle aged Brazilian couple who had a band, Samba Blue, composed of young Brazilian boys. I don't believe anyone can beat the Brazilians as sociable, happy, fun loving people. We performed on the same bill and became good friends. I kept in touch with them for years after they left show business as they went back and forth between their home in Brazil and Naples, Florida, where they worked for years as an au pair. Eventually we lost contact and since they were older it's probable that they passed away. We miss them and I regret that we didn't get together through the years.

We had a contract for two of the large hotels for the Oberoi chain in India, one in New Delhi and the other in Calcutta. Unfortunately due to a financial crisis in India, the contract was canceled.

— — — — — —

I had a good friend, George Gonzalez, born in Spain but who, after serving in the US armed forces, became an American citizen. George lived near Madrid with his wife from Luxembourg. They had a large German Shepherd named Kaiser. Jill and I would drive out to visit them fairly often. I gave Jill her first ski lessons in their back yard. Being a trained dancer she learned rapidly.

George Gonzalez was visiting us at the Hotel Sace in Madrid. I mentioned that we had some time off. Jill and I were talking about going to Formentera but never seemed to get around to it. George commented that I spoke frequently about going to check out the island and since Jill and I had the time, it might be a good idea to take advantage of the opportunity. We didn't leave then but soon after we were in Barcelona with a few days to spare before our next contract in Belgium before leaving for the island. I don't remember if we took the ship, eight hours overnight or the plane to Ibiza and from there a boat to Formentera.

Jill, I and the children were leaving Formentera returning to California. Our flight arrived behind schedule at Heathrow Airport. We were afraid we would miss our connecting flight. Before landing, there was an announcement over the loudspeaker "Will the Kiefer family please deplane first." We were surprised to find a limo at the foot of the steps waiting to whisk us to TWA for our stateside flight. We were thankful for the kind considerate service. We were traveling economy class with no idea that we would be able to catch our plane for the final leg of our flight. I doubt if this type of service would happen these days except for some VIP.

Chapter XVII
Formentera

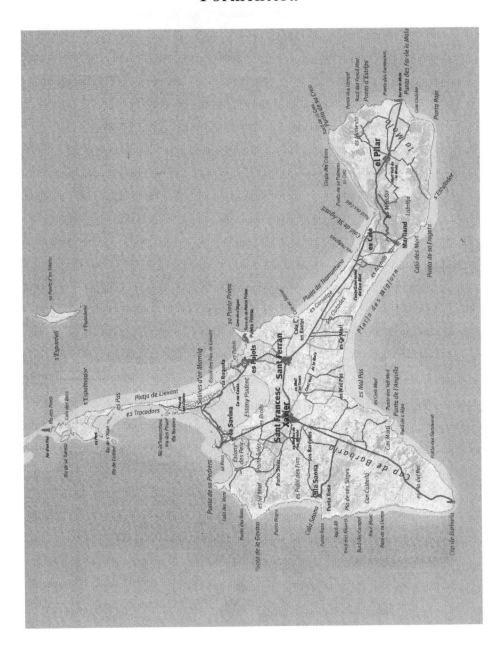

It was a miserable cold and rainy day. The boat was equipped with a small diesel engine and could seat six to eight people. The pilot and only passenger, aside from us, was Louise Gardener, an American who lived with her American husband Bob and their three children on the island. The rough, rainy crossing took almost two hours and the fare was twenty cents US each. The fare one way now varies between five euros for local residents and thirty euros for non-residents.

It was a very disappointing sight arriving at the Formentera port of La Sabina, a dreary, desolate, rocky landscape, a few small buildings, a small old bus, waiting for our boat to arrive. The driver in a shaggy overcoat, collar pulled up, hat pulled over his eyes against the drizzle, an unlit cigarette hanging from his mouth was standing at the side of the bus by a nearby lone scraggly, dead or dying palm tree. We drove uphill to San Francisco Xavier, the largest town and capital on the island, consisting of a half dozen small one and two story buildings. There was only one inn, Fonda Campillo. The family was very friendly and hospitable and invited us to eat supper with them. I can only recall the main dish of rice with "tordos," small birds abundant in Spain. Sr. Campillo was originally from the province of Murcia.

We were both tired and Jill had just come down with the flu. Before going to our room I asked if they had hot water bottles to take the chill out of the lumpy, damp cotton mattress. They gave us six empty cognac bottles filled with hot water that were clinking against one another in the bed. The bedroom was on the second floor and the outhouse was outside at the back of the building. The following morning was glorious, warm and sunny and everything that was ugly the day before was magically transformed to the vision of the island that I had always imagined. I believe that was the day I first fell in love with Formentera. Even Jill felt better and both of our spirits were lifted once again. As we had a contract coming up in Belgium our intention was to spend only a week in Formentera but we canceled the contract and stayed a glorious three weeks before having to return to the mainland to continue working and clearing up matters in Madrid for our future move to the island.

I gave up my apartment in Madrid when we began to travel. When Jill and I were in Madrid between contracts we stayed at Hotel Sace where we met Bert Schwab, Paul Lukas and his Dutch wife Anna, Norma from England and a few others. Bert worked for an airline in California and lived in Palos Verdes just a few miles from our house in San Pedro. Paul was a well known actor having made many films, one of the most notable was Watch on the Rhine that earned him an Academy Award as best actor. They had American friends, ex-airmen from General Chennault's Flying Tigers who settled in Son Vida, a new upscale complex on the outskirts of Palma de Mallorca.

The island of Formentera appears as a small dot on the map at 38.5 degrees north latitude and 1.47 degrees east longitude. It is separated from the larger island of Ibiza by a distance of eleven miles through the strait of Es Freus. The Balearic archipelago consists of the largest and main island of Mallorca, Palma being the capital and another smaller island, Menorca, its capital, Mahon. Both Formentera and Ibiza are also referred to as the Pitiusas, from the Greek, Islands of Pine. They are approximately 100 miles east of the Spanish Peninsula and about the same distance from Mallorca to the north and 130 miles south to the North African coast. In my earlier years in Spain, I was surprised that many Spaniards were unaware of Formentera's existence. Some confused it with Cape Formentor on Mallorca.

Before the influx of tourism the island's main source of income was salt, the only product that was exported and the major source of employment. There is a very extensive system of salt flats on the northeastern part of the island that still produces salt.

I inquired about buying land and was directed to Antonio Tur, the telegrapher. He accompanied me all over the island. We went on foot and by bike almost daily for two weeks. I covered the complete 42 mile long coastline and many of the other areas that I was interested in more than once. There are many coves, some almost inaccessible except by boat. The island is twenty five kilometers (14 miles) long and from one to eight kilometers wide and rises the last five or six kilometers at the southern part to an elevation of two hundred meters. That part of the island is called the Mola, flat on top surrounded by high cliffs with a lighthouse at the southern tip. The other southern tip to the west, separated by the beach of Mitjorn, is the Cap de Berbería. Some of the old timers claim that on an exceptionally clear day one can see the snow capped Atlas mountains of North Africa from the lighthouse. These peaks are two hundred miles distant. There are six strategically placed Moorish watchtowers on the island remaining from the eight century Moorish occupation of most of Spain.

I finally purchased six acres of cliff-side land for five thousand dollars with a private contract with Francisco Ferrer Marí, our nearest neighbor, who lived three hundred meters from us. He was a barber but as almost all Formenterans, farmed, hunted, and fished. It was a self-subsistence way of life. Francisco was a slight man extremely humped and bent over. Years later, even at his advanced age, he had a surprisingly successful surgery which miraculously corrected his spine. As a physical therapist I was amazed that he was able to walk erect after so many years of deformity.

After securing permission to build a one room abode, I contacted a few contractors on the island who were involved in building and decided on hiring Joan Mayans. His foreman, Joan Cordeta was a tall, gangly man, very strong and ingenious. Jill was unable to catch a small mouse in the house but Joan was very quick and scooped it up in a split second. Eventually during the seven year period to finish the house we used three or four different local contractors and laborers.

Construction methods in those days were limited as were many of the more modern techniques and materials. I had the choice of cement block or natural stone and chose the latter. Our land was almost all rock so we had the material at hand although block was faster and cheaper due to less labor involved. Our walls were two feet thick, parts of our roof were flat and the majority of the roof was slanted tiles and all the floors and bathroom walls tiled. There is a bathroom upstairs with a regular bathtub, rarely used, as water has to be conserved, another with a shower downstairs and an outdoor shower in the back patio. Windows were made by the carpenter, the frames all wood with glass panes, exterior slatted wooden shutters, solid wood panel inside shutters and solid wood exterior doors. Our house is 2400 square feet not including the two enclosed outdoor patios. We used butane for light and cooking and water from our underground cisterns. I took it upon myself to gather a few tons of rocks before starting, thinking that would save some time and money. When the workers arrived they said that surface rock was no good for building as it was exposed to the elements and partially deteriorated. We ended up using these undesirable rocks for a low wall adjoining the house but not connected to the structure. I worked with the workers every day from dawn till dusk, six days a week, twelve hours per day with two hours for lunch. I was busy mixing and supplying cement and concrete on a flat rock for two to four masons. We had no mixer, all was done manually. It was hard supplying and keeping up with two or three masons with enough cement or concrete. My hands and feet were blistered and cracked.

One day while working with the builders Jill and the children were at the beach. I received an important letter that I wanted to show Jill. I hesitated to leave the workers but biked to the beach and while we were distracted with the letter we noticed no sign of Linda, who was four at the time. I spotted her limp body, face up with a vacant stare in her eyes, in three or four feet of water. When I got her to shore she began coughing. An unknown lady rushed up trying to wrestle Linda from my hands, wanting to start giving her some sort of artificial respiration until I thanked her and said that our daughter was OK.

During the hour I wasn't at the house they were to put up the supporting wall partition between the kitchen and the living room with a large opening that I specified for a bar. I returned only to see a small opening about two by two feet which is common for passing trays, plates, etc. from one room to another. They had to tear down most of the wall to enlarge the opening to eight feet long by three feet in height as I previously specified. The lesson I learned, unless you have detailed blueprints and the the foreman has an understanding of what's to be done, always be around when someone is doing work for you.

Years later when we started to add to the house which we did over a period of seven years due to having to leave to fulfill our contracts and save money for continuing the construction. Eventually we had one of the larger homes on the island at the time.

The only tools we had for digging the cisterns were hand chisels, sledge hammers and dynamite. It was solid rock. The foreman said they didn't even find one fissure or crack consequently they had to use a lot of dynamite. It took weeks of constant blasting until they could cover the whole interior with a coating of cement and a special sealer that was made from a red earth found on the island. Our property is solid rock and we could feel the strong vibrations of every explosion. We had two large underground cisterns with a capacity totaling 36 tons of rainwater from our roof and the two large patios and a stone walk-way around the house. Eventually we acquired electricity and an electric pump as these became available.

Jill and I drew up our own plans from start to finish. I'm sure we also had input from friends. The final plans, filed with the municipality, had to be drawn and submitted by the local architect for approval and registration.

When our section of the island was being electrified we finally decided to have it installed. From the junction box on the road at the foot of our land there is a distance of more than three hundred feet. They would have had to put up two cement pole-like towers for the cable. We opted to have the conduit and cable buried underground which cost seven thousand dollars to go through the solid rock but we didn't want anything to spoil the natural beauty of the property.

When I purchased the land it was quite barren except for three stone pine on the western edge of the property, some scrub sabina trees and lots of rosemary bushes. One reason that the land was barren was due to the sheep and goats that the neighboring locals would take wherever they pleased. Anything green disappeared. Most of the neighbors weren't happy when we put up barbed wire fencing all around except on the north which had a high stone wall from the road to the cliffs. I bought sixty, five foot fence posts of sabina from a farmer on the Cap de Berbería. He laboriously peeled off all the bark and delivered them seven miles in his mule drawn wagon for fifteen pesetas each, the equivalent of twenty five to thirty cents each.

Gary Neff, a retired lieutenant and alcoholic friend worked all day with me in the hot summer sun with pick, shovel and rock hammer to make deep and large enough holes in the rock to set the posts in concrete. We then drilled holes in the tough Sabina posts and pounded in galvanized staples over the four wire strands of barbed wire totaling seven hundred linear feet.

Jill bought a chicken from a farmer in Cala Mitjorn. I don't recall how Gary and Nanda, his Dutch girl friend, got involved but between all of us there was no way, in spite of baking, boiling, frying and roasting, that we could cook that chicken to make it tender enough to eat.

Antonio Guasch, our caretaker, neighbor and friend, knew that I would like trees on my property. During the winter he would gather pine cones and take out the seeds which he stored in bottles, a labor intensive, time consuming task. When it looked as if it might rain he would scatter the seeds in the areas where he thought they might have a chance of survival. Being all rock with few fissures and cracks, there was no way to actually plant trees. He did this for a period of many years. Usually the mice, lizards or birds would get the seeds or they would dry up and the winds carry them away. A few started growing but with the lack of soil and the lack of water most died. Little by little through the years some took hold and were able to survive. Pine roots have the capacity to slowly dissolve rock and often are able to thrive. We now have a heavily wooded area with a few hundred good sized pine trees that are so dense that it's difficult to penetrate the area. We also have a group of tamarisk trees near our cesspool and a eucalyptus near our compost pile both which I planted from neighbor Guasch's cuttings.

Jill's sister, Joy, and Basil, her husband, wanted to invest in helping us build two chalets on the other side of our property. When they came to visit again Bas smuggled 7,000 pound sterling notes in his boots and we had one chalet built but due to lack of funds only the foundation and the cesspool were excavated for the second chalet. This also was through sold rock and required jackhammers and dynamite. Pine trees and bushes eventually sprung up in the excavations intended for the proposed chalet and bordered by the remaining piles of rock.

I noticed in the hole for the unfinished cesspool, in one corner there was a tiny piñon pine growing in the solid rock. The pine on our island are Mediterranean stone pine not the usual Christmas tree or spruce shape. There are few piñon pine on the island and I was thrilled to have one on the property. The pit area is one meter by one and a half meters by one meter deep. Now and then I would take a look to see how it was doing when traipsing around my grounds. I began to water and deposit our human fertilizer and it slowly grew. I had doubts that it would live but it was over two meters high with small cones the last time I saw it. I have always taken pleasure in planting and nurturing trees. My daughter and son-in-law visit the island once a year and at my request take photos of the piñon pine and other features on the property that I like to keep track of.

Toni Guasch knew I wanted to plant a lemon tree. He asked me if I would like him to buy a lemon tree from a horticulturist he knew in Ibiza who he claimed had the best trees and would pick a special one for him. A few days later he appeared with this small Lisbon lemon tree. It was and is today, about forty five years later, a prolific producer of lemons. I planted it in a protected corner of our rear patio. On our windy, salt air coast it is very difficult and iffy growing anything. After various storms with gale force winds and salt spray that may last for days there were times that we were certain that the tree with all its leaves blown off and the tree looking dry and brown, was dead or dying but it always came back and flourished. It never grew more than seven feet tall and about the same width. It still bears a good crop on lemons almost all year long.

We thought of different names for the property and were informed that the locals called it Ca'n Manley and no matter who eventually owned that property, to the locals it would always be referred to that way.

As the island became more developed and tourism increased, City Hall zoned areas for urbanization and various zones for protection of the various species of flora and fauna and the areas of natural beauty called green zones. We are fortunate to have all our property within a green zone. Cutting any trees, taking stone or making any amplification or modification in the zone is strictly prohibited and enforced. No exterior additions or changes are permitted on any of the houses or any other existing structures in the zone.

I noticed some small century plants growing along the sandy roadside near Es Caló. I gathered a dozen or so to plant on our land. They eventually grew larger and disseminated throughout the property. I also brought a small arm of a night blooming cereus cactus in a shoe box on one of my first trips back from the states. I was lucky that customs didn't check. There was a small pocket of earth in our rear patio where I dug a hole and planted the cactus along with the entrails of fish that I speared. It grew fairly rapidly and was a thing to behold, especially at night in the season when the large white flowers bloomed. I never before witnessed hundreds of honeybees at the cactus at night. I was unaware that bees even leave their hives at night.

Toni's son, also named Toni, Invited me to go out one night to accompany him to catch bees from a swarm in a nearby tree. I stood a distance away. He knew that I wanted a beehive. He surprised me with a hive he made for me which I put in one of my trees with the swarm he captured. I believe it was too close to the coast and eventually the bees either died or disappeared.

Entering our one room house late one night my flashlight revealed a huge black rat sitting on our bed staring at us defiantly. It had eaten a hole through the nylon screen. Jill ordered me to get rid of it but I wasn't about to confront a cornered rat. I went to the garage to get my spear gun and when I returned I was relieved to see the rat jump out of the window and into the night. Fortunately we seldom saw them. They probably only venture out at night. The upper caves and crevices may be occupied by large black rats like the one that entered our room.

Two animals that are unique on our island and Ibiza are a squirrel-like rat with a long white bristly tail that chirps at night and an Ibicencan or Podenca hound with humanoid eyes, pink or flesh colored nose and similar to a greyhound in body. They are very intelligent and almost all the locals have one of more. They are primarily used for rabbit hunting. The rabbit hunters had a habit of leaving a rabbit or two hanging from the door knob as a courtesy for getting rabbits on our property. It is said that the origin of these dogs is Phoenician, undoubtedly from foreign ships that touched these islands centuries ago. We also have countless small lizards, mostly green, and geckos in the darker, moist places. Strangely enough, with my hearing deficit, I could hear the tiny-like, suction foot pads of a little gecko climbing up the glass surfaces during the night, or was it only my imagination?

We started to put our dirty dishes in the patio so the lizards would clean them, after which we washed them. David our youngest when he was about three or four was sitting naked in the patio when suddenly we heard a scream. A lizard had nipped the end of his penis. They have no teeth and don't draw blood. They seem to have an affinity for the color red. They'll even nip at finger and toenails with red polish. They can jump high in the air to catch insects but when food is plentiful, they don't bother

Throughout the years we had two other temporary additions to our family. About a year after Jill and the children returned from Formentera in 1981 to join me in San Pedro Jill was offered a six month old black curly haired bitch from someone in our local supermarket. She named it Suzy. It looked like a Portuguese Water Dog but I'm certain it was a mix, maybe with some poodle. If any stranger came to the house she would be at the full length glass windows, barking, snarling, baring her fangs and with her wide eyes glaring with a menacing look. She would cower if they came in face to face - - all show and no go.

After our divorce she kept Suzy and took her to England and later to Scotland where she lived in the countryside for a few years before returning to our house on Formentera to live. When Suzy got old she must have gone off the cliff or wandered off and was not seen since.

Shanti was one of a litter of pups from someone on the island. Jill liked one that was quiet and docile but the owner said "No, this one is for you" and picked a rowdy bitch. She was smart in taking the advice as the dog turned out to be a great companion for the family, a good watch dog and protector. Although Jill never formally trained any of her dogs they all obeyed and were house broken. I have no idea what breed mix this one was was but am convinced she had some Podenco (Ibician hound) but was sturdier and larger. It was an ideal dog. Jill always would walk with Shanti, usually twice a day every day for a few miles over the rocky terrain along the cliffs.

Shanti died of old age and our son Yale made a grave-site ten feet from the side of the house with stone markers and a head stone that he engraved. I don't think Jill is interested in another dog because of the sadness when the dog is gone. I'm sure most pet owners share those feelings upon the death or disappearance of a pet of many years.

Aaron and Karen were a young American couple, who had just arrived from Kampala, Kenya with their large but docile female Doberman. They wanted to go out for a few days and asked if we would watch the dog. We thought it was great to have this large watch dog although there wasn't much around our area except for a few distant neighbors farms. When it was dark we opened the door for the dog to go out but it promptly hid under the bed. Finally when we pushed it out it circled our property as fast as it could run and immediately came in and hid under the bed again. A small dog would have probably been less fearful and a better watchdog.

My parcel runs about 110 meters from one boundary to the other along sheer cliffs for a distance of 120 meters and compromises a total of 23.000 square meters or six acres. During the first years with the three tots we instructed them not to go near these dangerous rocky cliffs and ledges. They were very obedient and never wandered but as the children matured they were able to scurry down the almost vertical 150 foot cliff to the hidden cove in the rocks below.

Our cove was all rock. Two meters out in the water the rock gives way to a white sand bottom. Along the waters edge along the cliff it is ten to fifteen meters deep. There are many caves and underwater crevices for fish to hide or take cover when threatened. All our diving is free diving using a face mask, snorkel and fins. Diving along the cliff wall underwater suddenly my mask and snorkel were yanked off my head. For a moment I couldn't imagine what happened but soon realized a small octopus was the culprit and it paid the price by eventually ending up in our stomachs.

I cemented large eye bolts in the rock on the pathway down the steep escarpment to anchor a rope along the more dangerous places. The children used this method a few times before disregarding it completely. I sometimes would take them to help me locate fish and octopus. Their eyesight was keener than mine. I told them to look for any movement of the octopus as they blend with their surroundings and are well camouflaged. After spearing I would bite the the octopus behind the eyes to immobilize them to avoid their thrashing tentacles and bring them to the surface. Once out of the water, the method taught me by local fishermen was to invert the animal's cape or hood, remove the organs and beat it against the rocks for tenderizing. We discovered a method of preparing octopus by steaming it for ten to fifteen minutes which made it easy to slide off the grayish mucous membrane exposing the pink flesh which we then cut into small pieces and later cooked with the "sofrito," the sauteed veggies. Normally octopus can be quite chewy and even tough but this turned out very tender.

When there were bad storms there were occasions when small cargo ships and large commercial fishing vessels would seek shelter in the lee of the cliffs. On one occasion there was a Spanish submarine which we all ran out to watch. The visibility in the water is approximately 50 to 70 feet unless the water is riled by bad weather. Between Mitjorn and Cap de Berberia, a modern Italian commercial fishing boat sank during a storm. We would climb down the cliff to salvage items until the authorities had the local

Guardia Civil stop anyone from approaching. I believe it was later salvaged by the owners.

During those early years on the island there was only one doctor, José Peris, originally from the province of Valencia on the mainland. He was a charming homosexual gentleman. He would visit us socially now and then and taught Jill how to make the best paella and taught me many things about lemon and citrus trees. I think he was more knowledgeable in those areas than in medicine. He had a small restaurant near the beach at Pujols called Pinatar.

During good weather Jill frequently made paella over a fire on our land, before Linda and John on one of their visits built a barbecue in the large back patio. Jill learned well from doctor José Peris. I would gather dead rosemary branches and Jill would instruct me when to dampen and when to increase the flames. It is an art to make a good paella. We would use all fresh, whole raw shrimp, octopus, cuttlefish or squid, some chicken, rabbit, pork, black mussels, clams, peas, saffron, a special kind of rice, garlic, olive oil and probably a few other ingredients I can't think of at the moment. Many of our friends have asked Jill how but never seemed to get the same results. Preparing paella the old fashioned method was an intricate procedure but the results were well worth the effort. I don't think I've ever tasted better paella then Jill made.

Paella originated in the province of Valencia and has become a favorite of Spanish cuisine and throughout much of the world as well. It's important to use whole, fresh crustaceans to give the desired flavor as much of the flavor comes from the organs in the thorax.

In one of the rock promontories bordering our cove there is a small entrance to a cave a few meters above the water that was used many years ago for stashing smuggled cigarettes and possibly other contraband mostly from North Africa. The cave was five feet high, six feet wide and eight feet long carved by hand out of solid rock using picks. The walls, ceiling and floor are completely covered with the gouge marks. The small entrance was not noticeable except for a few of the neighbors. few knew of it's existence. All along and all down the cliffs are caves and indentations from small to large caverns.

I borrowed a small rowboat from my friend Pat Pringle, an Englishman who, with his Swedish-American wife Ingrid and two children, lived in a small old farm house. I anchored the boat in the middle of our cove with a rope from the bow and one from the stern each to opposite sides of the cove. A knocking sound woke me after midnight. Half asleep I realized it was probably the boat against the rocks as a strong wind had come up suddenly. I rushed out of the house in my pajamas and barefoot running across the rocky thirty meters and then down the perilous cliffs in total darkness. In my haste I forgot to take a flashlight and there were no moon or stars. The boat was already on the rocks but I was able to drag it higher in the cove where it was protected from the wind and the waves. I must have got there soon after it came loose and already on the rocky shore, as there were only some minor nicks and scratches.

My favorite spot for spearfishing was just around the bend in our cove. There was a wide, shallow cave three or four meters in length at a depth of ten meters but the mouth was less than a foot high so one couldn't enter and could spear only from the entrance. Infrequently, I would encounter grouper but many other species were almost always present. Groupers are not migratory so once taken, their cave may not harbor another grouper for some time.

I spied a rubber bucket on the sandy bottom 18 meters deep. That was about my free diving depth limit. I hyperventilated and dove. I grabbed the handle of the bucket and stupidly tried to get it to the surface not realizing that it would act as a sea anchor. I had to let it drop to the bottom, surface, regain my wind and dive again but this time bringing it up inverted to minimize drag. When I finally surfaced both my hamstrings cramped. Fortunately I was only about forty meters from the cliff and made it back, swimming painfully, towing the bucket with two cramped hamstrings.

When the sea was calm I would dive along the cliffs to Punta Prima. One afternoon rounding the punta I spied what I believe was a tuna. It appeared to be six to seven feet in length and big bodied. I tried to follow it and would have shot it with my spear gun but it slowly disappeared in the distance. I shook with excitement afterward. If I could have speared it, no doubt I would have lost my spear and maybe the gun also but I would have liked to have taken the chance. With a large fish, unless one hits a vital spot, chances are one wouldn't be able to land it.

Cala Embasté is a mile south along the cliff from our property and has easy access to the water. They are not cliffs but rather a gradual incline to the sea. I had just entered the water when I realized that I had forgotten my knife and immediately returned ashore. A few of the people nearby asked why I came out. When I replied that I'd forgotten my knife, I detected a faint sign of disapproval on their faces and the remark, "Don't worry, there is no shark problem here." I didn't reply. Divers and especially free diving spearfishermen, habitually carry a knife usually strapped to the leg. The main purpose is, if necessary, to cut any lines that might entangle and endanger the diver aside from being a useful tool for various applications. When diving around rocky outcrops and caves the nylon line holding your float attached to your weight belt could snag and prevent your surfacing. If you can't submerge again due to the lack of air to free the line there's no way you can free it without cutting. It's almost impossible to break no matter how hard you pull..

Due to the lack of local workers during the time of our construction there was an influx of construction workers, laborers and others from the Spanish mainland, mostly from the poorer areas of Andalucia and other southern areas. Consequently minor problems and clashes between the islanders and the Spaniards from the peninsula arose. Theft was practically nil before the influx of the workers from the peninsula. Many were uneducated and crude especially in the treatment of the island women. As the years went by and they intermingled and integrated, matters smoothed out and the local resentment of the outsiders grew less.

– – – – – –

My friend Howie Noodelman came over to visit us and installed a mahogany mantel over our fireplace and lined one whole wall of the living room with the same dark mahogany. We had to go by boat to Ibiza and buy a mahogany log imported from Africa, take it to a carpenter to have tongued and grooved, slats made and then haul it back by boat. It looked beautiful in contrast to the rock walls. Hearing scratching at night we discovered that there was a mouse or mice trapped in the wall. I assume they perished as the scratching ceased after a few days.

Howard was an avid reader and brought many books with him. At that time we only had the one bedroom and the garage that were habitable. Howie slept in the garage. He would light 10 to 12 candles to give him enough light to read before going to sleep.

– – – – – –

Many of the early years we spent on the island, I had my second hand Citroen two cylinder auto or my Peugeot station wagon. After I returned to the states and would return for visits, my transport was a bike. My oldest son Yale is the bike expert and any repairs I needed he would take care of.

Movies were shown in the church in San Fernando but the priests who ran the projector would do their own version of censorship in spite of the strict censorship of Spanish films for anything resembling or suggesting sex. They accomplished this by covering the lens whenever a kissing or other suggestive scene appeared. Consequently they were the only ones to see those scenes. It seems that now censorship is a relic of the past. In fact there is less censorship in Spain than in the US regarding sex.

The great majority of locals had farms and had their pig slaughtering ritual in the month of December inviting family, relatives and close friends to the one day festive and social affair. Usually only one large pig was slaughtered. The intestines were used for making the various types of sausages and other cuts cooked and served to all. The sausages and other other portions were saved for the family's use during the year. I always thought how great it would have been to have the ribs barbecued but they were boiled and rather tasteless. Our family attended a few of the neighbor's pig slaughtering parties. We had friends who've resided on the island many years longer than us who were never invited to their neighbors slaughtering and were envious that we were always invited. Jill didn't like to see the slaughter, blood-letting and rendering. I think the children were somewhat curious and aghast the first time but later unaffected by this fact of life practiced by many cultures.

On our early days on the island Jill went to the butcher who worked out of his house. It took a long time to cut the meat and when it was ready to be wrapped Jill was shocked to see it still quivering. At least we couldn't complain that it wasn't fresh. In our early years in Formentera, the early 60's, it was old Spain where one went to the butcher for meat, the baker for bread, the dairy for milk, the fish market for fish, etc. Now there are supermarkets and all the other modern amenities.

Supermercado Colmado Toni was our first mini supermarkets on the island. It wasn't very large and had limited varieties, nevertheless it was a welcome change. I'll always remember when he first imported avocados, which at the time were relatively unknown on the island. They were quite expensive compared to normal prices for avocados and they hadn't sold any for some time. The next time I went in I noticed that the avocados were ripe. When I asked Toni what he was going to do with them. He replied since they weren't selling that he would feed them to the pigs. I asked and he agreed sell me the ripe ones at fraction of the original price. Until the other shoppers got wise we ate avocados daily. We all loved avocados which were plentiful in California, so for us it was nothing new. I did promise the children that when we returned to San Pedro we could have avocados every day and I kept my promise and I still eat avocados daily.

A few years later a real supermarket, Syp, opened in San Francisco Javier. It was large market with a large variety of foods and drinks. Since many foreigners lived on and visited Formentera, Syp imported foods and drinks from other countries. There were almost always many shoppers and filled parking spaces. .To get a shopping cart, one put a euro in the slot and when finished slipped the cart back in the rack which released the coin.

Our three children attended school on the island at the three room schoolhouse in San Fernando. Their teacher was also the mayor. All schooling was in Castilian. They always walked together the one mile, rain or shine. Linda was punished, having to kneel in the corner on the cement floor a few times for talking in class. Yale graduated primary school with top honors at the head of his class. Later attending the only high school on the island in San Francisco Javier, having to walk or bike the two and a half miles each way.

I was driving David, Jill, her sister Joy to enroll David in the kindergarten. He seemed unhappy about the prospect of school and said in no uncertain terms, "I can't go to school, I don't know how to read," which we thought was quite amusing.

They always walked on the many narrow paths and old roads instead of the main roads to avoid the traffic. Our island did not have a good reputation for auto accidents. With the new prosperity from tourism many of the locals bought automobiles. Their lack of driving experience made our roads more dangerous. Foreign visitors during the tourist season added many new vehicles on the limited roads adding to the problem.

To not mention the famous Fonda Pepe in San Fernando would be an unpardonable omission of island life since the early '50's when the hippy element and young foreign artists, revolutionaries, etc. discovered this relatively untouched, primitive and very conservative culture. The islanders are very tolerant to what was considered obscene behavior of many of the new wave of young including some of the older foreigners.

Pepe and his sister Rosalia were very conservative, intelligent, simple country people but with good common sense. Maybe because of their tolerance this new unwashed element gravitated to this bar and restaurant. It was a tourist attraction for visitors and locals alike to view the odd and outrageous beings (people?) and their antics. It was also evident that drug use among these hippies was widespread. Eventually there were other bars on the island that had a following of what many of us living there considered undesirable. Whenever I returned to the island and even living on Formentera I made it a habit to say hello to my friends Pepe and Rosalia even though I rarely went into the bar. More information about Fonda Pepe and many of the people, places and events mentioned are on the internet and can be found on Google.

We invited Pepe's father, an old farmer, to eat with us in our home. Jill, my wife, said that he must have been awful hungry to have eaten the chicken bones. At the time she didn't realize in Spain and in many bars and restaurants alike it was customary to throw the bones, shells, etc. on the marble or wood floors or under the table only to be swept up later.

The early tourism to the island was mostly English and Scandinavian. As the German economy improved after the war a small group from Dusseldorf settled and began developing German tourism and real estate businesses on the island. I would often hear anti-Semitic remarks and comments which is not surprising since they many of them had been or were still Nazis.

I had banked at the Caja de Pensiones ever since it opened in May of 1959 at which time it was the only banking institution on the Island. Since all the employees were friends of mine on the soccer team and with my excellent banking history over a period of more than twenty years and with sizable amounts of money, I was favored and trusted . I could issue a check for thousands of dollars and get the cash immediately even though the bank policy was not to cash any foreign checks till the money was received by the bank. Later during one of my visits to the island, standing in line at the Caja de Pensiones (bank), I unobtrusively practiced some foot movements as we do in tango that I though were unnoticeable to others. My children were embarrassed and asked me to please refrain when they were present.

Chapter XVIII
Island People, Personalities & Friends

Formentera seemed to attract artists, hippies and other assorted characters. Americans Don and Louise Gardener and their children were rather infamous. He and his friend Jack Longini, another American, probably dealt in drugs. Don was a handyman and started a restaurant, La Tortuga, which was bought by a local after the Gardeners left the island.

Bella and Siuma Baram were well know Israeli artists who lived in an old typical island house on Formentera for many years. After they both died on the island an art museum dedicated to them and bearing their names was created on the main street in San Francisco Xavier, the island's capital.

Briefcase Hans was German or Austrian. He was not a tall man and rather stocky with short cropped, reddish-brown hair. When he went to Ibiza or dressed for any special occasion, he wore a black tuxedo, a Homburg hat, white gloves, fancy walking cane, a monocle and carried a black briefcase. He was a sight to behold on a small, rather primitive island.

Bob and Karen Isely were friends. He is an American ex-serviceman and Karen, his wife is German. They were frequent visitors to Formentera for many years but resided in Germany. Jill was perturbed with Bob at a get together in our patio to eat when he stirred the paella she was cooking for dinner in the patio. Jill was in the kitchen and Bob thought that it might need stirring.

Three priests had dubious reputations. The main priest in San Francisco Xavier was noted for having bottles of wine and liquor sent up to him in a bucket via pulley to the top of the old church in the plaza. The priest in San Fernando had the reputation of having fathered a half dozen illegitimate children with various women on the island. A new younger priest from the mainland, short, pudgy with thick lens glasses would sit at an outdoor cafe ogling the passing females through his newspaper while supposedly reading with two eye holes cut in the paper.

The following six couples were English: Bill and Sylvia Madders were possibly the longest foreign residents on the island and had one of the largest and most luxurious stone houses on the island on the most popular beach at Pujols. Sylvia started a restaurant, Sa Palmera, which she gave to the family that worked for her for many years when she became too old and could no longer do the work. Bill passed away many years before Sylvia, who died in her nineties, both on the island. They donated their house to the local fisherman's club and did many beneficial and charitable things for the island. They were loved by all. They were instrumental in getting together with the local officials to help oppose big money interests from outsiders wanting to build modern hotels and other complexes. The local council then passed a moratorium on large scale commercial building and other enterprises, which is still in effect prohibiting large commercial construction, even by the locals. After seeing what "progress" did to Ibiza and the other nearby islands most Formenterans were interested in preserving their more natural, tranquil life style rather than acquiring monetary wealth. Pat and Ingrid Pringle and children were also long term residents of the island. Pat was a writer. When the earpiece fell off of his eyeglasses he used a safety pin to attach it to the frame. I'm certain he enjoyed looking odd and attracting attention. Ingrid was Swedish, a large woman who breastfed her two children until each reached four years of age.

Frank Jackson and his wife Mary also resided many years on the island. He was a cabinet maker. He was on the frail side and I believe he had tuberculosis. He passed away and his wife Mary continued working as the librarian in San Francisco Xavier.

John and Helen Tunks and children were permanent residents from England. They were poor but worked hard, admirably succeeding in becoming well accepted and part of the island society.

Our closest neighbors and friends were the Dowse's, John and Mona. They were a few years older than us, John was a retired engineer and helped us with many things especially maintaining my Citroen by cannibalized car parts from the junked cars. After John died, Mona sold their property, occupying and taking care of our house and property in our absence.

Joyce and Bill Braden lived for a short period on the island. Joyce was English, a painter, and Bill, an American, was a technical writer and part time alcoholic or an alcoholic and part time technical writer. Joyce gave us a large four by eight foot composite abstract painting she did in the style of the Swiss painter, Klee, with a theme of the port and the old castle fortress of Ibiza and elements from the port of San Pedro. It has been hanging in our living room in San Pedro for more than thirty years.

Nigel and his local, or is it "loca" lady, Mercedes were both boozers and characters. These seemed to be common traits with many of the foreigners on the island.

Mario Prinz from Holland and his wife Ana Marie, a Jewish lady and concentration camp survivor, were residents of Formentera for quite a few years. Mario had a reputation of being somewhat crazy and weird. Their house was a large, block like building surrounded by a high wall. I would guess he was about fifty when he died. I don't know the circumstances of his death.

Xiquet and Margaret, his German wife, operate a restaurant and pension hotel in Pujols. They have invited us and vice versa a few times. I also went spearfishing with Xiquet who often, like many of the islanders, goes fishing in his boat. We've always enjoyed their company.

Bob was a tall, thin, soft spoken American gentleman whose profession I believe was a librarian. He had a tiny book store in San Fernando, adjoining my old clinic, where he loaned and sold from his amazing number and variety of mainly used books. One could find books on almost any subject and in many languages. Almost all the foreigners and locals alike patronized his establishment.

Eileen Corduroy was an English writer with two young children, living meagerly in a small rented room. On Christmas day we went to visit them. Eileen was upset. She had saved three thousand pesetas, approximately $80 US for presents for her children, but needed the money for food. I went to Fonda Pepe and asked Pepe for a loan of 3,000 pesetas. He said if I needed 10,000 that it was no problem. I loaned the 3,000 to Eileen and wasn't concerned if it was repaid or not. Since then she referred to me as el caballero rústico (the rustic chevalier). She later did pay me back.

One of the benefits of island living is that the locals soon determine who is trustworthy and a true friend. We would have been able to go to any one of the islanders who knew us for any favor including money had the need arisen.

I don't know if this is a practice in other places than Formentera and Ibiza, but if a lost object is encountered along any of the many roads and paths bordered by the low stone walls, locals will place said object on the wall in plain view for the owner unless they know and return it to the owner. They are inherently distrustful of turning it in to the police, the church or officials, many of whom were not originally from the islands; otherwise they may post a notice for the owner to identify and claim his property.

We were continually filling out forms for military permission (these islands are classified as a military zone under the jurisdiction of the Spanish government) and a hundred other forms necessary to acquire a legal deed or anything of an official nature. Being foreigners even complicated matters worse. We were constantly going through the myriad of official documents, payments and other bureaucratic red tape which seemed unending. In spite of constantly trying, it was thirty years later before we finally received our official deed to the property. Many foreigners who were there as long or longer than we were, never did get deeds and unfortunately without a deed the legality can pose big problems. There are gestorías, specialized agencies that do the official paperwork for a price. Using them is expensive and may still take a long time for results but they continue charging nevertheless. It's an exasperating time consuming task dealing with the Spanish government. It may be simpler now or at least, take less time. Now it is much simpler for members of the European Union.

Ca'n Manley, Formentera

Downstairs living room of our house in Formentera,

back row – Jill, me, Yale *front row* – Linda, John, David
Formentera 1997

Returning from one of the many trips I made to Ibiza for official and other matters, I arrived in Formentera on the boat on a dark winter night. It was pitch black with no moon or stars visible.

I didn't have my flashlight and walked the seven kilometers home stumbling much of the way. Most Formenterans dislike having to take the boat to Ibiza. I would only go when absolutely necessary and when possible, a common practice was having a friend who was going, do your errands. A friendly, convenient and reciprocal arrangement.

A common sight at the dock was older local women in their black Arabic-style cloaks and head covering carrying an empty bucket for the children they were taking on the boat to Ibiza. They would explain to the children how to use the bucket when they get sea-sick and vomit. In most instances the power of suggestion would take effect and the child would need the bucket.

Often the crossings were rough and our old faithful boat, the Joven Dolores, would rock and pitch. There have been crossings when I and others, took off our shoes in the event that we had to swim. Many of the local men were seamen and fishermen and most is-land men had boats. Years ago there was little opportunity on the island to make a living, dispersing many of the men to the far cor-ners of the globe. Their women and children would stay behind to do the chores. Eventually almost all returned to Formentera. With the passing years changes and modernization have made it pos-sible for more of the inhabitants to earn a living without leaving the island. The many vessels that now make the crossing between Formentera and Ibiza include large motor vessels and ships that can carry a hundred or more passengers along with large vehicles, including buses, heavy machinery and cargo. There is frequent service especially during the tourist season with rapid passenger boats, including double hulled hovercraft.

— — — — — —

I had two episodes of illness during some of my early years in the island when I was in my forties. One day I felt ill but the next day felt better and I spent many hours lying in the warm sun in my bathing suit. That night I was worse and for the next week I was bedridden. Jill wanted to contact doctor José but I had little confidence in his medical expertise and medication. I thought of taking antibiotics but foolishly thought that with time I would be OK. After eight days I was able to get out of bed and gained my strength back very slowly. For a period of months afterward I felt like I had iron bands around my chest restricting my breathing. I can only conclude the probability that I had pneumonia.

I don't recall how it started but my fatigue syndrome began around this time. I was extremely fatigued and exhausted. I spent a lot of time either lying or sitting. I had difficulty falling asleep nights and often could barely drag myself out of bed. I did not feel sick or have any pain or discomfort. I had a good appetite. I consulted with various physician specialists in Ibiza undergoing many lab tests that showed no abnormalities. All in all, no one seemed to have any idea of my malady. I seemed to recover slowly after a week or two. I would have exacerbations from time to time but as the years passed the episodes became less frequent and less severe. I'm convinced that this was viral. I still have recurrences lasting for a day or two. Resting a few days seems to abort a full blown attack. If I get too tired without much rest this often brings on an attack that may last much longer. Through the years I more or less know how to cope with this problem. This has been diagnosed when I returned to the states as chronic fatigue syndrome which seems to be a vague and questionable diagnosis of the medical profession.

— — — — — —

I spent many days throughout my years on Formentera at my favorite beach. This was a nude beach that was frequented by primarily Germans. During my early years on the island nudism was prohibited in Spain and often the Guardia Civil would enforce the law but through the years with increased pressure from German tourism primarily, it became more difficult for the authorities to control and since the Balearic Islands are dependent on tourism the officials became more lax and eventually tolerated the nudism.

I'm not certain if it is still illegal on the statutes but it continues to be widely practiced.

Busom Buddies – Formentera (Baleares), Spain

Woody Flo & me – Formentera (Baleares), Spain

I enjoyed the earthiness and naturalness of being among naked people. I met many lovely ladies there. It was a new odd feeling going completely nude and approaching a nude woman to get acquainted. At first at the nude beach I found it somewhat unnerving to approach a women that you didn't know, each of us with nothing to hide. After awhile one becomes accustomed. No one seemed bashful or timid and for the most part were receptive and friendly.

The island is interspersed with tiny coves, immense stretches of beach and low rocky to very high cliffs. The sand is more granular on the beaches of Mitjorn and finer and lighter on the other beaches. This seascape lends itself to nude bathing, which is becoming more prevalent to some degree even in the more populated beaches.

As the years pass, more Italians, French and locals come to the nude beach. I noticed that most of the Italian women and men wore thongs or bikinis. I believe that most nudists resent others who don't abide by our informal rule of being completely naked. My wife and the children never go to the nude beach.

My friends, Flo and Woody visited us on the island on three different occasions. Woody wasn't too keen about going nude but Flo reveled in that ambiance and would be half undressed in the car before we arrived at the beach. She loved to flaunt her sensuous body but commented that no one stares or even pays attention, they seem to notice you more when dressed than naked. Europe seems to be quite natural and relaxed with nudism compared to the Americas. An English couple, John and Susan frequently sat with us. Susan was getting dressed to leave, slowly and daintily putting on her all white undergarments: panties, bra, nylon hose and petticoat and head scarf. Woody and I couldn't keep our eyes off of her. We agreed that it was the most sensuous and sexy dress tease we ever witnessed and even Flo commented how erotic it was. I'm certain that a professional striptease wouldn't have been nearly as exciting. I am certain that it was unintentional and that Susan was completely unaware of the sensuous effect she was causing.

When one went to a cabaña or restaurant on the beach to eat they would don the bare essentials. What surprised me in later years at the beaches, many of the local youth were nude. Most of the older local islanders didn't go to the nude beaches. They may have stood nearby as looky loo's. There were many other beaches where people went nude along the long stretches of isolated sandy beaches interspersed with cliffs and coves, making available many different possibilities to go nude and also have privacy.

Of the many ladies I became friendly with, I was fortunate in meeting Bernadette from Belgium and Marion from Germany, both beautiful ladies who were also good Argentine tango dancers. We arranged one evening to go to the chalet of a German friend of theirs and dance tango, converse, eat and drink. There were eight German men and women and although they all spoke in German they would speak to me in English. Most educated Germans speak excellent English. The tile patio floor was damp from the evening dew which made it rather sticky for dancing. Not all the Germans are beautiful. Some of the middle aged "hausfraus" are quite heavy, not much of a turn-on at the nude beach. Many others, even older ones, keep themselves in lovely shape. It's not unusual that many of the German visitors that arrive in the summer with their northern European pallor spend most of the day sunning and end up looking like cooked lobsters. One would think they would end up in the hospital or at least stay out of the sun but surprisingly they're seen sunning the very next day. Most of the European visitors look slenderer, and in good shape compared to their American counterparts.

The sea is transparent, the almost white sands of the Balearic Islands invite going in the water. Some of the unsuspecting women suddenly scream without warning. Periodically there are tiny fish an inch long with sharp teeth that bite and nibble on any scratch, infection, scab or just plain skin.

A landmark restaurant is the Sa Palmera, on the beach at Pujols, founded by Sylvia Madders in the early 60's and taken over by her long time employees of the island, Jaime and his wife Lourdes upon Sylvia's retirement. Her death, was a great loss to the many of us who knew and loved her. Sa Palmera has an excellent reputation for food, price and service on the island. It's one of ours and many others' favorite eateries. My mother always ordered the filet of sole which overlapped both edges of the large plates on which it was served.

— — — — — —

On the 25th of May, 2007, on a Sunday morning, there was a knock on the studio door. I shouted "Adelante," expecting my son Yale (we primarily speak to one another in Castilian Spanish). I waited but there was no answer so I opened the door in my pajamas. An unknown man stood in the doorway and I invited him to come in and since I didn't know him we began conversing in Spanish. His name was Wilfried Wedehn, 70 years old, tall and athletic. He was German and spoke fluent English so we continued chatting in English. He was an excellent biker, skier and probably a lot more. We talked for a half hour. He talked about and we discussed many mutually interesting subjects. He retired years ago as a ship's captain on cargo vessels.

He has and continues to travel extensively throughout the world. We talked about and discussed many topics. We have a lot in common and I feel like we're kindred souls in spite of our brief encounter. I was hoping we'd cross path again in the future. It's was very unusual that anyone known or unknown to us would stop in without an invitation. He said he was walking along the cliffs observing the birds and nature and thought that I knew his sister Christine with whom he stayed on his various visits to Formentera. She has lived on Formentera for many years. I wanted to find out if I knew Christine. He described where she lived and I was under the impression that I knew her well years before. Later I went to the house he indicated and met his sister who was not the woman I knew.

Chapter XIX
Performances & Performers

Tito's night club in Palma de Mallorca was one of the most elegant clubs in the country, situated high above the ocean with an impressive view of the ocean and the illumination of the city lights when darkness set in. The stage was quite elevated and with the additional height of our table prop and with no roof and open to the sky, It must have been breathtaking for Jill if she would have looked down, but she knew better. She has to always fix her gaze on a point of reference for balance.

Sr. Serrats, the owner of the Emporium nightclub in Barcelona asked me to come to his office after our performance. He was sitting with three American GI's and wanted me to translate. They complained that their bar bill was very high. They had quite a few beers each aside from inviting some of the women present. I had to explain that as drinks were expensive in Spain when going to a nice club the average person nursed one drink for hours or for the full evening while they watched the show, danced etc.

While in Ciudadela, Menorca performing in an large old palace-like stone theater in our dressing room Jill was standing in front of a mirror putting on her facial makeup when I inadvertently pulled her chair away to put my foot on to tie my shoe, not realizing she was about to sit down. When she sat down and there was no chair she landed on her coccyx (tail bone) on the hard stone floor just moments before we were due to go on stage but she bravely endured the pain and as the trouper she was, went out and performed.

An experience returning to Spain from France during the winter. We bought quite a bit of French Camembert cheese to bring back. When we arrived at customs at the border and opened the window the customs agent held his nose and waived us on. Having the cheese in the car various days with the windows closed can really get raunchy, like a dozen pair of sweaty tennis socks and shoes.

After awhile one gets accustomed and doesn't notice but let someone who's just come in smelling that pungent and disagreeable odor can be overwhelming.

At the casinos in the French and Italian Rivieras, between shows, Jill wanted to try the slot machines and won small amounts of change which encouraged her to try her luck in other places. Much to her disappointment she finally realized that it was a losing proposition.

On the same trip driving along the Spanish Valencian coast in our Peugeot station wagon, night was falling and we were very tired from driving. We pulled off the road into a pine forest not far from the sea to sleep. Jill was changing and getting ready for bed when I heard someone outside and thought they were looking in our window. I went out and saw two men in the darkness who I confronted. I came on quite aggressively. They showed me their badges, they were plain clothes police. It was a little late for being nice on my part after practically accusing them of peeping toms and they reacted antagonistically. They finally accepted my rational explanation that seeing two unknown men in the dark of night in a deserted pine forest and my wife undressing in the van was a little disconcerting to say the least. I was worried for awhile but things worked out OK. Spain has many plainclothes police and if they desire they can make things difficult.

Sergio, Bob and Fritzie were an Italian dance trio. We were quite friendly with them. Sergio saw some of my photos of the Ten Commandments. He asked if he could borrow them. Being the naive American I loaned him the photos. I'm certain he used them for his publicity as we are similar in looks and from a distance they would probably suffice. Needless to say, I never saw them again. I was upset, having no way at the time of replacing them. Fortunately, as I mentioned before, years later I went to see the movie for the first time at a small movie theater in Golden, Colorado and was able to replace the pictures.

New Year's eve during our performance in O Coliseu in Lisbon, Portugal, Jill fell from quite high during our performance and hit her head. She was rushed by ambulance to the hospital emergency room, a busy place on New Year's eve. Later she related that all the doctors and attendants were constantly with her ignoring other patients with serious gunshot wounds and knife wounds. That's one of the perks that goes with the territory for gorgeous women. I'm sure that if I were the patient it would have been vastly different.

She still was hurting and undoubtedly apprehensive about the next performance but in spite of this she finished the next performance. I too was worried knowing that some of our routines could be dangerous and Jill had never done that sort of athletics before I trained her. Consequently I was always concerned and felt responsible.

We were about twelve different acts, mainly from Europe. To celebrate the new year we chose to have the whole group in our hotel, the Suizo Atlántico, as the rooms were very large. We bought two dozen bottles of champagne for the equivalent of eighty five cents a bottle for the twenty people. I'm not accustomed to drinking and drank six glasses as if they were water. I didn't realize that one should sip not gulp. Since that night I have never liked champagne.

Legal gold in Portugal is nineteen and a quarter carats versus the 18 carat standard. We walked along the street Rua do Ouro with its numerous gold shops where I bought three massive identical gold rings, one for my father, one for my brother, one for myself and a gold bracelet for my mother. I dropped my ring while dressing and being almost pure gold it was soft and flattened one of the corners. I never wear jewelry so it remained unused. Eventually both my father and brother told me that the rings were so big and heavy that neither of them wore their rings. Years later, my friend Howie sold the gold for me at a good price.

After our contract in O Coliseu in Lisbon we had a two week

contract in the Casino de Estoril. This was a very elegant, upscale establishment on the beautiful Portuguese coast. It is the largest casino in Europe and noted for stories about spies, other notorious characters and the James Bond movie, Casino Royale.

Jill and I, in our spare time during the day (our performances were at night), would often travel up and down the coast. In the charming coastal village of Cascais we were intrigued with a beautiful multi-colored woven woolen blanket in the display window of a small artisan shop. We made quite a few visits and enjoyed talking and haggling with the owner, finally we made the purchase on what we considered a good price. This blanket-tapestry still occupies our home in Formentera.

The years we were in the Iberian Peninsula, not many spoke English but now English spoken in almost any form of commerce. The Portuguese seem to have an advantage over Spanish speakers in being able to speak other languages with little accent, whereas this isn't true for Spanish speakers. Reading Portuguese is not a problem for the Spanish but speaking and understanding Portuguese is more difficult for the Spanish than Spanish is for the Portuguese.

THE MANLEY BROS.

Manley Brothers (with George Patten)

Manley & Jyl - Madrid

I have to admit that Jill was very brave to do some of the more risky stunts, there were falls and minor injuries along the way. For the routine of Manley & Jyl it was more of a problem for Jill as a dancer but less of a problem and danger for me as a handbalancer and gymnast. We contacted a Spanish choreographer from Madrid by the name of Diego Larrios who helped us develop an act with a theme and some comedy instead of a purely acrobatic number. Our rehearsals took place in the gym Moscardó and often while rehearsing many of the members would watch. It's doubtful they were looking at me.

I sent Vicente, my Cuban friend, a plane ticket to join us in our act as a trio. I thought that with his talent as a Latin dancer and his ingenuity we could have developed a novel and interesting trio. He went back to Cuba to see his father who was dying. We never heard from him nor did anyone else that we knew that might have known of his whereabouts. When I went back to Minneapolis in 2003 my ex-partner George Patten and I made many inquiries of people who were close to him, without success. We tried to contact Chiki Piazza, a lady he often danced with, but were informed she had advanced Alzheimer's and others had passed away. It is disturbing not knowing what happened to close   friends. I really missed him as did others.

— — — — — —

My left elbow became painful, undoubtedly due to the physical strain of the act and my exercises. I believe that my elbows were very vulnerable as they had both been injured when on a courier run a year or two earlier returning to Madrid from El Ferrol, a thirteen hour drive. I was dozing in the front seat when suddenly I was abruptly awakened when I heard the sound of gravel hitting the chassis. The driver evidently having dozed, suddenly awoke and slammed on the brakes. I braced myself with both hands against the cowling of the dashboard and had pain in both elbows for weeks afterward. The company's insurance paid all the medical bills.

So the driver wouldn't get in trouble we made up some excuse to relieve him of any responsibility, otherwise it would have probably meant his job. I always had good rapport with fellow workers and enjoyed their mutual companionship. Sometimes they took advantage of being away from home, staying out late and not getting enough rest after a long trip resulting in not being up to par to drive on the return trip.

It began to be very painful performing the various lifts with Jill and my own handbalancing and exercising. When it became worse I visited a few doctors with no success. I tried everything I knew including advise from others to no avail. After visits and treatments from other doctors with no results, my friend José Torres the instructor and coach from the gym, suggested contacting Doctor Felix Cabot Bois, a renowned Barcelona orthopedic surgeon and rheumatologist and the treating physician for two of the world top soccer teams Real Madrid and Futbol Club de Barcelona.

When we were in Barcelona we arranged an appointment with doctor Cabot. We were fortunate to have recommendations from the right people as his office manager said that he rarely took on clients off the street. His clientele consisted primarily of star athletes and of the elite. We tried various modalities without success. Finally he said we'd have to operate to remove the olecranon bursae bilaterally. The doctor ordered a general anesthetic but I opted for a local. Under the overhead surgical light surrounded by mirrors I could observe the procedure. The initial incision and final suturing of the skin were painful but otherwise I could only feel the painless movement of the cutting and scraping. Both arms were heavily bandaged from the wrists to the shoulders with the elbows flexed at a right angle.

The doctor ordered the nurse to give me a light lunch. I told him I was hungry and with only a local anesthetic there shouldn't be a problem. He relented and I was brought a regular full course lunch. A few hours later Jill came to visit. I told her I was starved in spite of having eaten two hours before and asked her to go out and get me two pepitas, steak sandwiches, which I proceeded to devour.

When Jill left a few hours later it was still warm and sunny in the late afternoon. I found my way to a flat roof on the second floor and began to do some arm waving exercises, stretching and flying or jumping squats. A few minutes later from a window across the way the nurses were shouting at me to stop and go to my room at once or they would report me to the doctor. I paid them no attention and continued my light workout. The doctor understood and told them that I was capable enough to regulate my own physical activities.

It was a while before Jill and I could resume performing our routines. I had to be careful with my therapeutic exercise and other activities. It was a very slow laborious process. I had gradually increased the resistance knowing that once we resumed doing our act there would be strain. There was still varying amounts of pain off and on. Rehearsing and performing but gradually along with continuing therapeutic exercise both elbows recovered almost completely. I still have occasional twinges in my left elbow when exercising excessively.

Toward the end of our performing days we were about to add a flamenco number, Alegrías de Baile, with me on the guitar accompanying Jill's dancing. To prepare for this we contacted one of the most famous old time gypsy flamenco dancers, La Quica, for private lessons for Jill. After the first lesson La Quica was surprised how quickly Jill learned the footwork. The next time we showed up at the rehearsal we were overwhelmed seeing many of her students and professional flamenco dancers who she invited, seated in a circle, to watch Jill rehearse. Our flamenco routine was only for performing outside of Spain, but it was never used as we terminated our act before returning to the states.

Chapter XX
Physical Therapy & Massage - Formentera

I'm not certain exactly when I decided to practice my profession of physical therapy on the island but eventually I rented space and equipped my clinic in San Fernando in a small building that belonged to our neighbors and very good friends, the Guasch family. I believe that my decision was reinforced by the fact that Tony Guasch who at seventy six had agreed to look after our property in our absence and who also helped me with certain chores, told me that he has suffered for years with sciatica. In spite of his condition and age he could lift heavy stones and work hard without rest for hours. I gave him some treatments at home and an exercise regime to follow. Frankly at his age with a long standing chronic condition, I didn't think he could look forward to much improvement. To all our amazement, within a relatively short period, he said that he was never bothered anymore with his sciatica. Good news spreads rapidly in a small community. I eventually was referred to as having magic hands. I have always emphasized massage and exercise for almost all treatments in conjunction with many other useful modalities and procedures. The locals' praise was almost embarrassing but at the same time flattering and encouraging.

It was also very professionally gratifying working with the locals as patients. Unlike many of the patients I had in California who for the most part weren't very diligent in doing their part and only seemed to improve when they got reimbursed, all my clients on the island followed the instructions and followed through with the home exercise programs I set up for them. They invariably did more than I prescribed. Their objective was to get functioning as soon as possible, a necessity for their survival. There was little if any compensation awaiting them, rather the contrary. Spain has a comprehensive national health system but not being a part of this, my patients paid me for their treatments. I never had a patient miss or arrive late for an appointment and they insisted on paying for each treatment. My rates were very reasonable and with each treatment I spent a minimum of a full hour and often considerably more.

As a general rule according to my observation and experience in California, treatments usually ranged from twenty to forty minutes and were performed mostly by an aide rather than a registered therapist. Many facilities were taking shortcuts and doing incomplete treatments, what was commonly referred to by the therapists as "shake and bake," that is, putting on a hot pack, giving a light massage and maybe doing one other short procedure or modality.

I attempted to have my US professional credentials accepted in order obtain permission to work in Spain as a physical therapist but their prerequisites for becoming a physical therapist required that first, one was either a nurse or a physician's assistant before acceptance in a school of physical therapy. Not being able to proceed and after much bureaucratic red tape I did manage to get a work permit as a masseur. Most of the islanders either knew I was a therapist or, more important, heard that I got results. There were occasions that I would refer a patient to see one of the two doctors on the island for some condition I thought might warrant medical attention. I know the doctors had resentments about my successful results. In all the years I practiced there they never referred a patient to me.

I practiced on the island, from 1962 to 1979 except for the times we were off the island. Presently there are quite a few therapists and related healers from outside of the island. Licensing restrictions have been somewhat relaxed especially for members of the European Union.

A new hospital and medical facility was established with permanent staff of physicians, nurses, etc. and specialists that come in regularly from Ibiza and Mallorca. In emergencies that can't be handled on the island, there is a fast ambulance speedboat and also a helicopter emergency service to Ibiza twenty kilometers distant.

The emergency services are very rapid even in remote parts of the island and probably superior to these services in many large cities worldwide.

In my late seventies I thought about the possibility of retiring on the island. I inquired about health insurance and was informed that unless one was insured before the age of seventy that health insurance was unavailable. Whether this was a factor in my decision to live in California or not I'm not certain.

By pushing wheelbarrow loads filled with stones totaling up to five hundred pounds over a rough rocky terrain, I demolished three heavy duty steel wheelbarrows. Most of this heavy work was done when I lived permanently on the island. The latter years of my visits I wasn't nearly as strong. My last visit to the island was in 2009 mainly to arrange the closing of the sale of the chalet and land. When Yale saw me struggling with large rocks he said that I did my share of the heavy lifting for the many years and he would carry them for me and looked forward to carrying on in my place. That made me feel very proud. I was quite strong due to my lifetime of gymnastics, handbalancing, weightlifting and bodybuilding. I was really surprised how strong Yale had become and realized that I wasn't capable of doing nearly as much physical work.

When I left Formentera for California, Jill said she would get the workers to finish my wall. I told her that unless I finished it, it would remain as is. Actually it needed only some leveling at the top. I worked on the wall off and on for a year. It is over two meters high, 65 centimeters thick and 10 meters long. This wall encloses the southern enclosure of our rear patio and adjoins with the studio. The nice thing about building with stone aside from the natural beauty is that it's for a lifetime or an eternity, especially if constructed using mortar or concrete as filler for the joints. I finally completed it on one of my latter visits. Many of the stone edifices and walls than are made without any filler and if well built will last for many years. The filler used by the locals was mud and later some used mortar for a more durable bond. I enjoyed making things from stone and rock such as walls, one of which I made myself from large stones. For the higher sections of outdoor wall construction the locals and the masons often used smaller rocks as they weren't as heavy and were easier to work with, but for appearances.

I could never get over the glorious feeling of surveying my domain. I knew every tree, bush, cactus and rock on my six acre parcel of land on Formentera. It was a very satisfying and glorious feeling to watch the sunrises and sunsets, the full moon and the cloudless night sky of sparkling stars that appeared close enough to touch.

— — — — — —

When Jill and I were teaching tennis at Hotel La Mola the management requested that I move my office to their hotel. I gave up my office in San Fernando and installed myself in the sport area of the hotel. Even though the hotel was rather distant for many of the islanders they came for treatments.

Aside from physical therapy I did a majority of full body massages as most of the hotel's clientele was German and very massage conscious. I brought disposable paper gowns but as most of the massage clients were women who soon informed me that they were accustomed to having their full body massages in the nude. Consequently the gowns were never used. I normally would work only three to four hours in the morning and help Jill teach tennis a few hours in the afternoon. I must say that Jill was an excellent teacher and all our clientele adored her. Many of the guests inquired if she would be teaching the following season so they could book their reservations and count on taking lessons with her.

One of my massage clients was a lovely German lady who came with her husband. He asked where he could wait. Instead of having him wait outside I seated him in our small room with his newspaper. I was finishing massaging his nude wife, when she asked if I could massage her breasts more. I complied but felt uneasy with her husband a few feet away. My American hang-up. Most of the Europeans I came across didn't seem affected with nudity and nude massages.

A German lady doctor came for a massage and asked me what she should take off. I replied, whatever is comfortable for you. She ended up in her panties, the only German woman that I didn't massage in the nude.

A young Belgian man said he'd never had a massage. He was very up tight and couldn't relax which in turn made me more tense. Not a pleasant experience.

Before we worked at the hotel some of us would rent the tennis courts to play when not in use by the hotel guests. We may have looked good but a good tennis player could readily see that we were not good tennis players. One day the hotel manager came out to ask Jill if she would be interested in teaching tennis. She was hesitant but the manager was encouraging so she accepted. It began with only a few hours three days a week but rapidly increased and it was too exhausting all day in the hot Mediterranean sun. Jill asked me if I would her help her teach. I usually had only a few hours massaging and some therapy so I could help and give her some relief. We kept all the fees we earned for our work both in tennis and my physical services as the hotel basically only needed the services.

It was embarrassing when class "A" German tennis players would ask me to practice with them. I had to apologize and tell them that my level of proficiency wasn't adequate to play on their level. When my eldest son Yale heard this he would tell them that he would like to play with them. He was only fourteen and really wasn't good enough but they seemed to enjoy his company. Yale never lacked confidence and I am convinced that he always felt he could accomplish whatever he wanted.

It worked out great having the children there and being able to keep an eye on them while we worked. Meanwhile they could entertain themselves taking advantage of knowing the various instructors and staff in the sports area. Linda, our daughter, took swimming lessons from the German instructor, Wolfgang. She won most of the swimming events even among many of the older children. The two boys used to play soccer with the others. We all played tennis.

— — — — — —

The only time I "punished" Yale was one day Jill told me that I have to punish him for something he supposedly did. I asked Jill if she witnessed him doing it. She replied that a mother knows, which I rightly interpreted as her not having seen him in the act.

I took him in the bedroom and asked if he was guilty. He said he wasn't and I believed him. I've never known Yale to lie. I took down his pants and I'm sure when my hand made contact that it didn't hurt and I told him to holler so his mother would be satisfied that I spanked him. That was the only time I ever laid a hand on anyone in my family. I really felt that our children were very obedient thanks to their mother's discipline and didn't require or deserve any punishment from me.

Jill, Linda, John, Yale, David and myself went for supper, buffet style, to the local Indonesian restaurant in Jill's car. I don't recall and probably didn't hear what went on but whatever it was it came to a head in the parking lot after dinner when John stood up to Jill who was critical of Linda for some reason or other. I do remember that we all agreed that John was in the right. Jill got into her car and left in a huff and we had to walk the four kilometers home in the dark.

I and most of my family and friends, realized that Jill and I had constant communication problems. I tended to avoid conflict and arguments which in turn infuriated Jill. We were probably both at fault.

My mother and father visited us twice and my mother three times. My mother was a walker since childhood. There was rarely a day in her life that she didn't walk. Jill and I and the children would either bike or drive the ten kilometers from our house to work at the Hotel La Mola. My mother walked back and forth many times. Once she walked the six miles with the children. From then on they either biked or drove with us. She would walk with them the mile to school and later accompany them home almost daily.

Formentera had a good soccer team and won many of the competitions with the other teams we played against in Ibiza. For a few years I donated my services as the trainer taking care of the injuries on and off the field. The management of the team invited me to take the children to our games all expenses paid at various venues on the island of Ibiza. My two sons enjoyed the camaraderie of the players and often practiced with them. Yale, my oldest son was an excellent and strong midfielder and I'm confident that if he had continued he would have done well professionally.

It was almost a ritual when our Formentera soccer team played in Ibiza. First, off the boat, we would all go to Ortega's to eat pepitas, steak sandwiches. Sandwiches were normally made using hard buns instead of sliced bread. Our soccer field was hard pack and gravel instead of the grass turf, consequently we were not accustomed playing on grass. Nevertheless we were victorious in most of our games unless the field was muddy. Our Formentera team, except for a few of our players who were originally from the peninsula, had no experience getting down and dirty in the mud. Little Patiño from Andalucia was a one man scorer but not a team player. Pepín and his brother Jesus from the island were the intelligent players and we had a fabulous goalie. Others players were Francisco, Paco, etc.

— — — — — —

When Yale was twelve he came down with type A infectious hepatitis. We felt isolated on the island living two kilometers on a narrow, rough, rocky road to the nearest town. Doctor José gave him an injection of gamma globulin and had me continue giving him injections. We worried but eventually he improved and recovered completely.

Chapter XXI
Voyage

I'll miss the closeness and friendships when in Spanish speaking cultures, especially in the smaller communities and islands where I always felt accepted and that I belonged. We were fortunate that we adapted and blended readily, whereas most other foreigners we knew only managed to be involved with the local population to a limited degree. Undoubtedly being a family with children was also a factor in our acceptance.

After nine years Jill and I left Spain for Denver in early March 1964. We boarded the small cargo passenger ship with the now defunct steamship line, Trans-Atlántica Española in Barcelona. We docked in Vera Cruz, Mexico after 28 days with full day stops in Valencia, Alicante, Almería, through the Straits of Gibraltar to Cadiz, Tenerife, Canary Islands, to Santo Domingo (it may still have been called Ciudad Trujillo at the time) and Puerto Plata, both in the Dominican republic, La Guaira, Venezuela, Curacao, San Juan, Puerto Rico, disembarking in Vera Cruz, Mexico. Quite an adventure for the price of $223 each. If I had decided to stay and settle in the US I had two places in mind, either San Diego or Key West. Knowing what I now know my choice would have been San Diego.

Our vessel, the Virginia de Churruca, was sixteen thousand tons and we looked like a tug boat when we were docked near the Bremen, a German passenger liner. Our steel plate swimming pool was about six by nine feet and four feet deep with the water sloshing over the deck when we had water. The after-deck had hundreds of cages of fighting cocks destined for various ports in Latin America. There was a constant crowing and an odor depending on the prevailing breezes. On deck were barrels of capers and other sundry items. One could roam freely anywhere on the ship, engine room, pilot house, look at the radar screen, etc,. etc. Enjoyable as that was I think that is a poor policy and could lead to problems.

Other ships that I've been on from other countries were quite strict and limited where passengers were allowed.

We had a physician aboard as maritime law requires an MD if there are more than twelve passengers. Our ship accommodated up to sixty passengers. Being primarily a cargo vessel, ports and destinations depended on the cargo commitments and one can't be sure of the exact schedules or destinations. Most of our passengers were Spanish emigrants or travelers boarding and departing at various ports along the journey.

At times Jill and I would find a sunny nook with no one around and sun bathe in our bikinis. As I recall they may have shown a Spanish movie or two otherwise we passed the time reading or socializing with the other passengers and going ashore when in port.

One of the interesting ports of call was at the Dominican Republic, the Capital Santo Domingo was renamed Ciudad Trujillo after the dictator at the time. It later went back to its original name. I walked the streets alone and noticed few people except for patrolling vehicles with six armed soldiers sitting in the open back. There were many large signs throughout the city, "Yankee go home" and others, not an inviting atmosphere. I did go skindiving for a short time at the breakwater of the port with some of the young black boys who were intrigued by my equipment, the spear gun, mask and snorkel, fins and dive knife.

The three times I have been to the Dominican Republic I never fail to order their national refreshment, Morír Soñando (to die dreaming). It's somewhat like an Orange Julius made with tropical orange juice, milk, sugar with granular ice. I forego the ice. Some add rum but I like it virgin. In other countries I have run across Dominicans employed as maids in hotels and invariably when I tell them I'd like a Morir Soñando they smile and never fail to bring me some of their home made beverage before I depart.

Puerto Plata on the other side of the island was a small African appearing village with thatched huts and a large open air market. During the few hours I spent on Puerto Plata, aside from the passengers on our ship I didn't see one white person. There were three young American men, passengers on our ship, who bought a large bunch of plantains to eat on the journey thinking they were bananas only to find out they were plantains and weren't to be eaten raw.

In November of 1967, just after our ship entered the harbor at Willemstad, the capital of Curacao, the large bridge spanning the port collapsed killing 16 workers

According to modern standards the food aboard ship was typical low class Spanish fare, what the average middle or poor class ate at the time which consisted of everything over cooked in a low grade olive oil and served tepid or cold. Breakfast consisted of tea or coffee and a roll. We requested from the purser if we could get some of the vegetables raw instead of cooked. He said we could get whatever we requested and accompanied us to see the ships larder. We asked for bacon and eggs and a few other things for breakfast and steak for supper. I should have known that this was too good to last. After a few days other passengers made requests and our special privileges came to an end.

I have also made this trip two other times by myself. The last time I brought my Peugeot 203 sedan transported on deck and covered with a tarpaulin. On this voyage, disembarking in Vera Cruz, I brought a collection of replica Spanish swords, armor and multi-colored woven woolen saddlebags (alforjas) as samples, intending to go into business with my friend Howie. I arrived in customs at 10:30 am and was told by the inspectors that I would have to pay duty. I replied that by international law if those items were recorded with my passport and presented when I left Mexico, that they should be duty free and exempt from taxation. They refused to let me pass and I went back and sat on the bench with my luggage till 3:30 pm when they all left and I walked out without any problem.

It's common knowledge that in Mexico, government employees and officials are paid little and supplement their income by asking for a "mordida" (bite or bribe) both to foreigners and locals alike. It seems to be a disliked but an accepted practice, actually a part of their culture.

On that same voyage with my auto I met another American gentleman on the ship who asked if he could share a ride with me to the states. It was a pleasure having company. My companion helped share the gasoline and also the driving. On a stop in Tlascala I met a group of Mexicans my age in a cantina. They all bought rounds of alcoholic drinks as is the custom in many countries. I explained that I didn't drink alcohol pretending that it was for medical reasons so as not to offend. Things were getting a little too boisterous and I thought it was a good idea to leave.

When we arrived at American customs at the border in El Paso the agent waived me through but a hundred yards into the US he ran out and called me back. He assumed that I had entered and exited Mexico with the vehicle from the US as do most American visitors but then realized that the car had a Spanish license plate. They charged me a small fee for duty and we continued on our way. I don't recall where I let my passenger off.

On the previous return to the states from Spain by ship, I took a bus from Veracruz to El Paso, changed to an American bus line and went on to Denver. I never could understand why the first class buses I've taken in Latin America were so much more modern, better scheduled and more comfortable than the American buses I've taken.

An interesting quirk of one bus trip in Mexico. The driver would state a time to leave from a meal stop and a few minutes before that time he would drive off leaving everyone panicky running after the bus. He would drive around the block and wait in his original space at the designated time to the relief of the worried passengers. I don't know if this was a prevalent practice or just this driver's prank. That was the only time I experienced this sort of thing.

Chapter XXII
Topolobampo

Back to my story about returning from Spain in March 1964 aboard the Virginia de Churruca. Jill and I met and became friends with a young Mexican gentleman, Julio Liparoli, recently graduated from a Spanish medical school and returning to his home in Topolobampo, Sinaloa to practice medicine. He was intrigued when I mentioned that I was an ardent spearfisherman and encouraged me not to miss going to Topolobampo, assuring me that it was a marvelous spot for spearfishing. He insisted that I look up his father, don Julio Liparoli and meet his family.

Docking in Vera Cruz, Jill and I continued on to Mexico City where we visited a friend of mine, Mario Reed, a taxidermist whom I met when he was in Denver attending a taxidermy convention.

Arriving in Topolobampo we met Julio's father, an older gentleman, who invited us to his large spacious home on the edge of town for a lovely evening of a delicious supper and animated conversation. I find the Mexican people, rich and poor alike, very friendly and generous. Don Julio came from Italy as a young man and was the founder of Topolobampo. He has been very prominent and active in local community affairs and politics.

Jill and I rented a room in the home of a woman, Doña Marta, who was fluent in English. Jill came running out of the bathroom trembling after seeing a large four inch long cockroach ambling around on the floor.

I was talking to a retired American gentleman staying in a caravan area near the water with other Americans and their recreational vehicles or caravans. His one regret was not taking his retirement earlier before he had a stroke a few years later. Something to think about.

Walking along a railroad track, my way was blocked by a surly, older armed man in uniform with his hand on his holster. He told me I was trespassing and threatened to have me arrested. I assumed that he wanted a "mordida". I told him that I am a friend and guest of don Julio Liparoli. He almost fell to his knees begging my pardon and offering to personally escort me to my destination which I politely refused. At times there's nothing like having important, powerful friends.

I met two local boys, Cerrillo and Mejo, who worked at the local shrimp cannery. They showed me how they spear fish on the banks of the estuaries by lying face down on the surface or submerged with our spears extended waiting for schools of fish swimming against the strong, murky current. It was a simple matter spearing the hoards of fish that passed within a foot or two from the tip of your spear, like shooting fish in a barrel.

Paul Herring, his father and uncle, from Texas, were camped nearby. Paul is a qualified scuba diver and free diver. His father and uncle fished from a boat with rod and reel. They were kind enough to invite Jill to go fishing when Paul and I were doing our thing. Jill had never been fishing and I asked her how it was when she returned. She said it was tiring, constantly reeling in fish one after another. I never heard any fisherman air this complaint. Sea life was plentiful and available in this fisherman's paradise.

Cerrillo and Mejo invited Paul and me to dive at the Farellón, a huge rock pile of an island 20 miles off shore. After a long uncomfortable trip in a Panga, a long, narrow canoe, we arrived at the island. The top was covered in guano from the countless number of sea birds and the rugged shoreline with hundreds of nesting sea lions and elephant seals. The silence was broken by a cacophony from the chattering birds in concert with the barking mammals on the rocks below.

We waited in these unknown waters for our companions to initiate the diving. To our astonishment they had never fished in this area. Paul and I decided if we want to fish, we'd better get wet. We jumped in leaving our guides in the boat. We were diving up to twelve meters, a little less than forty feet. Our first dilemma was trying to decide which fish of the many fish should we shoot. One kept sighting larger and larger targets. My first few dives I didn't shoot as I couldn't decide and had to surface to breathe. Finally we both got down to business and started spearing fish. Most of the fish were groupers, red snapper and a few other species. I don't believe our local buddies went in the water. We were concerned as the playful female sea lions did their fancy maneuvers very close to us occasionally zooming in front of us or nipping at our fins. They posed little if any danger but we were careful not to get between the larger bulls and the pups. We loaded the canoe with our catch almost to the gunnels and had a hairy, rough ride back with water sloshing into the boat. It was calm when we left but the seas were rough on our return and we were a little uneasy until arriving back in town.

We unloaded our catch which our friends sold to a small restaurant run by an Indian lady, doña Temicha. We didn't accept any money as our friends furnished the boat and the gasoline.

One of my pet peeves is, on the west coast of the US the selling of cod as red snapper in place of the true tropical red snapper, known as "pargo colorado" or "huachinango" in Mexico.

Jill and I took the trip on the Chihuahua Pacífico y Ojinaga Railroad that was recently initiated, the route through Barrancas del Cobre, or Copper Canyon. The trip is 900 miles from Los Mochis to Chihuahua and return. The cost at that time was eight dollars each. There were two Fiat passenger coaches. I won't go into details of that fabulous journey as details are available through various sources. Prices at present are $130 each.

Los Mochis is only a few miles from Topolobampo. Jill was upset at the fact we were on the way to Denver to meet my parents, she was pregnant and we weren't married. We went to the city hall in Los Mochis with my two Mexican fishing companions as witnesses and best men in a civil ceremony at the court house. The ceremony was performed by Judge Díaz. Since Jill didn't understand much of what was said and the judge asked if she agreed to the marriage, I told her to say "Sí". I later translated our Mexican marriage license to English and had it officially registered in California.

Chapter XXIII
California

In early 1964 I returned with Jill, pregnant with our first born, Yale, We stayed with my parents in their house on Ivy Street in Denver.

California like many of the states now had licensing by examination to become a registered physical therapist. I studied while working part time at a lower wage in the Physical Therapy Department at Colorado General Hospital where I had studied and worked eleven years earlier. I'm sure that Herb Levy was instrumental in getting me approved as I was no longer licensed. After studying in my spare time I passed the state exam in spite of my long absence from the profession and felt very lucky as there were many new graduates and others that didn't pass.

Later that same year I met Irwin Paris, a physical therapist from California, who was attending a national physical therapy conference held in Denver. He offered me a job working with him in various clinics and hospitals he contracted with in the South Bay and Beach Cities in the southern area of Los Angeles county. Hugh Pendleton, a colleague, worked with us.

I wanted to wait till Yale was born but Irwin needed me sooner. I left Jill with my parents in Denver and left for Manhattan Beach where Irwin generously invited me to stay with them in his home with his young children and his Mexican wife. Soon after, Yale was born, a six pound preemie of six and a half months born at General Rose Memorial Hospital, Denver. I sent for them to come to Los Angeles. We rented half of a duplex in Hermosa Beach. The other half of the duplex was occupied by Andy and Billie Fischl. Billie was a wonderful lady. Andy was a big, strong and Jolly Dutchman, a fisherman by profession. They were both simple, loving people and we felt like family and as if they were our children's grandparents. It was a wonderful period in our lives.

I met Helen Hunter in a travel agency where she worked in Hermosa Beach. Her husband Henry was dark, tall and good looking. Henry and I became good friends, played tennis and socialized through the years we were in California. They later visited us in Formentera various times. Henry's father was an officer in the English Army and stationed in India, his mother was from India. Henry worked as an engineer at TRW. He was also a ladies' man.

We often went to their condo six miles up the coast from our house just before Marineland. The condo complex was complete with tennis courts, swimming pool, spa, recreation room, gym, etc. as were many of the upscale condo complexes on the coast. Helen is a gourmet cook and we would have delicious meals. When they came to our house Jill would usually make her delicious paella with gazpacho and flan for desert. I will always remember when Helen prepared a platter of sole, lots of prawns and a sumptuous chocolate cake with many trimmings, followed by a special coffee with Cointreau, chocolate, whipped cream and probably other ingredients. I rarely drank coffee but that was really a dessert, a real treat. Years later I asked for the coffee recipe but she never did find it.

Some time later she served a similar supper with the sole, shrimp, etc. but this time to my disappointment it was prepared with curry. That was my introduction to curry and I did not like curry. I realize that curry is very Indian but often have wondered if I made a pig of myself the first time without condiments and maybe Helen thought with the curry I wouldn't feel I had to finish everything. I sincerely hope that wasn't the case.

Back in California we used to go often to Burt and Uta Schwab's home. Our homes were only a few miles apart. Bert was a gentle, immaculate person. I recall the times he worked on my car in a white shirt with not a spot on him, whereas I didn't get near the car and usually ended up with grease on my shirt, hands and arms.

Burt and I were driving along the dark coast road the to my friends house at about 10 pm, when suddenly in the headlight beams appeared a naked figure walking on our right side of the road. As we approached we saw it was a woman carrying a handbag and shod in high heels, nothing more. Burt said for god's sake don't stop I've got enough female problems. If we would have had a cell phone we could have called the authorities but if we would have stopped it might have presented a problem for many possible reasons.

Burt wanted a divorce from his wife Uta when he discovered she was having affairs, and one of the affairs was with this same friend. Burt asked me if we could talk to my friend to give evidence if needed for the divorce. My friend did agree to help Burt as a witness to Burt's wife's infidelity in his divorce case. I found out years later that Derek, Burt and Uta's son, who played with our children, died of a drug overdose.

— — — — — —

Before we moved to San Pedro we moved to an upstairs apartment on Calle Mayor in Torrance Beach just south of Redondo Beach, one short block from the beach. No matter where we locate we seem to have access to the beach. Linda was born there and my parents came out to spend some time with us. They relieved us of having to be up much of the night changing diapers. It was amazing watching my father with his cigar in his mouth and a face mask, in the wee hours of the morning, changing diapers on a four pound, seven month preemie little girl. He used to walk with Jill pushing Linda in her buggy. There was a Foster Freeze a few blocks from the house. Jill always looked forward to her soft ice cream cone.

On the day Linda was born I was working at a clinic and Jill had her appointment with the obstetrician in the same clinic. In the middle of my treating a patient the obstetrician interrupted and asked me to take Jill to the hospital delivery room in nearby Little

Company of Mary Hospital in Torrance. I replied that I would finish my patient and take her. He said "now".

My parents were concerned about the steep long stairway to our apartment on Calle Mayor so we rented a house on 37th Street in San Pedro for one year, two blocks from the beach. We did have stairs but as not many.

I later signed the contract to purchase a house on Starline Drive in Palos Verdes but later was able to annul the agreement I signed. I was unhappy with the lack of a window in the downstairs bathroom and a long crack in the wall over the fireplace. The Realtor was kind enough to annul our contract. My parents found our present house. I really didn't like it at first but that changed with time. My parents made an excellent choice.

Since my father was knowledgeable in real estate he managed all the dealing with the owner and the Realtor, Libby Di Bernardo. The asking price was $37,500. My father agreed to the price if we could assume the original loan, to which they replied that it would pose no problem. The loan wasn't assumable so in order to make the sale the owner and the Realtor paid the $2,500 loan fees.

During the period when we lived in the beach cities I would go spearfishing with a friend who lived nearby. We often went off the King Harbor Redondo Beach breakwater. Although it was not permitted to fish on the inside we usually got away with it. The outside was normally rougher with poorer visibility. Many times we would spear our limit of calico and sand bass. My friend speared an illegal salmon which he didn't recognize at the time. Salmon are not common in this area. We also dove off Catalina island's west end for abalone. I would clean, tenderize and prepare the abalone slices and Jill would saute them 30 seconds on each side in butter and almondine sauce. Abalone and lobster are only reveries now.

We were about to enter the water at Paradise Cove west of Malibu.

The sea was rough with large surf raking over the rough, mussel-shelled rocks. My friends went in. I stayed ashore. I wasn't worried as much about going in as coming out. My friends had a bad time with the heavy surf on their return but they finally managed fight their way over the rocks their wet suits were ripped and they had multiple cuts.

I took advantage of an advance scuba class sponsored by the County of Los Angeles Department of Parks and Recreation Underwater Unit. There were a series of twelve, one hour classes in a pool. The classes consisted of a wide range of subjects including helmet diving with mixed gases and finishing with six ocean dives at Catalina Island. I received my certificate December 3rd, 1965. I seldom ever used scuba gear for spearfishing as I prefer free diving without the hassle of lugging the bulky heavy tanks.

I had a renewed interest in Flamenco guitar and also the dance. Inesita invited me to attend her flamenco rehearsals in her garage studio on Sundays, usually with Stamen accompanying her on the guitar and at times there were other flamenco enthusiasts present. Inesita still performs professionally on occasion and I look forward to her presentations. Although I've seen her many times I remain impressed with her authenticity of traditional flamenco as we knew it. Many music and dance performers have introduced a fusion, which may be progress, but some of us prefer the dance and music as performed during our times.

A friend, Yvetta Williams, who plays flamenco guitar and a few others including our friend Anna Konya and myself began classes in flamenco dancing with Raúl de Alva who danced with the Pilar Lopez Ballet in Spain. Anna is the sole proprietor of her business in San Pedro making exquisitely beautiful gypsy style multicolored skirts.

We were interested in all the components of the dance but two of the men insisted on footwork only. The few of us remaining dropped out and the class disbanded. Raúl's son David became an excellent guitarist and accompanied many dancers.

In the mid 1950's I attended a flamenco show with José Greco & Company performing in Denver. It was inspiring and I was especially impressed with a young gypsy dancer, Juanele Maya.

I went quite a few times with friends to El Cid, the Spanish restaurant in Los Angeles that had flamenco shows and was known by most of the flamenco aficionados in the area. I saw José Greco who was watching one of his sons and his daughters perform. Yvetta and I had a chance to converse with him briefly. Greco was a world famous flamenco dancer, born in Italy, moving to New York at ten years of age. The Gypsy in my Soul, was his autobiography. Surprisingly, in his book he mentions names of women with whom he had affairs. One of the women mentioned happened to be sitting at the bar in El Cid just a few feet away from where we stood. I was disappointed in his uncalled for braggadocio, probably to impress us of his female conquests. At the very least he could have left out their names. Since then I watch his performances with less respect for him as a person.

José Greco (in white) and Yvette Williams on right.

— — — — — —

On my birthday, February 22nd, 1969 David was born at South Bay Hospital in Redondo Beach, another four pound, seven month preemie. Who could ask for a better present? Jill was always impatient to get things done.

Linda, Yale & David
circa early 1970

After David was born, Jill's obstetrician advised me to get a vasectomy as it would be dangerous for Jill to have more children. I arranged an appointment with the urologist for the surgery the following day. When I arrived at the clinic he said his nurse had to leave early but if I could assist him with my surgery we could proceed. I had no problems and drove home with little discomfort.

After terminating my contract with Irwin Paris I continued contracting my physical therapy services with other clinics and facilities in the area.

Doctor Gary Hathaway was an all around athlete in his mid thirties. I performed physical therapy services for various hospitals and clinics in the South Bay area where he was on staff. One incident was in a small hospital in Hermosa Beach where he ordered a massage to a breast and pectoral muscle of a woman in her 30's. I have no idea what the treatment was for or whether the patient asked the doctor for a massage in that specific area. It certainly was not a usual request. The ward consisted of four curtained off cubicles, all containing women in that same age group.

I draped the patient, as protocol required, but the patient removed the covering before I began. As I was treating (massaging) her breast she was intentionally making remarks along with sounds of pleasure in an audible voice so the other women patients in the adjoining cubicles could easily hear. It was apparent and we all knew this was done purposely to elicit the remarks and laughter from the others.

Ms. Poteet was the supervising, head nurse in Los Palos Convalescent Hospital. We usually had a friendly chat when I arrived to treat patients. I noticed she was upset and she related the incident that occurred earlier that afternoon between a male and a female patient. He, a 65 year old wheelchair bound and she a 47 year old former swimmer with either Sydenham's chorea or Huntington's Chorea (St. Vitus Dance). It was known that they were in the habit of being together alone in his room on various occasions but this time they were in the vestibule with her performing oral sex, him sitting in his wheelchair, meanwhile the other LVNs and aides were standing around the periphery, watching and evidently enjoying the sensuous spectacle.

Seacrest Convalescent Hospital was on the same block as the aforementioned Los Palos facility. I was giving a back massage, as ordered on a well endowed 70 year old woman with gray hair in a long braid to the middle of her back. As the massage progressed she was getting aroused and I had a difficult time from keeping being dragged on to her bed.

Even sick and older people have desires of intimacy and it's a shame that the rules of most institutions prohibit the more intimate sensual and sexual activity of their patients, nevertheless, I do understand this could be a serious social problem.

We spent a few years in San Pedro before I decided to give up my physical therapy practice and return to Formentera. Jill adapted nicely to the lifestyle here never having had access to so many activities and material things. She didn't want to return to Formentera but I said as the bread winner the decision was ultimately mine. My decision may have been partly because I liked the adventure and simple life style of the island and that we all had more time together. It was an ideal place to raise the children who have always been grateful for the experience of having lived and grown in those exotic and relatively primitive circumstances.

In the late seventies my friend and physical therapy colleague John Monlux and his wife Barbara came to visit us on the island. It was August and I recall that afternoon we had the heaviest rainstorm that I've experienced in my lifetime. We were standing in our patio when suddenly the downpour came. One could hardly breathe for fear of drowning. Fortunately it only lasted a short time and the run off from our property is very fast with no danger of flooding.

John was interested in electromyography, a diagnostic procedure performed in the states only by specialized physicians, primarily physiatrists and neurologists A small nucleus of physical therapists were attempting to legally enter into that field and finally after years of battling the medical bureaucracy were permitted to practice on equal terms with the physicians, providing we could pass the difficult test to be licensed. John tried to encourage me to began studying and prepare to enter the field when I returned to the states but at the time I had little interest.

We had been friends for a few years and would go skin diving, play tennis, etc. They had a home in the small gated community of Three Arch Bay near Laguna Beach. We visited a few times and had Jill and Barbara, John's wife, make a paella on the beach.

John was competitive by nature. I recall the instance when his son Steve first beat him in tennis which seemed quite upsetting to him and I'm certain he was waiting to play again and hoping to regain his status. I personally was always proud of my children when they could out perform me.

My thanks to John for encouraging and helping me to become one of the early members of our newly formed physical therapy group to obtain professional status in California in the field of electro-neuromyography on an equal status with the physicians specialized in this field. More about this in Chapter XXX.

The following year after my return to San Pedro in late 1979, my buddy George Patten came to visit me. We were in dire need of a new roof on our house. George said let's go out and buy the materials and we'll re-roof the house. I was dubious because I knew little about actually applying the roofing even though years ago I helped George and his dad with their house but George has done a few and we decided to start. We had the materials delivered, elevated and unloaded on the garage roof. Total cost of materials $926. We had to scrape off the old tar and stone roofing before putting on the new roof. Nancy Smith, who rented our house while we were in Spain, actually helped do some of the roofing. She was quite athletic and hard working. Also a neighbor's nephew Bobby, a stout red headed boy of 14 also wanted to help. He was quite strong for his age. I don't recall what he was helping with but we were impressed with how hard he worked. I could not have done it without George's know how and help and would never have undertaken that task without him. I did get a new roof a year ago for approximately nine times the price, even though the old one still looked good, it was overdue after thirty three years.

During some of my visits back to Minneapolis I usually stayed with George Patten or in latter years when George and Lee had moved to a smaller condo, I stayed with Norman Oakvic, except for the time that Marisa Riviere invited me to stay in her home near Lake of the Isles.

George Patten had a habit of giving me the grand tour of the Twin

Cities whenever I would visit. On one of my visits we parked in front of our old house on Xerxes Avenue. The house looked the same as I remembered. I went to the door but no one answered. We waited a while and I noticed that on the other side of the street facing Theodore Wirth (Glenwood) Park, there were quite a few new homes where none existed before and where we used to have a pristine, panoramic, unblocked view. After a brief time, a car pulled up and parked in front of the house. When the three black passengers got out of the car and started up the steps, I told them that I used to live there. We chatted a short while and they invited us in, but George was due home so we didn't go in.

When I sent for Jill and the children in Formentera at the beginning of 1980 I wanted the house in good shape so I decided to paint the inside myself. I'm not the world's best painter and have a tendency to put too much paint on the roller or brush and most of the time have it dripping down my arm. As long as I was going to do it, I'd better do a good job as Jill is a good painter and very particular. I even took off the door handles, hinges, electric socket plates, etc.

Two minutes after they stepped into the house Jill looked down the long hallway and remarked that there was a line on the linen closet door where the paint was a little thicker in a vertical drip line. To me it was hardly noticeable. I never offer to paint anywhere she will be.

Phil and Nancy Smith were close friends of ours. Nancy and Jill played tennis together. Their children, Michael and Christine along with our three children would accompany them to the tennis courts. We had a friend Ramón from Mexico who also was a tennis player and would entertain the five children in the large playpen our wives brought along while they played and not have to worry about the kids. Nancy was an excellent tennis player and competed in the A league.

We all went on a camping trip along the Kern river. There quite a few other campers in the campground. We set up our tents and during the night the five of us, rolled together during the sleepless night. I didn't realize that the ground wasn't level when I set up the tent.

Eating outside was a problem because of the swarms of wasps attracted to the food. If we ate breakfast early and supper late we could avoid this. For lunch we would just snack on the run so as to avoid the nasty stinging critters.

We enjoyed swimming in the river but constantly had to swim to bring back the children drifting down river in their inner tubes

One night we heard loud growling coming from the other side of the river. Both Phil and I got out of our tents and with our powerful flashlights scanned the opposite river bank. We saw two pair of yellow eyes and assumed they were bobcats or other small wildcats until we saw their tawny bodies with long tails. We followed along the river until they were out of sight. It was a heady experience. The next morning I spoke to the park ranger and told him about seeing the two mountain lions, also called cougars or pumas. The ranger told me that in all his years in that area he had never seen any there. He said they probably were young lions that came to drink as there was a drought at the time.

Phil and Nancy divorced at the time we were in Spain and sold their house. We rented our house to Nancy and the children for $200 per month.

Years later when I returned permanently from Spain in late 1979 and Jill and the children in early 1980. We were pleased that the property was so well maintained and indeed fortunate to have a tenant like Nancy and her children.

Upon arriving in San Pedro I first went to the house to visit Nancy one evening. She was watching TV with her boyfriend Al Corsini, the chief pharmacist at our local hospital. They were eating popcorn while watching a porn movie, a new phenomena for me. It was the first I've seen after having lived many years in Spain, a very conservative and censored society. It was titillating but at the same time embarrassing for me with another male present. Immediately following was a short documentary of two elderly, nude couples playing tennis outdoors in Ojai. It was hilarious. I liked Al from the start. They were later married and moved to Minden, Nevada.

I was working with Irwin Paris doing physical therapy and setting up gyms and health spas. Jill did some part time instructing in one of the gyms.

Chapter XXIV
Mexico

When Yale, my oldest son, graduated from high school with top honors my mother gave him a generous check with which he purchased his dream of a '69 Chevrolet Camaro Z 28. He did a beautiful full restoration. To pick up this used vehicle, he asked if I could drive him to Orange County. When we arrived he asked if I would drive the Camaro and he would drive my car home as he didn't have that much driving experience before we returned to the US. I had never driven a powerful muscle car before and the way it accelerated almost scared me.

Yale was a very correct, law abiding citizen. While we were driving on the freeway he noticed that I changed lanes often trying to get ahead. He said he drove this route to the university every day and found that if he stayed in one lane, he arrived just as soon as the cars that constantly changed lanes. Leaving the house, just out of my driveway, Yale asked me to please fasten my seat belt. I told him I'd do it in a minute. He said "You know dad, most accidents occur near home." I respected his point of view and took his sensible advice.

March of 2007 I received a call from Yale in Spain. While biking with a few of his biker friends in the foothills of the Pyrenees in northern Spain, he skidded on black ice on a curve and crashed into a ravine. They called for an ambulance that rushed him to the emergency room of a local hospital where he remained for a few days before being released. He sent me the X- rays showing fractures of three ribs, the left scapula and clavicle. I spoke to my cousin Tom, a physician, who said it wasn't life threatening but would be very painful for six weeks more or less. When I spoke to Yale a week later and asked how he felt and if he was taking anything for pain, he said he didn't have that much pain if he didn't move around too much and he wasn't taking any medication since leaving the hospital. It wasn't long afterward that he was biking again.

I had Vonage telephone service and could call most countries at no cost and occasionally spoke to Yale. I received a call from him assuming it was from Spain but he was on vacation for three weeks in Mexico City. He invited me to join him and do some traveling. I took the Blue Line from Long Beach to Florence Avenue. I have never been on that train and was unaware that you bought your ticket before boarding. I asked a policeman standing on the platform what the procedure was and he directed me to get on the train. I sat next to a young Spanish speaking man and his young daughter. While conversing I asked about how one buys a ticket. He was about to get off and gave me his ticket. Often things work out for the best. I was informed that there are penalties for boarding without a ticket.

There are a few Mexican national bus lines that have offices and buses at Florence and Pacific avenues. I took a first class bus to Guadalajara where we were to meet. The trip took thirty six hours. These bus lines are almost exclusively used by Mexican laborers and of the three times I've used these buses I've never seen another Anglo or heard a word of English. Mexicans seem to be the only ones that even know of these local services to Mexico. It was very comfortable, with TV, air conditioning and seats that almost reclined flat. I enjoyed speaking with fellow passengers and seeing the countryside and villages that I knew many years ago. We arrived at the Mexican border at Nogales at midnight and I asked some of the other passengers if passing through customs and immigration was any problem. Sometimes they can give you good advice or helpful hints. Entering Mexico there were two adjoining lines one leaving and the other entering. On the side leaving, a Mexican official stood with his back to us checking the passengers leaving and entering the US. Entering we passed by him by inches. No one stopped us or even looked our way as we walked through into Mexico.

From the bus terminal in Guadalajara I took a taxi to the hotel where we were to meet. Yale was waiting on a street corner a block before the hotel. He saw me in the cab and hailed the driver to pull over and stop in the middle of the street. We stayed three days in Guadalajara in a small hotel owned by a Spaniard from Galicia. He was thrilled that we were so familiar with Spain and invited us to dinner. It was an enjoyable dinner and I'm certain that he enjoyed talking with us and probably had few occasions to converse with anyone about Spain.

There was a small outdoor swimming pool in the hotel where we would exercise and talk to the girls.

In Guadalajara I always make it a point to go shopping or browsing in San Juan de Dios, the main outdoor market occupying two square blocks. In the many times I've been there I don't think I've ever left without buying a pair of huaraches. There are probably twenty different stalls in that market that deal exclusively in huaraches. I also bought a pullover shirt with Guanajuato on the front. I forget what Yale bought.

My Mexican friends in Los Angeles said we must go to Tlaquepaque on the outskirts of Guadalajara. It was too touristy for our taste, the streets lined with tourist shops and eateries. All our travels were with public transportation and a lot of walking, no taxis. We ate in some good restaurants and in some primitive stalls with room for only a few people. We both enjoy being with the locals and frequented public places and the lovely gardens and plazas. Next we went to Guanajuato a city that impressed me for its colonial style and surrounded by mountains. We happened to be there during the soccer competition between Mexico and the US team. Mexicans are avid soccer fans and we spent some interesting nights watching the games on television with the locals at some of the cantinas and in the main plaza where there were always mariachis, my favorite music. After walking all day we would climb the countless steps a few hundred meters up hill to our lodging. I was too tired to leave again to explore in the evening but Yale would take off for another three or four hours. He told me about visiting "La Valenciana," the mine that sent more riches to Spain than all the rest of the treasures Spain acquired in the Americas. Our next stop was Dolores Hidalgo famous for "El Grito" or the shout by the priest Hidalgo that initiated the uprising for independence against Maximilian. We visited many of the historical museums and landmarks. When traveling, the most interesting aspect for me is being with and social intercourse with the locals.

Yale was great in checking all the schedules. I was to leave from León to Mexico City. Yale found an inexpensive flight on the computer for me to Los Angeles. As we went to the indicated gate to catch the bus, we saw a bus leaving, a hundred meters ahead of us. Yale took off running and I was sure there was no way he would catch and stop the bus. He must have run a block before he waved the driver down to stop. It wasn't my bus, mine came later. I arrived in Mexico City at 4 am next to the subway station and waited till 5 am when the gates opened and I was on my way to the airport. I caught my flight and was fortunate to have a beautiful Mexican model and movie actress for company until she deplaned in Monterrey, Mexico. All of Yale's instructions were precise. I don't think that I would have fared as well without his help. I would look forward to his company traveling almost anywhere.

Although Yale is as fluent as any well educated Spaniard he is not as familiar with the Mexican dialects and expressions as I. He is a pleasure to travel with and takes care of his old Dad. He actually invited me and paid for most of the trip. After I left he continued on visiting more places in southern Mexico before returning to Spain.

An incident in San Pedro long before this Mexican trip on my way to the mobile home park to play tennis mid afternoon I saw this bicyclist wearing a helmet pulling up to speak to me. I didn't immediately recognize my son Yale. I asked where he was going and he replied that he was going to our house for a haircut from his mother. I asked if he'd like to play some tennis when he finished. He said he'd like to but wanted to return to his place in Burbank before dark. His route was 53 miles each way.

– – – – – –

On one of my trips to visit friends and family in Denver and Minneapolis in the fall of 1988 I was staying with my good friend Norman Oakvic. Norm was in our group of gymnastic, bodybuilding and handbalancing friends. He was a top notch skier specializing in the Nordic events of cross country and jumping. He had a berth on the '56 US Olympic ski team but due to an industrial accident while working in Seattle he was unable to participate. Norm also is a good west coast swing dancer and we would frequently go to a swing dance in St. Paul. He leads an uncomplicated life and has always eaten healthy, basic foods. He also is an avid biker. I hadn't been doing much aerobic type exercise since my heart attack in '82. I was still leery about doing too much physical exertion six years since my heart attack. We went biking 14 miles that day around the outskirts of the city. I hadn't biked since I was a teenager but from that day on I started a biking program aside from my other exercises and kept a log of each ride. I maintained that log for 24 years. I bought a bike upon returning to San Pedro and rode from the back gate of the mobile home park to Pacific Avenue and back. A distance of five miles. I tried to bike two or three times a week between five and fifteen miles depending on how I felt at the time. I still bike eight to twelve miles each ride but at a more leisurely pace.

Norm flew to visit me in San Pedro in the mid 90's. We went on a two week trip in my '84 Ford Econoline van to various ski areas in Oregon. When passing close to Mount Shasta, Norm commented that the many times he's passed this mountain this was the only time he was able to see the whole mountain as it's usually cloud covered especially the upper portion. We both slept in the van except in Bend, Oregon, where Norm had a lady friend so those nights he slept in the house and I slept in my van. On the way home we stopped at Mammoth Mountain in late April for some spring skiing. Instead, a cold storm hit that afternoon. We bundled up in our clothes, ski clothes and sleeping bags to keep warm and try to sleep in the van that night. In the morning the water in our water bottles was frozen solid.

Years later I went to meet and pick up my friend Norm arriving on a charter flight from Minneapolis at the Imperial annex of LAX. I met him as he deplaned and as we were walking this beautiful young lady that also was on the flight from Minneapolis, threw her arms around me and kissed me. I was taken aback having no idea who she was until she told me that she was Denise, my second cousin whom I hadn't seen since she was a child.

At one of the swing dances in St. Paul I met a lovely lady, Eileen Reagan, who was one of the best local all round dancers. She is a concert pianist by profession. I looked forward to seeing her when I was in Minneapolis or when she would visit her mother in California. She is a beautiful redhead. I liked her very much and maybe we could have had a real relationship had we had been geographically suited. I took Eileen to my 50th high school reunion in Minneapolis at one of the large hotels. We probably had two hundred alumni, family and friends in attendance. The band was a well known local band whose members all happened to be from my same school during the same years so we all knew one another. I think Eileen and I made a good looking couple. We received many compliments and I noticed everyone looking at us. I'm sure it was because of Eileen's attractive appearance. I was not one of the noticeable students in school and didn't participate in any of the social activities, nevertheless I looked forward to our reunions and have attended our 60th reunion also. I feel much closer and more comfortable with everyone as the years pass.

Elke was a shapely lady I met with her Italian girlfriend at the Elk's pool. She took care of and lived in a home owned by an

Italian family who resided most of the year in Italy. Elke and I were good friends and we eventually married as her visitor's visa was running out and she wanted to stay in the US. I was invited to dinner when the Italian family was visiting and they hinted at the possibility of us getting married so Elke could get her green card. Elke was too embarrassed to ask. I said I would but would accept no remuneration whatsoever and clarified that it was for convenience and we would divorce as soon as practical. She tried that before with a man who she had paid in order to get a green card but the judge wouldn't approve it. Everyone was surprised that we were approved immediately. I was very fond of her but was not interested in marriage nor being a couple. Elke paid for all the expenses to Las Vegas and took care of the divorce. We are still friends and speak on the phone occasionally.

Soon after we met Elke invited me to to her house one afternoon. I remember she was impressed with my appearance in my form fitting matching yellow tennis outfit consisting of brief shorts, T shirt and socks. I remember purchasing this outfit and another tennis outfit at el Corte Inglés in Barcelona. Both have lasted me for more years than I dare say. I still have pieces of both outfits that I just stopped wearing and had to throw out after four decades, believe it or not. In those days, even in Spain, things were made to last.

When Elke remarried I attended her wedding party at the groom's house in the valley. Elke was telling his family and everyone else about our wedding night in Las Vegas. Very embarrassing.

Her sixteen year old son Thomas was visiting from Germany. He wanted to see Las Vegas. Elke couldn't go so he and I drove. I played my flamenco tapes all the way and found out later that he hated listening constantly to the singing. In the hotel lobby I told Thomas to sit and watch our luggage while I checked us in. When the clerk asked for his last name I shouted to him to ask. It didn't dawn on me for awhile what the people must have thought, a 58 year old man not knowing the last name of his teen aged companion sharing the same room.

He later returned to the states to live and married a lovely Mexican girl and has a successful Mercedes dealership with thirty six employees. His mother mentioned that he had no possible future in Germany.

— — — — — —

A few years later I saw this beautiful lady with long platinum hair lounging at the mobile home park pool accompanied by a nice looking gentleman. I would have loved to have met her but under the circumstances I didn't think it was proper. The next year I saw her alone at the pool. I'm not timid talking to women but she was so striking I took awhile to decide. I introduced myself and found her very pleasant and receptive. We chatted for a few hours and before leaving she mentioned that her children were grown and she began to dance again and was taking lessons. I commented that I was thinking of taking lessons but I'd never danced before. She asked if I would like to accompany her and if I felt like taking the lesson or just watching, whichever was more comfortable for me. I certainly wasn't going to miss the chance to be with her.

Lou Schreiber was giving dance lessons in some South Bay venues. We primarily danced west coast swing but also other ballroom dances. Later we went on to other teachers. I think Lou was very arrogant and I didn't have a very good impression of him but he was instrumental in starting many people dancing.

Virginia and I went often to the Alpine Village in Torrance for swing dancing. Since she was a much better dancer and a beautiful lady she was asked constantly to dance. She realized that I sat most of the time not being confident in my dancing and asking very few ladies to dance. She suggested that we limit our dancing to one dance only with people we knew and no sensual dancing with other partners. This worked out very well and we ended up dancing together much more. I really appreciate Virginia's consideration in dancing and other matters. Another incident which favorably impressed me was when we were on the sofa talking. She asked me what I thought of the idea when she spoke to me that I repeat back what I thought she was saying because often there is a lack of real communication between people especially between men and women.

We had a twenty fifth year high school reunion for our Minneapolis high school attended by alumni from classes over a span of a ten year period held in a large hotel near the Los Angeles airport. Many former students relocated out west, there were two hundred people present. Virginia and I had been doing quite a bit of west coast swing dancing, we attracted a lot of attention, both with our dancing and Virginia's striking looks. She was always noticed both by men and women. I have been lucky in having such beautiful women in my life.

Virginia & Me.   Boston

We began taking group dancing classes with Candice "Candi" Davis. Candi was one attractive, charming, beautiful woman. I can't believe anyone wouldn't be enchanted in her company. I was quite fond of her and possibly the feeling was mutual. Being of a very jealous nature Virginia mentioned and was suspicious of the apparent closeness between Candi and myself. In Virginia's presence I had to curb my attentions toward Candi. Years later Candi began teaching classes at our local Elks lodge. Although I didn't take but two classes in the years she taught there I would make a point of greeting her when I would be a the Elk's gym which was next to the dance area. We always greeted with a close embrace and a chat. I've known Candi off and on for twenty five years and believe that most of that time she was in a relationship, otherwise I would have liked to have been romantically involved with her. Her affection toward me may have possibly been more of a friendship than mine toward her.

Me & Candi Davis.

I happened to encounter her accidentally in Long Beach after one of her classes. She took my breath away clad in a body hugging silk oriental style split leg dress. While Martín Vaccaro was living with me around the year 2000 we invited Candi for a free tango lesson in my small home dance studio. I'm always amazed how quickly a trained dancer can learn. I recall that Candi and I did go dancing on a date.

Virginia and I were married twice. The down side of Virginia's and my relationship was her unfounded jealousy. We had many disagreements because of this and often without a valid reason. One example was the night before we were to be married a second time dancing in the skylight room in our San Diego hotel. I could sense that she was angry and she wanted to leave the dance. It took quite awhile before she would tell me, accusing me of flirting with some woman sitting nearby. I had no idea of what or who she was talking about. It turned out that she said I didn't do any turns as I usually do so I could look at that woman. I said that maybe I was tired. I was completely unaware of what she thought was going on. After awhile she relented and said maybe I wasn't guilty of flirting. Before we went to bed I finally said that an apology of "maybe" wasn't enough and I wouldn't go through with the marriage with those doubts at which point she apologized and things smoothed over. Our two brief marriages were in Lake Tahoe and the other in San Diego. At our San Diego wedding Tom Payne my good black friend and colleague came down to join us for dinner. We discovered that there was an international chocolate festival in the hotel ballroom. Unfortunately we were full after dinner and couldn't take full advantage of all the enticing delicacies.

I took Virginia to Formentera but she didn't like to go out of the house if there was any breeze that would get her hair out of place. She was always well groomed and preened, definitely an urban type. Virginia and I went on trips to the northern Sierra with my mother, to Minneapolis to be with the family and to Boston where I attended a medical symposium and meeting where we had dinner at famous Legal's Seafood Restaurant with my best friend Dr. Spamer who also attended the professional confab.

During my separations from Virginia I met another lady named Virginia C. and another Virginia M. a Portuguese opera singer. With the three Virginias in that time frame I didn't have to worry about saying the wrong name at the wrong time.

We separated various times before and after we married. We lived together and later, during the marriages a total of five or six years. We divorced amicably, at least on my part. I petitioned for divorce after Virginia said one evening when we were both sitting on the sofa, "I'm really not comfortable living together." In my mind that was reason to separate. She later mentioned that I was awful quick to divorce and that we should have waited and discussed the matter first.

After breaking up with Virginia I was fortunate enough to meet up and become part of the group of dance instructors and other dancers who took me under their wing. To name a few, there were Shari and George Block, Richard Jetter and Pat, Alan and Leslie Scott, Vera and Gene, the flamboyant Cassie who I tried my best to follow when she dragged me onto the floor for a tango and a few others I cannot recall at this moment. Everyone was very helpful in assisting me to learn to dance. Most of our dances were ballroom dances, Latin and west coast swing, street style without the flourishes of the international competitive style. West coast swing distinguishes itself from regular swing in that the dancers confine their dancing to a slot and not all over the dance floor as in regular swing or as we refer to it as, east coast swing. Also west coast swing is danced to a slower beat and east coast swing to big band music.

Casa Escobar in Marina del Rey had a small Latin combo of musicians and Ernie the DJ. There were nights only a few people showed up and our group was anywhere from six to ten. Consequently we had Ernie play our requests and we had the floor to ourselves all night. After the dance we would order potato pancakes at a diner a block away.

Shari and I would practice together often. Some of the venues our group frequented were: Alpine Village in Torrance, San Pedro Elk's lodge, the Mayflower ballroom in Inglewood, Casa Escobar in Marina del Rey and a hotel in Burbank.

The San Pedro Elk's Lodge 966, two blocks from my house, located at the foot of the Palos Verdes hill with a magnificent unsurpassed view of the port, the Pacific Ocean and much of Los Angeles and Orange Counties is one of the larger Elk's lodges in the country. There are three tennis courts, a large pool complex, body building weightlifting gym, bar and restaurant, three salons, etc. I don't play tennis any longer nor use the pool but I do work out regularly at the gym. I have been a member of our local lodge for thirty three years. As a thirty year member, one can become a life member with the annual dues a third as much as the regular dues.

I feel very fortunate to live in San Pedro. Our house overlooks the ocean and all of Catalina Island. We are on a slope to the ocean a half mile distant at an altitude of 600 feet. The prevailing winds are onshore, tempering the climate, cooling in the summer and warming in the winter except when the undesirable dry offshore Santa Ana winds pass through the city with its contaminated air on the way to the coast. Fortunately they are not too prevalent.

Much of downtown San Pedro is composed of many older buildings which are gradually being replaced but many of the old time residents that have been here for seven and eight generations are resistant to drastic changes preferring an old town atmosphere. San Pedro with Long Beach and Wilmington is probably the largest port complex in the US. San Pedro retains much charm and has similarities reminiscent of older European cities with a multi-ethnicity of Croatians, Italians, Portuguese, Spanish and others.

There is a local saying, "Nobody goes through San Pedro," that is to say it's a destination and there is no reason to go through San Pedro. Actually it's a peninsula surrounded by the Pacific Ocean and to the north by the Palos Verde hill (altitude 1,500 feet above sea level) and to the east, Terminal Island, Wilmington and Long Beach. The drive along the coast from San Pedro along the Palos Verdes Peninsula to Redondo Beach is not to be missed. On the way just a few miles from San Pedro one passes through a mile of the active Portuguese Bend landslide. This area is constantly moving down slope toward the sea. There were many homes destroyed with existing visible evidence of slanting structures and undulating sections of the coastal road. Our beautiful Paseo del Mar had a large section of cliff that fell into the sea last year and it's doubtful that the extensive damage will be repaired. There is a detour through the nature park by foot or by bike.

I frequent Cabrillo Beach and belong to the Polar Bear Club at the bath house where we have our own gym and club rooms. As a member we have free parking privileges. I previously rode my bike along Paseo del Mar until the cave-in and now ride in the large beach complex and to the end of the fishing pier for 60-80 minutes followed by a walk a few miles barefoot in the sand along our beautiful half mile long beach with the crashing surf, the seagulls, pelicans, seals, dolphins and other sea life along with the clean, fresh air that has purified itself after crossing more than 5,500 miles of open Pacific Ocean.

Years ago, it was quite difficult to have any business or commercial venture in San Pedro unless you were from or related to the older generation of residents and their ethnic groups. This has slowly changed through the years.

— — — — — —

My cousin Bob's son Reed was having problems of pain in his legs and elsewhere. Bob's brother in law Jack is a doctor and suggested that he ask me to perform an EMG and nerve conduction velocity tests. After hours of extensive and painful testing my results, I thought were consistent with a diagnosis of Guillain-Barré syndrome. It was verified and confirmed in the hospital at a later date as Charcot-Marie-Tooth, a hereditary neuropathy.

After my divorce from Jill and from Virginia I rented a room with a women in Palos Verdes Shores mobile home park where I had previously lived with Virginia. I couldn't return to my house which I had leased to Virginia's ex-husband, John Cuffel. Even before I met Virginia, I had friends that lived in the park and I often used the facilities, tennis, pool, health club, sauna and recreation room.

I also rented a room from my friend Ray Falk's mother-in-law's house on Almeria Street. Ray was president of the Polar Bear Club at Cabrillo Beach of which I've been a member for many years. She was called Birdie. The back yard was a virtual jungle. There were many edible plants and Birdie would cook very healthy meals. She later died of lymphatic cancer in her 80's.

John Cuffel was a contractor and changed many things in the house. He did make a nice dance studio in which I had wall to wall mirrors installed. He wasn't a dancer but many of his friends were dancers and he would have parties with many people. He would do all the cooking, etc. He was an alcoholic and heavy smoker and died soon after.

Chapter XXV
Argentine Tango

After my last divorce I continued dancing. I had a good friend Audrey who was an excellent dancer until she and other dance friends after months of cajoling finally convinced me to go with them for lessons of Argentine Tango. I finally consented after months of pleading and telling them I had no interest in tango. The place was Rusty's Hacienda in Hollywood. Mark Celaya promoted and taught. That night I didn't dance once with my partner which was upsetting for her, ending our relationship. I met many interesting people and was hooked on the dance. Hadassah "Das" Silverman was sitting with others in a booth and when I was introduced. I mentioned that Hadassah was a beautiful name. As I was jotting her name down she said she would spell it for me. She was surprised when I mentioned that I knew how it was spelled. Presently Das, whom I've often referred to as our Gran Dama del Tango is presently in her mid nineties and is not well. She is a very intelligent, generous and classy lady. We all miss seeing her at the milongas.

Bill with Hadassah "Das" Silverman

Two distinct things I recall with Das. At the Casa Argentina in Santiago, Chile, I kneeled to help Das adjust a heel strap and upon arising I asked her to dance. She looked at me and said, "Manolo, aren't you going to wash your hands before we dance?" Embarrassed, I immediately went to the wash room. She was also adamant about not calling her before noon. I just learned that Das passed away at 96, fifteen years after I first met her. She will be missed by many.

I resisted learning tango at my friends constant urging but after the first lesson I was determined to concentrate and become a good tango dancer in six months. I've now been dancing tango almost exclusively for fifteen years and still feel that I have so much to learn. I believe that Argentine tango is the most difficult of all the social dances to master. American or continental tango is much different from Argentine tango.

Charito is a Spanish Basque lady. I noticed this beautiful lady and attempted to speak with her but soon realized that I wasn't making any headway, she acted rather cool toward me. It wasn't until months later at a dance that she asked me to dance. To my delightful surprise she said that I danced like maestro Orlando Paiva and she would like to dance more with me. There is nothing anyone could have said to me that would have been as flattering. We were friends and went together for a short while but our personalities were too different. Her attitude seemed to be based a person's lineage, education, class, financial and or social position. Not my style. We did enjoy a romantic evening at an Italian restaurant and danced tango , alone on the floor, to the beautiful music of the string trio.

Flo, Unknown, Victoria & Me

Orlando Paiva and me

We met again at another milonga and danced. I was taken aback when she commented that I didn't dance to the rhythm and she pointed to a mutual friend and dancer, Norwood, who was a very rhythmic dancer. I said "Charito, I agree and I think you should dance with Norwood." Many years have passed with very little contact between us and I was surprised that she contacted me with her renewed interest in tango inviting me to go tango dancing. We talked about meeting at the dance sometime but I've managed to not make any commitment and would only dance with her if we happened to be at the same dance which is very unlikely as the dances she attends are not my favorites.

Michael Espinoza and Yolanda Rossi had a milonga at Tango Alley, in Hollywood, a, long narrow room with only one exit. I believe it closed because of the fire code. A fascinating night was the impromptu dancing of Orlando Paiva with Sandor, both men professional dancers. To many of us new enthusiastic tango aficionados anything relating to tango seemed to have a magical aura. Mark Celaya's milonga at Rusty's Hacienda was across the street.

Driving home in my 1984 Ford Econoline extended van after my first night of tango on April 10th of 1996, I dropped off my dance partner Audry, at her home and as I neared the end of the Harbor Freeway a little after midnight, a section of the freeway that was poorly lit, I suddenly noticed directly in front of me an old dark van stopped without lights in the center lane of the three lanes. There was a vehicle in both my left and right lanes. I slammed on my brakes knowing that at fifty five miles an hour there was no way I would stop in time. I chose to go to my left, hoping I wouldn't hit the car that was slightly ahead of me in the left lane. As I pulled over to the left about to pass the stopped van, the driver rushed from in front of his van to open the door on the driver's side to get in his van. I took off his door and hit him squarely. What I didn't realize, that he was in front of his van with the hood raised and evidently heard my screeching brakes and saw my headlights and desperately rushed to get into his van.

I pulled over to the left side got out and examined the body. He was dead. An off duty police officer passing by stopped to help me drag the body to the left side of the freeway. Evidently someone phoned in a report immediately as many police units converged on the scene and closed the freeway. One of the officers asked if I'd had anything to drink that evening. I said only a glass of cranberry juice. I guess he was satisfied as they didn't give me any tests of any kind and he said, that I chose the correct course of action, otherwise it would have likely caused a multiple vehicle accident. I had to wait for the coroner to arrive before I could leave. The officer offered me a ride home but my van was still driveable and I told him I was OK to drive. I arrived home after three am and went to bed. I fell asleep immediately and didn't wake up until after eleven the next morning. I was surprised as I've always had trouble sleeping. I've never had any regretful thoughts after the accident. There was nothing else I could have done. I was at the wrong place at the wrong time.

The deceased was a young, twenty year old Mexican national who borrowed his uncle's van to celebrate his birthday on the that very same night. Later the results from the police laboratory showed he tested positive for drugs and over twice the legal limit for alcohol. I had to go to court for a wrongful death hearing with my insurance company's lawyer. The judge asked me what percent of the accident was my fault. I replied, none. Again he asked if maybe ten percent was my fault. I replied again, absolutely none. My attorney said he couldn't have handled it any better himself. The family was awarded $40,000 instead of the $100.000. I felt bad for the family and wished the insurance company would have given them the hundred thousand. Since I was faultless my insurance company didn't raise my insurance premium.

The DMV contacted me for a special driver's test. I believe this is done when there is an automotive fatality. This was a very long extensive test but I felt very confident and comfortable of my driving ability.

Another incident occurred a few years later driving home after practicing tango with Woody and Flo at their home. From Long Beach, in the wee hours, over the bridges on a two lane, one way road with a concrete barrier separating the road going in the opposite direction, I was in the left lane and in front of me in the right lane was a Ford Explorer with five passengers. There appeared an opening in the barrier and suddenly without warning the Ford turned in front of me to go through the opening to return in the other direction. I was driving fifty miles per hour and smashed into the middle if the Explorer. Everything happened in an instant, I didn't know if I was going to come out alive. My car filled with smoke and I was sure it was on fire. I had difficulty releasing the seat belt and the door was jammed shut. Finally after a few hard kicks it flew open and I jumped out and distanced myself from my car. The "smoke" was from both airbags bursting. I don't know what would have happened without the airbag between me and the steering column and the windshield. I had no idea at that moment if I was OK or not. I hurt in a few areas of my upper body for a few days afterward. When the policeman approached me he said after seeing my totaled 1997 Toyota Camry he expected to see bodies. Fortunately that wasn't the case. The other vehicle was caved in at the middle but miraculously none of the five passengers of that Mexican family were hurt. Their vehicle was a rental. Again my insurance company did not raise my rates. A tow truck was called and I rode home with him.

— — — — — —

Aside from Orlando Paiva, the few Argentine disciples of his that teach or have taught locally are Martin Vaccaro and Claudio Omar Rubio and his wife Veronica, all originally from Rosario, Argentina. Claudio hasn't been back for years. Orlando's unique, original and difficult style is fluid and elegant. He was one of a kind and to this day there are few that still dance that style. I continued taking group and private lessons and going to milongas (tango dances). Once I began to take lessons with Orlando I took very few lessons from others except from Martín. Orlando moved back to Rosario but made frequent visits to teach in California. His partner, Susana Levrini also from Rosario, often accompanied him along with Martín, her seventeen year old son who also helped with the lessons.

At a group lesson with Orlando in a church in Pasadena I met Flo and Woody who are still my close friends. I began practicing and dancing with Flo. We went to all of Orlando's classes sponsored by Michael Espinoza and Yolanda Rossi, a local couple that taught and sponsored tango dances. Yolanda also studied and partnered with Orlando for the three tango videos they produced. I always enjoy dancing with Yolanda. I have to admit that I find it some what uncomfortable to dance with some ladies who are either not experienced with many styles of tango or have not been trained by Orlando Paiva or by his few disciples.

Orlando's style lends itself more to slow melodic romantic tangos such as those by Osvaldo Pugliese, Di Sarli and a few others. I even like a few by Astor Piazzola to which many Argentines refuse to dance. The term milonga is used to designate an Argentine tango dance venue. It also is a different dance and different rhythm then tango or waltz. In my opinion Orlando's style is beautiful but limited and doesn't do justice to fast heavy beat pieces, milongas or waltzes. Consequently I dance when I like the music and with partners that I feel comfortable with. The rest of the time watching the others dance, listening to the music and chatting. This can be entertaining as well. Occasionally there is Candombe, similar to milonga and a popular folk dance, Chacarera. Whenever you see the word tango, unless specified, will refer to Argentine tango only.

I believe I was instrumental in urging the playing of sets and the serving of vegetables at our local milongas. When Mark Celaya and his partner Joan Yarfitz had the most popular milonga at the Realtor's Hall in Burbank, I suggested some vegetables instead of the potato chip, crackers and peanut fare. I wrote a treatise on tandas (sets) and cortinas (curtains are short intermissions between sets) as played in Argentina. At the milonga in Downey with Miriam Larici, Hugo Patyne, John and Betty Tice. John told me that Miriam wanted to continue playing random songs as before. When Miriam and Hugo were out of the country performing I urged John to give it try and it's been tandas ever since. Tandas are now used in most of our local milongas. At present almost all the milongas locally follow this accepted Argentine protocol. There were only one or two milongas each week in the Los Angeles, Orange County area when I began tango. Presently I estimate there are more than a twenty each week, too many for the number of dancers.

I just received word that a friend and tango dancer, Francesco Tarantino, passed away. He was Italian and was one of our old guard, a distinctive character known by all. He had been ill for quite some time before his death. We were close friends in our tango world and never failed to greet one another with a hug and kiss. He will be missed. He always called me brother and playfully introduced me as his brother.

A few years into tango, either in San Diego or Los Angeles I met Jorge Nel from Manizales, Colombia, a professional tango dancer from childhood. I believe he organized the first milongas in the Miami area. He invited me to visit him in Florida and I spent a very interesting week as his guest. I spent the days either at the beach nearby or the pool at the apartment complex where he lived. There were two ladies at the pool every day with whom I would flirt. One was visiting from Bogota, Columbia the other, an older lady with an age wrinkled, but a very shapely body.

I accompanied Jorge and his partner to Key Largo for an engagement to perform at an upscale club. It was an outdoor venue and they performed exceptionally well considering they danced on a four by six foot piece of plywood on the sandy ground. After the performance I asked Jorge how he managed to perform under such adverse conditions. He replied that if he was paid he would even dance in a swamp if necessary.

Jorge was an excellent master of ceremonies and entertainer. One of his enticements to the audience was playing a recording of music he assumed no one was familiar with and offering $5,000 to anyone who could come up with the title. No one could identify the song but by sheer coincidence I just happened to know the title, "En er Mundo," a Spanish paso doble. When I mentioned that afterward he was amazed. I don't recall collecting the $5,000. If by chance someone did come up with the correct title I'm certain that Jorge would manage to somehow gracefully wiggle out of it.

Aside from performing and teaching around the world he has a line of tango footwear manufactured by his brother in Manizales. It's always a pleasure when I run across Jorge now and then during his travels. He and his partner have stayed at my house a few times recently.

Margareta is a Swedish woman approaching seventy. She has for the past dozen years devoted herself to Argentine tango and goes to Buenos Aires yearly. The first time I saw her was at one of the large popular milongas, Los Consagrados. She was seated in the front row. She was rather nondescript on the heavy side at that time and evidently she was unknown, probably one of her first milongas in Buenos Aires. The night went on and I noticed that no one invited her to dance. I finally thought she probably was not a good dancer so I would do her a favor and give her the accepted nod. I am not a good dancer so I thought nothing lost. I was amazed how well she followed and went over to tell my friend Howard Barsky to dance with her. When he came back he said, "Don't tell anyone how well she dances, they'll monopolize her and we won't be able to get many dances before they find out." Howard likes to tell that he was the one that discovered her. Not true. She has become one of the accepted and most sought after dancers and has recently published a well documented book, Tango Passion, thoroughly covering the many aspects of the dance and the emotions involved in this very special tango world.

How could I forget my old friend and salon tango dancer Howard Barsky. Howard is probably one of the best known and popular dancers in the LA area and well known in the Buenos Aires milongas. An accomplished painter, great joke teller and charming personality, his tango blogs are up to date and contain a wealth of tango information, venues, comments, etc. Always great seeing you, Howard.

My tango scene cannot be complete without mentioning Dee. She is a beautiful, statuesque lady, one of the dancers whose presence makes for a lovely ambiance at the milongas and parties. She dances almost every dance, always smiling and a pleasure to be with. She is very generous in dancing with everybody and rarely lacks a partner. Dee and her husband Gerry have a fabulous party for their tango friends every summer for 15 to 20 people. There is no dancing because this is purely social and dancing changes that atmosphere. I have followed that premise for my tango patio parties and find you get to know the people more intimately than at the dances. I, like most, always look forward to my dances with her.

Kent and Sheryl Johnson studied with Claudio and Veronica. I look forward to dancing that style with Sheryl. They are one of the most sociable, well liked couples at the milongas.

Bill and Ann Frond, a charming couple from England, take advantage of living near Palm Springs in the winter months and returning to their home in England during the summers. It's always a pleasure to be in their company and watch Bill's personal, entertaining style of dance. They are excellent tango dancers.

Speaking of parties, my dear English friends Gerry and Marion Leighton had lavish tango dancing New Year's parties which we all looked forward to. The variety of wonderful cooked and cold foods and a blues band made for a fabulous party. I attended three successive years and those were the only ones they gave that I'm aware of. Naturally I'm the designated driver of my friends for most of these affairs.

I would like to comment about a few of the local tango dancers that impress me regarding their style, courtesy and floor craft. Tall David and his beautiful Argentine wife, Gloria and Hector and Cecilia his lovely Argentine partner. They all dance a very smooth and lovely tango. Both ladies are excellent followers. I am especially impressed how well Cecilia follows. Although they are capable of fancy show steps they walk their tango as social tango should be done.

Larry Burnett, originally from South Africa, hasn't been dancing that long and so far sticks to basic and walking and to me he looks like a polished salon tango dancer, mainly due to having a smooth nice walking style. I'm not sure he believes me when I tell him how good he looks.

I certainly cannot omit my good friends Bill and Patricia Blakeney who were dancers and two of our teachers of Orlando Paiva's style. They held an informal get together in the recreation room of the apartment complex where John and Phyllis lived in Orange County. There was a free half hour lesson before the dancing attended anywhere from ten to twenty dancers. We were all friends. I miss that atmosphere of camaraderie of those sessions.

There was a ten day international tango festival in Amsterdam that Bill and Patty were to attend. A few nights before, at Cesar's Sunday milonga, they took me aside and told me that Bill at the last moment was unable to take time off of his job and if I would accompany Patty, all first class expenses would be paid. It was such an unexpected and shocking proposal that I wasn't sure how to answer. I made some lame excuse about the weather that time of the year in Holland. Patty was personally insulted that I could turn the offer down and frankly I would have gladly accepted the company of that tall, beautiful lady had it not been for the circumstances of being with the wife of a friend. If the opportunity arose again, I certainly would accept.

After a large group class with Orlando Paiva a few us were chatting with him. Next to me was Patricia from Chile who looked surprised and said that she didn't know I spoke Spanish, to which I replied that I didn't know that she spoke Spanish. Patricia's lovely appearance is very Anglo Saxon with blond hair, etc. We've known each other for all the years I've danced tango.

Flo and I took a few classes in tango waltz with Julio and Corina Balmaceda at Norma Gil's home. I ran across Ernesto Balmaceda, brother of Julio and his partner Stella at Niño Bien in Buenos Aires. He invited me to join his group class in waltz at another venue. He was leading a class of about fifteen students but I vacillated until he convinced me to take his class. We followed behind him and suddenly stopped and said, without turning around, that someone was dragging their feet. That somebody was me. Some styles have contact with their feet on the floor at all times, others do not. The Balmaceda family including the father are well known tango waltz luminaries.

Los Angeles is very fortunate to have Miriam Larici, her partner Leonardo Barrionuevo and her father, Bruno, all have resided here for many years. Miriam is undoubtedly one of the best performing tango dancers in the world and has developed Leonardo into a great partner. They constantly perform throughout the world. She has been the leading female dancer in many of the important tango revues. They started the milonga, El Rincón, my favorite milonga.

John and Betty Tice took over the milonga as Miriam and Leonardo are traveling and with their performing and teaching had little time, although they always perform at and attend the milonga when they are able. I'm not that interested in the ordinary performances of show tango after having seen so many, but watching the eternally young and gorgeous Miriam and handsome partner Leonardo is something very special and artistic. They are beautiful, friendly people to all, inside and out. And they are very modest and low key. They get many students for their classes, performances and tango cruises.

John Tice does the presentations, MC and DJ. In my opinion, for my dancing, he plays the best music: Pugliese, Di Sarli and many slower romantic tangos. Betty is very musical and together they choose which songs they will play. Betty, ever since she was a child has had the uncanny ability to memorize a song and lyrics hearing it only once. When she was a girl she thought that everyone had this talent. She has an extensive repertory and is a virtual encyclopedia of Latin American music lyrics. Along with Betty's daughter Bridgette, the three of them cater, organize and do all the non stop work from before the milonga starts until after the end. Tragically Bridgette's husband suddenly passed away. I sent my heartfelt condolences. We've missed seeing you, Bridgette.

My good friend Henrik is actually everyone's friend and the most courteous dancer and person I know. It's always a pleasure to see him. He is also one of the dancers who generously dances with all the ladies.

Jo Ann Travis and I were driving to a milonga with Henrik in his car when we had a flat tire on the freeway. We pulled off the freeway to a side road where Henrik phoned for assistance. He started to phone for a taxi to take Jo Ann and me to the dance while he waited until his flat tire was changed and would join us later. We said that we preferred waiting with him which we did and all went together. The consideration for others is very typical of Henrik. Henrik is always on the beat, a competent dancer.

Sad news, another old tango friend, Ruth Jaramillo, wife of Marcelo died after her two year battle with breast cancer. I always remember whenever she would greet me she would kiss me on each cheek, Spanish style, whereas most Latins kiss on one side only. May she rest in peace.

A memorable dance experience at Luba's milonga in Costa Mesa a few years back was my encounter with Bill and Terry Ott. This was the first time I saw them. I noticed that Terry wasn't dancing so I asked her to dance to a slow tango. I was amazed how well we danced the first time. This was the first time that I was so at ease and that a partner followed me so beautifully. I actually felt that I was an excellent tango dancer. Amazing the effect that can have on ones psyche. Terry is a complete dancer.

I recall that they won a trip to Buenos Aires at the first International Festival in Las Vegas that I also attended but I didn't know them at the time.

At that time Bill Ott didn't dance social tango with his wife although they performed other choreographed dances together. They were a good looking couple and Terry is an exceptionally beautiful and sensuous lady with a figure to die for. Bill told me that she enjoyed dancing with me and to ask her for more dances, a rather strange request I thought at the time.

I only saw them a few times and only at Luba's milonga after which, they seemed to disappear for two years. Dancing at Luba's the other night, Luba mentioned that they had been there the last few times. I was hoping they would show up that night but that didn't happen. Last night at El Rincon milonga at the Downey Elk's lodge it was a pleasant surprise to see them and the pleasure of dancing again with Terry. I look forward to seeing both of them and hope it won't be as long as before.

I had an unexpected bumping into and embracing Johanna in the middle of the aisle on a plane returning to the US from Buenos Aires about ten years ago. I remember a tango performance in one of the Los Angeles milongas by Guillermo Alió who chose Johanna as his partner. He knew she was one of our best tango dancers.

I went to get acquainted with Guillermo Alió in his studio in La Boca on Magallanes street. I ended up spending most of the day chatting with him and a magazine editing friend of his. Aside from tango he is a well known artist and a friend of my friend Mirta Rosenberg another recognized artist from La Boca. On another occasion the three of us happened to meet at Alio's studio. There is an ice cream parlor El Vesuvio on Avenida Corrientes. I was with a date when we saw Guillermo perform. Another time at that same locale, we were surprised when someone tapped me on the shoulder. When I turned around Elizabeth Kopecky was there. She was also performing singing Peruvian waltzes, her forté.

Woody, Flo, me, ? Ann Shaver

El Vesuvio, an ice cream parlor on Corrientes, had performers, both amateur and professional dancers, singers poets, anything related to tango on Tuesday evenings.

Flo, Das, Patricia, Paula, Woody, Sala Cha 3, Madrid
Bill, Ana and me.

A group of our tango devotees consisting of Flo and Woody Woodruff, Patricia and Bill Blakeney, Das Silverman, Ana Rossell and Paula Ardilla met me in Spain in 1998. We started in Madrid where we spent a few days going to milongas every evening and night. Some of our favorites were La Carreta, Sala Cha 3, Gomila, Palacio de la Gaviria to name a few I can recall. We stayed in Hotel Paris on Alcalá adjoining the Puerta del Sol. Much of our days were spent exploring and noshing on Spanish bread, cheeses, olives and wine, aside from our meals. We were fortunate to attend the premiere of the movie, Tango, by Carlos Saura. After waiting in the long line and looking for our numbered seats it ended up that I was next to Ana Rossell and I should have been between the others that didn't speak Spanish as there were no subtitles and I could have helped with any translations.

From Madrid we flew to Barcelona where we stayed at the Continental on the Rambla de las Flores. The few days in Barcelona, as in Madrid, we went to many milongas. A memorable one was El Molino Rojo that had the perfect bordello like atmosphere for tango. The only drawback at that time was the rough cement floor which was later replaced by a wood floor. Ana Rossell fell in love with Barcelona.

Patricia had planned all the details and made any reservations we needed. She knew every detail of our trip and would actually tell the Spanish taxi drivers which streets to take. I don't believe a professional travel consultant could do as well.

Except for Ana, Das and Paula, we all went to Formentera for a few days. Jill was a gracious hostess as always. Bill was amazed that Jill picked up, in a brief time, the basic tango he showed her, which isn't surprising with her extensive dance background.

The following year Woody and Flo came back to visit us in Formentera. The Punta Prima Club Hotel had their end of the season party. They invited all the guests, staff and employees and most of the island locals. There was probably in excess of two hundred people attending. Many finger foods were served including hors d oeuvres and jamon serrano, a true Spanish delicacy of raw, naturally cured ham aged by hanging under certain controlled conditions for many months. This type of ham is graded according to the letter "J" followed by the numbers from one to five, the latter number indicating the highest rating. I didn't like the odor and didn't like cured ham in the beginning. The smell reminded me of the days spent in the anatomy lab dissecting cadavers preserved in formaldehyde. I now enjoy this Iberian favorite when it is good quality.

The younger crowd was dancing to the modern music played by the DJ with recorded music. At about ten in the evening the band composed of six older musicians had just arrived from the Valencia and began to play music for the adults. I asked if they knew and could play Argentine tangos. They said yes. I exchanged a doubtful glance at Flo figuring that it wouldn't be an authentic rendition. When they began playing it sounded quite good and danceable. She asked Woody, her husband, but he didn't want to dance in front of so many people so she grabbed my hand and we went to the middle of the floor and we danced through my whole repertory of steps. We danced by ourselves, alone on the floor continually for a medley of three tangos. I closed my eyes most of the time and had one of those rare moments of being transported to another dimension, a feeling I've only experienced a few times since I've been dancing. Everyone applauded for quite awhile and approached us to congratulate us on our performance. Flo was amazed at how perfectly everything went and that I was so completely relaxed and confident. Maybe if we could see a replay now we might not be so impressed, nevertheless it was unforgettable night. It was one of those too few glorious episodes of the ultimate sensation in dancing one experiences during a lifetime.

Many of Jill's dance students raved about our dancing exhibition for days afterward and she was quite upset about the situation. She refused to attend the party with us and maybe it was better that way. People on the street and at the beach would stop to compliment us for days afterward.

Argentine acquaintances of mine living in Formentera had a restaurant-night club on the beach at El Pujols called Caminito, which later was moved to a much larger more elegant site with a swimming pool and outdoor barbecues for preparing Argentine asados. The proprietors were four Argentines from Buenos Aires living on the island. I told my friend Jorge, one of the owners, whenever we go there we only wanted to hear tangos not other music which they sometimes would play for the non Argentine clients. When we ate there Flo and I would make a spectacle of ourselves dancing tango among the diners. Woody was more discreet and reserved. Jorge said his father- in-law was a great old-time tango milonguero and Flo couldn't wait to dance with him. One night Jorge brought the old gentleman. It was arranged that he and Flo would dance. It was a disaster, he was absolutely a terrible dancer.

Flo & Me

One of those times at Caminito, which Flo doesn't like to hear me talk about, was the only occasion I've witnessed where between the wine and champagne she was tipsy. We started dancing and she was quite unsteady to say the least. When we finished Flo commented on how well we danced. I couldn't believe she was serious as we just didn't dance well and I cut the dance short. This was the only time in the many years I've known her that this occurred. I don't believe I've encountered any woman that followed better than Flo. I suppose that's one of the reasons so many men are anxious to dance with her. It's not uncommon to be at a milonga when Flo isn't present and have many of the men ask, "Where is Flo?"

The last trip Woody and Flo took to Formentera in the autumn of 2000 or 2001. Our friend Ann Shaver, with whom I previously practiced and danced tango, accompanied us, the three of them traveling from Los Angeles to Spain. Woody really doesn't participate as much as we do in the island's beach activities and said he would like to take a trip on the mainland if they were to come to Formentera again which I promised to do. I really did not look forward to more traveling on the mainland as I had done such extensive traveling throughout the whole country when I worked as a courier and with Jill in our act for a total of eleven years. I don't believe there are many places or areas in Spain that I haven't been numerous times.

After two weeks on the island, in mid September, we flew to Barcelona where we rented a car and proceeded south along the coast without an itinerary nor any reservations. The tourist season was coming to an end and there was little traffic and no problem encountering lodging. Woody did almost all the driving with Ann as the navigator with Flo and I in the back seat.

We visited many wineries both large and small family operated ones. All were different and unique experiences. I decided to go inland from Valencia to areas that tourists rarely visit, mainly in La Mancha, where we also visited other wineries and a small family olive oil plant. Everywhere we were shown through the facilities except one wine bottling factory where the owner said it was their busy season but to feel free to wander wherever we wished throughout the plant. We didn't run across other tourists during most of the trip.

In Valdepeñas we stopped at a hardware store to buy duct tape to patch Ann's suitcase which was coming apart. At the same time we stopped in a small charming local restaurant for supper. Ann ordered a local dish with no idea of what it was and the rest of us ordered standard fare. Hers was delicious and we all dug in and ate most of it before Ann could finish it.

Off the highway we were impressed with a large iron structure of Don Quixote on his steed Rocinante and Sancho Panza at his side. Nearby we stopped at the reconstructed ruins of the historic castle of Chinchilla in the province of Albacete, enjoying exploring all the nooks and crannies. That was the time that my camera malfunctioned.

At the foot of the hill where the castle was located was a small village where we went down the stone stairs of the local wine cellar where we purchased some beer and soft drinks to go with our sandwiches bought nearby. We sat on a stone bench in the sun eating and chatting.

After seven marvelous adventure filled days we arrived in Madrid where we turned in our rented vehicle and stayed in the Hotel Paris on Alcalá and Puerta del Sol. It was one of my very best trips. We all enjoyed and raved about our mutual adventure and will always remember and treasure those precious moments with dear friends.

It seems as though most of the times I've flown from the states to Madrid or Barcelona or returning to the US, the connecting flights to and from Ibiza entailed spending the whole night anywhere from ten to fifteen hours at the airport in Madrid or Barcelona. Flo, Woody and I went through this on one of our return flights from Ibiza to Madrid. We arrived at Madrid about 9 pm and our flight to LA was scheduled to leave at 8 am the next morning. We were unable to get a room in Madrid as it was October and their peak convention season. I checked with a female employee at the airport who told us about a lounge in another section that we might find comfortable. It was a large lounge with many cushioned chairs, an all night bar with sandwiches, nearby washrooms and large tinted windows facing the tarmac. We were able to put our suitcases between two lounge chairs almost in form of a bed so we were quite comfortable.

In all my other similar trips since then that lounge no longer exists at Barajas, the airport at Madrid. The only alternative is to spend the night, is either go into Madrid which isn't really practical from a time and economical standpoint or sleep on the hard, cold tile floors as many do, or sit at the all night bar in the terminal. Prat de Llobregat, the Barcelona airport was smaller than Madrid and had hard chairs and benches and no bar that I was aware of at night. I seldom can sleep under those conditions although I can rest and occasionally doze. That is one of the reasons I dislike air travel and plan to avoid it in the future if I have my druthers. If I could fly business or first class it may be more tolerable but my only time traveling in first class is on my way to the coach section.

When I flew in and out of Ibiza in the 60's the airport terminal was a large Spanish style chalet with various large rooms, alcoves and balconies decorated with amphorae as vases for various flowers and plants. There were many comfortable chairs and lounge chairs among abundant multicolored bougainvillea vines. Presently it is a large, cold rather sterile building as are many of the modern airports. I miss the charm, warmth, simplicity and comfort of many of these older bygone things no longer around.

Chapter XXVI
Tandas (sets) & Cortinas (curtains)

There must be a reason why all the milongas in Argentina and most of the world use this system. The following concepts are only from my limited observations and interpretation. Most tango dancers and aficionados who have danced tango in Buenos Aires and other venues are familiar with this system and related codes of conduct.

Basically this system consists of sets (tandas) of three or four songs of the same ilk, tangos, milongas or vals. Other sets of social dances may also be included such as chacarera, paso doble, swing, tropical, etc. If so, they are normally done only one set during the dance (milonga). At the beginning of each set the listener knows that all music in that set will be of the same genre and does not have the discomfort of an abrupt change of mood and pace in the same set. The advantages are obvious.

After each set and curtain the couples leave the floor and separate. It was not considered proper to dance with the previous partner for a consecutive set nor for more than a few sets with the same partner during the milonga. Couples are not obligated to observe these codes. Except for Saturday, usually a couple night, most milongas are attended by singles (no reference to matrimonial status). More dancers have a chance to dance and are not able to monopolize anyone observing this protcol. It seems in our milongas there are dancers who will keep their partner on the floor for numerous dances. This is especially noticeable toward the end of the evening when many of the ladies leave early and many of the men hold on to their partners. Consequently, others are left waiting or leave for the lack of available ladies. Since we are a relatively small tango community and known to each other some of the ladies do not want to offend their friends by not continuing to dance and may want to dance with others. She may have to resort to having to go to the bathroom, being thirsty, or tired. If this is the case, she doesn't want to insult the gentleman by getting up and dancing with someone else until a few songs have gone by so she's obligated to sit whether she wants to or not.

El cabeceo (the nod or the eye). This is a man's subtle invitation to dance but the woman has the option of not responding. That way both parties save face. It is not proper for a gentleman to ask and definitely not for a lady to ask. If a gentleman walks over to a lady and offers his hand or grabs her hand she is almost obligated to accept or bluntly reject him. It is not an accepted practice. I personally do not recall seeing this in Buenos Aires among the local milongueros. I think it might be interesting to use the cabeceo where practical for the purpose of familiarizing one's self, especially when at milongas where this is the accepted practice. Although at our local milongas I realize that we usually are familiar with most of the dancers and the cabeceo isn't a necessity and seldom used, but I like to keep the habit and often continue the practice.

These codes are not always observed or adhered to especially by foreigners (non Argentines). Also these codes are evolving and becoming less strict with the passing time and influx of foreign dancers.

Being accustomed to tango both here and in Argentina I am sometimes confused here when one partner says "Thank you" before the tanda (set) is finished. In Buenos Aires it is an indication that they wish not to continue and the couple leaves the floor. Thanks are only proper at the end of the tanda or when leaving the floor.

There was an anecdote I heard about a middle aged foreign couple who went to Buenos Aires and looked up an old famous tanguero to ask how long it would take them to learn basic tango. The old tanguero asked if he meant for the man or for the woman. The man asked if there was a difference and the old man said yes, there is a difference. The gentleman asked how long for a woman?

The old man replied, if shes has some talent and is in good shape then scratched his chin and thought for awhile before replying, two years. The tourist said that was a long time what about for the man? The old man replied, under the same conditions, seven years. There is probably a lot of truth in this.

How I miss that marvelous, elusive feeling of being transported to another unreal place. This hasn't happened more than two or three times that I can recall during the fifteen years I've been dancing Argentine tango.

I, for one, would very much like to see our milongas conform more to the Argentine style, realizing that some of the concepts may not work the same in our locale. All I all, I do think it would be more satisfying for the majority both socially and for the dancing once the dancers understand and become familiar with the way that tango is danced in much of the world.

I'm certain there are those who prefer the "status quo" in our milongas but it might be interesting to get other viewpoints and comments.

I am taking the liberty of using a copy of an article by Polly Mc-Bride, author and tango aficionado from Portland, Oregon, which is well worth reading by anyone in the world of tango dancing.

"A...n...t...i...c...i...p...a ...t...e.   A definite NO NO.

"What is it about wai..........ting that is so difficult?

"One of the most essential skills for Follows is to "listen." In other dances we keep moving and have learned to follow by continuing our motion in order to reach the next count with our partner and the music. Not so in tango. The lead has the option of altering the timing and/or direction each time we collect. Even if we know what the next step will be, as in practice situations, we are to w....a.....i.....t. Our upper body should be absolutely silent, no wiggles, jiggles, or sways. Firm, alert, quiet. The quality of our following is directly associated with axis alignment and our ability to wait. (Leads discuss this about us). We are not to assume, ever. The more skilled our partner, the more options available and if we move before receiving the invitation, we have inadvertently confiscated the lead.

We hover in collect position between steps, legs and knees together, until we receive the indication to continue. In forward and back ochos (figure eights), for example, we step and wait. The Lead may next indicate a rotation, or a forward, side (open) or back step. In molinetes we are lead in specific timing by the Lead, and are guided by the rotation of his chest and shoulders. If we change weight or shift our balance before invited, the lead follow connection is diffused, (Some instructors teach that the Lead may expect us to continue with molinetes or ochos until indicated otherwise.)

Allowing ourselves to yield completely and to pausing on a step are essential to developing good following technique (incorporating embellishments is a different aspect).

"Good Leads are well worth the w w a a a i i i t t t ....t t t."

- -

A few of my personal comments on Argentine Tango; a difficult dance to learn, an addiction, often pleasant, sometimes not. Being a very sensuous dance with close body contact and romantic music, for some there are dangers of jealousy, temptation and other emotions. In the case of couples, if one dances and the other doesn't, that can be a problem. If they both dance with others, that can be a larger problem. I don't think this needs elaboration.

Chapter XXVII
Buenos Aires

I was very aware of the large Jewish population in Argentina especially in the large metropolitan areas. It's not uncommon to see Hasidic Jews in their black suits with their long sideburns and black hats. Many others commonly wear their yarmulkes at work and on the street. Many of the businesses are Jewish owned. I happened to be in a small lock and key shop. The owner once in awhile would interject a Yiddish word in the conversation. When he knew I understood and that I was Jewish, we had a long friendly chat. He invited me to celebrate the Passover Seder at his house with his family but I couldn't make it. Similar things have happened to me more than a few times in Argentina.

Some of my tango friends went with Linda Valentino on a tango tour to Buenos Aires. Woody and Flo, Das, Ray Katz and others were in the group. I didn't start tango dancing until a few years after they began.

One of the first tango dances (milonga) that Flo and I went to in Buenos Aires was called Re Fa Si. Before I left the US, maestra Daniela Arcuri, a friend and teacher, advised me to watch for the good women dancers and not to dance with poor dancers. I saw this lovely girl dancing and she looked to be a good dancer. I nodded inviting her to dance. I knew immediately that things were not going well. I should have never asked her to dance. I knew that I was terrible. She was kind enough to stay with me till the first song ended before she thanked me which I knew was protocol for not wanting to dance anymore with me. I felt so bad and so embarrassed and inadequate that I went to stand in a balcony facing the street. I didn't dance anymore that evening. Flo also had a difficult and demoralizing time and we decided never to return to that locale.

Linda Valentino imported some of the best tango dancers, singers and orchestras from Argentina for weekend affairs in first class hotels in the Los Angeles area. The first one that I attended was a decade ago at the Crowne Plaza Hotel in Redondo Beach. The last extravaganza was in a Long Beach hotel. I distinctly recall the famous Argentine tango orchestra, one of my favorites, Color Tango.

On my right sat a gentleman, Daniel Rofman, a tango impresario from Rosario but living and conducting business in Buenos Aires. He spoke little English and we instantly became friends and have gotten together a few times in Buenos Aires. His office was only blocks from where I resided. As it happened, a pure coincidence, at the empty seat at my side came Loreen Arbus. There were eight at a table and maybe three hundred people attending. I was always interested in this attractive, exotic looking lady and have had the pleasure of dancing with her at various times. She has always been pleasant but I never did make any headway with her. I was danc-ing at El Arranque, one of my favorite milongas, in the Nuevo Salon Argentina near Callao and Bartolomé Mitre in Congreso. There was a normal crowd of about two hundred people when I saw her enter. I was lucky to get to her first for one set before the old timers who tend to monopolize the beautiful foreign women who are good dancers. Loreen danced professionally with Alberto Toledano and group. Theirs was one of the early local professional tango groups in California.

Alberto Toledano was one of the local pioneers in the the tango arena in the Los Angeles area. He was a Moroccan Jew from Tang-ier. He was an engineer by profession and I understand he was a genius in mathematics. Except for a few friends, he was a loner and not easily engaged in conversation.

His long time partner, Loreen Arbus, an exotic, voluptuous wom-an, composed one of the first professional tango duos in the area. Karlo Abouroumieh, an Iranian, joined the group later.

I remember one of Alberto's last performances with Li (la Japonesa) at the milonga El Rincon when it was temporarily in Long Beach. I thought their performance surpassed that of the well known, better Argentine dancers that performed that night in the same exhibition. Soon after he passed away, much before his time.

I danced with Loreen at one of Linda Valentino's milongas. Loreen had just returned from Buenos Aires, looking exceptionally stunning with black leather, skin tight slacks and low cut top, defining her ample bosom and hips and accentuating her slim waist. Her beautiful dark hair hanging down past her waist and good looks provoked an erotic sensation. I've danced with few women with hair that long where one had to be aware of his right hand on the ladies back not getting entangled in the long tresses on the lady's back. When I saw her leave I asked if I could accompany her to her car, which she gratefully accepted. I was hoping to linger and talk with her but that didn't happen.

I didn't have any special place to stay on one of my arrivals. Flo was staying at Hotel Castelar. I got one of the few remaining vacant rooms. Talking to the concierge, he asked me if I realized that the room I was occupying was the same room that Rubén Darío the Nicaraguan poet occupied when in Buenos Aires. He mentioned that Darío preferred that room because the balcony had a lovely view of the Avenida de Mayo. Later I noted a small bronze plaque on the facade of the hotel attesting to what the concierge had related to me a few nights before.

Most of the Argentine hotels and guest houses have very strict rules about who can enter. I've seen well known tango professors denied entrance to see a student. I believe this limited access to non residents of the hotel is more of a security issue than one of morality. I also observed this during my first years in Spain and Portugal although I never experienced that in other European countries I visited.

At a Sunday afternoon milonga at the gazebo in La Glorieta del Belgrano, upon starting to dance, I almost immediately had a sudden, intense reaction to the woman's perfume and told her I had to stop. My pulse was over 100, almost twice my normal rate. I sat on a park bench for twenty minutes before I felt OK. I'm certain she was offended, so later after recovering I tried to explain but she still couldn't or wouldn't understand as she replied that at least I could have finished the rest of that number.

At times I've had problems when I've been exposed to certain odors. Being asthmatic I have had occasions of sudden allergic reactions to strong perfumes, acetone in nail polish, polish remover and other essences. Very often the women don't understand and feel offended if I tell them that I can't continue dancing and have to stop immediately.

One of my favorite tango venues in Buenos Aires was the old Club Español right off 9 de Julio, the world's widest street, not far from Avenida de Mayo. I saw this attractive gray haired women and gave her the "nod". We met on the dance floor and between the songs we chatted during the short intermissions. Her name was Marisa Riviere. I inquired where she was from and she replied she was from Buenos Aires but lives in Minnesota. I asked where in Minnesota and she asked why I wanted to know. We were speaking in Spanish and she told me later that she thought I was also Argentine and probably didn't even know where Minnesota was. She was from Minneapolis. I told her I was also from Minneapolis. For a few minutes I think she had her doubts. I think most Latin women are dubious about many things that unknown men tell them and probably with good reason.

Marisa Riviere.

We have been friends since and I have visited her a few times and she has visited me for ten days in San Pedro.

About the same time I met Marisa in club Español, I met Clara Carlssen from Sweden. She was tall and shapely, a head above most of the others in the room. She looked my way, I nodded, and we met on the dance floor. We hit it off from the beginning. We spend the next week and her remaining time in Buenos Aires dancing together.

We made plans to meet in Barcelona, where we stayed at Hotel Peninsula, Sant Pau, 34. I wasn't very impressed with the four milongas we attended in Barcelona. Years before I had really enjoyed many good milongas there. Our five days there did not go well. From the first day I felt a distance and coolness about her. I discovered that she had contracted crab lice and she blamed me, thinking it was from our time together in Buenos Aires. I went to my urologist and tested negative. I can only assume she was infected elsewhere. I never contacted her again.

I met María Eugenia Yanzón soon after I became involved with tango. Flo and I had a private lesson the same day she and her mother had their lesson at Armando and Daniela's temporary garage studio in the Valley. For a period of several years, María who is Argentine, resided in Malibu and Santa Monica and for a short time had her own milonga in Santa Monica before returning to live in Buenos Aires. She is an architect by profession and has traveled widely having lived also in Spain and Brazil where she has property in both. I am well acquainted with her family. She recently purchased a nine room apartment in central Buenos Aires on Corrientes, the main thoroughfare of the city, which she remodeled as a tango guest house called Tango Paradise. It's conveniently located between Riobamba and Ayacucho. located one block from the metro B stop My daughter and son-in-law also stayed there on their trip to Argentina.

Two ladies and I, Bunny Schumaker and Carol Knight, were her first clients. I have stayed at her house various times for up to a month and she has always been a welcome guest at my house.

On one visit her main rooms were occupied but I used a small room that would eventually be prepared as a guest room. María bought a safe to be installed as she has in all the other guest rooms. In the meantime I locked my valuables and passport, etc., in my suitcase. I returned one night to find that my wallet, passport and more than $2,000 were missing. My room and my suitcase were both still locked and everything else was untouched. Her new maid had access to all the rooms and was confronted by María. I went to the local police station at 10 pm that same night to make a report but there were so many people waiting and the officials are inefficient and slow. I returned to my room and went back to the police station at 3 am and didn't have long to wait. I later read their report which had many errors and omissions. I knew that it would do no good but it is important to make an official report for legal reasons. I went the following day to the American Embassy for a new provisional passport and spent the entire day waiting and doing the required procedures, returning a few days later when the passport was ready. I wasn't too demoralized as I always say that things could be worse. I felt bad for María as I know she felt responsible even though it was not her fault any more than mine. She always offered to safeguard my valuables but I didn't want to inconvenience either of us. She reported the maid to the police but there was no proof. We were certain that the maid was involved by opening the outside and inside doors for an accomplice, opening my door and picking the simple lock on my suitcase. Everyone was out, making it a simple matter. I was dismayed when María told me that the maid filed suit and caused my dear friend María legal problems. I don't remember if she told me how it settled or if I was too embarrassed to ask.

A more pleasant memory took place in the milonga at Club Español. Between sets, with everybody seated, María looked my way a few times and smiled. I didn't know if it was a friendly smile or an invitation to dance. It must have been the latter because during the brief intermission with everyone seated she stood up and walked over to me across the empty floor. I have to admit I was pleased that all the others in the room saw this lovely lady come to get me. My friend Jo Ann Travis, another beautiful lady, always commented on María being the most beautiful lady in the world.

Other tango friends in Buenos Aires are Cherie and Rubén who teach tango, Graciela Giorgetti, a tango dancer and shiatsu practitioner with a graduate diploma in shiatsu from Japan. She is sought for treatments from prominent professional athletes and Japanese diplomatic personnel in or visiting Buenos Aires. Patricia, the dark eyed beauty, hostess at Club Español and Lo de Celia milongas. I always looked forward to seeing and flirting with her and the fact that she always would seat me in a choice section among the better dancers in spite of me not being one of the good dancers. There were times when she would have to shuffle a few dancers' chairs to slip me into the front row. I also want to acknowledge the many other friends that I may not have mentioned.

Howard Barsky, Dee Schwartz & me
at El Congreso. Avda. de Mayo & Callao, Buenos Aires.

It was always nice to be among friends from home, Flo, Dee, Howard Barsky to name a few. I must mention John and Betty Tice, who at the many crowded milongas would always arrange a seat for me at their floor side reserved table. I really appreciated that act of kindness. Often I would go to a crowded milonga and be seated far back where it was difficult to even get to the dance floor through the maze of tables.

Club del Vino was like a small theater with tables in the balcony for food and drink. They had different performances by known tango artists, primarily musicians and singers. Patrons were usually of a more well-to-do class. We always have enjoyed the ambiance of this dressier and more elegant venue. A memorable performance was that of the tango duo of Horacio Salgán, pianist, and his accompanying guitarist Ubaldo de Lio. We three, Flo, Adriana and I were the only privileged ones permitted in their dressing room after the performance and had the pleasure of chatting with them.

Flo, Adriana and I took the ship from Buenos Aires to Colonia, Uruguay and back, a four hour trip each way. All the shops were closed that day but we managed to have a good time traipsing through that charming little town.

Adriana and her friend, Flo and myself were strolling through one of the many neighborhoods of Buenos Aires on a Sunday, when we unexpectedly came across groups of people dressed in various strange costumes doing sort of a dance. After watching awhile, Flo and Adriana's lady friend joined in the dancing and had a great time; meanwhile Adriana watched while I took many photos of the activities.

We were informed this was called murga, a popular musical theater type of group dancing in Uruguay and Buenos Aires during carnival. Of the five rolls of film sent in for processing, that roll of 36 color exposures was completely destroyed, crushed under a cart in the developing lab in Long Beach.

I went by myself by bus to Iguazú falls. I paid eighty six dollars for a six day excursion special on sale at a Chinese travel agency. I was the only non Argentine on the bus. It was a fourteen hour trip each way with stops to see the ruins of San Ignacio, a precious gem mine, the mate plantation Tarraquí and restaurant stops. The seats were very comfortable and reclined to 160 degrees. There was a lovely young girl and her mother in the next row and many other people to talk with. The tour guide had me stand up in the middle of the bus on both the lower and upper decks and introduced me individually to each passenger to shake my hand. I'm constantly made aware of the warmth and congeniality of most Latin cultures, especially the Argentines.

I had my own hotel room and all meals included, three days of guided tours of the immense, extensive complex of falls and cataracts. What made it even more impressive was the spring runoff of the exceptionally heavy rainfall that winter. Standing over the Garganta de Diablo, the Devil's Throat, was mesmerizing. Most of the falls are on the Argentine side but there are marvelous views also from the Brazilian side. Going to the Brazilian side was included in our travel package but I didn't want to take the chance crossing over to Brazil since US citizens require a visa. Iguazú is on the northern Argentine, eastern Paraguayan and southern Brazilian border. If I ever have the opportunity to visit Iguazú again, I would certainly want to be with someone to share this exotic adventure. Everyone I know who has visited there has flown. I think they miss the real adventure. Today, ten years later, that excursion would probably cost at least ten times as much.

I've gone four times to Santiago, Chile, twice by bus and twice by auto over the Andes. I left the Retiro terminal in Buenos Aires late afternoon. I wanted to take advantage of the night during which time the only scenery is the flat pampa and I could sleep until the foothills before arriving in Mendoza the following morning. We changed buses in Mendoza and our bus was stopped in line due to a sudden snowstorm at the border to pass through both Argentine and Chilean customs and passport control. We walked through the deep snow for over a hundred meters arriving in an unheated barracks where we waited in line shivering from the cold. Most of our feet were wet from trudging through the snow. The road is narrow over the high Andean pass with few barriers to protect vehicles from going over the vertical drops of thousands of feet straight down. Often the wheels are very close to the edge. Few people I know are willing to take this perilous, adventurous route. Flying is less emotional and faster.

I often spent time with one of my favorite couples in Santiago, Miro and Elizabeth Kopecky. On one of my visits Elizabeth took me to two milongas and afterward in the wee hours to a quaint locale where professional and some amateur musicians and singers performed and had jam sessions. I think I was the only one or maybe one of the few that wasn't participating. Elizabeth gave me to date, three of her CD recordings of tangos and Peruvian waltzes. At our parties and milongas we sometimes have the pleasure of hearing her lovely voice. Both Miro and Elizabeth dance tango. She is an accomplished dancer in both tango and Argentine and Chilean folk dances.

Miro & Elizabeth Kopecky.

Elizabeth, Miro and I attended a performance of an Easter Island dance group at one of the theaters in Santiago where they invited Elizabeth on stage to dance one of their folk dances. We also went to a free concert by the Buenos Aires Tango Orchestra given in one of the large theaters in Buenos Aires. Many concerts and other popular events are made available either free or at a nominal cost to those who may not be able to afford to pay.

Torquato Tasso is one of the older authentic tango venues at 1575 Defensa, bordering Parque Lezama in San Telmo. Flo and I, along with some other tango friends attended a beautiful musical concert with only a guitarist and a bandeonista after which there was dancing. There were only three couples on the floor and they were playing the candombe, Tango Negro, a favorite of mine. When Flo and I finished we were greeted with applause which was flattering considering most of the patrons were local tango aficionados and dancers. Either they appreciated our efforts or they were glad that we finished.

Chris Wenham is one of our tango friends. He and Flo are very good friends. I've known Chris for ten or more years. I've always valued him as a friend and am impressed with his views and knowledge about the world. He has lived and traveled in many parts of the globe. He is a no nonsense, serious person. We haven't spent much time together due to the distances between us but I always look forward to his company and conversation whenever we have the opportunity. He recently moved to Berlin where his daughter Kara, a professional tango dancer, is now living after both having lived in Buenos Aires quite a few years. One of his interests is studying the culinary arts of various cultures in different parts of the world.

A year or two before, was when our tango friends Bill and Patty Blakeney, Paula Ardilla, Woody and Flo, Hadassah "Das" Silverman and Ana Rossell, were in Madrid and Barcelona where we attended many milongas and later went to our home in Formentera except for Das and Ana. Bill Blakeney taught Jill a few tango steps and was amazed how fast she caught on but with her extensive professional dance training and experience it wasn't surprising.

Ana and I both discovered Argentine tango dancing years ago and have been together in groups going to Spain and Argentina for tango. She is a member of CITA, a tango dancing organization in Buenos Aires. Some of these events have previously been mentioned in earlier chapters.

We all stayed in the now, non existent Hotel Paris at Puerta del Sol in the heart of Madrid. In Barcelona at the Continental Hotel on the Ramblas. My favorite milonga was in Salon Cha 3 at San Pol de Mar on Sundays from twelve noon to three pm, close to the Manzanares river in Madrid. A young Argentine dance couple were the gracious hosts and played good, danceable music. During my visits to Formentera I would stop in Madrid for a few days to go to milongas especially to my favorite one. On my last visit there toward the end of the dance I noticed a young man and a woman on the floor and was pleased the way they danced even though I could see that he was a relative beginner. As he was changing his shoes to leave I crossed the room to tell him I enjoyed their dancing. He was beaming and said he really appreciated my comment as he really didn't have much confidence in his ability. I also went to where the lady was seated to say the same to her and I asked her to dance. She followed me beautifully so I asked her how long she had been dancing tango and was surprised when she said only two years. On following visits to Madrid I would phone her and we would get together on Sunday for the dance and dinner afterward. Her name is María Jesus Valladares.

I was in Buenos Aires five days before Penny arrived the day before a cruise we were taking. That night we walked a few blocks from María Eugenia's house on Corrientes where we stayed, for one of my favorite milongas El Arranque in the Nuevo Salón Argentina on Bartolomé Mitre just off of Callao. Normally the DJ on that night is Mario Orlando whose music I've always liked. That night the owner's daughter played the music. I thought is was especially good, possibly it was Mario's recordings she used. It was one of those perfect nights, great music, not too crowded and we felt we really danced as well as we ever danced. It was something that doesn't often happen but when it does, it's a great feeling.

Chapter XXVIII
Rosario, Argentina

I took trips by myself to Rosario to see Orlando, take lessons and dance. Susana and her son Martín were like family. Orlando also traveled to Santiago, Chile, to teach. I would accompany him to many of his classes. There I met Jack and Patty Schmitt who live in Santiago and in the Chilean Patagonia and Miro and Elizabeth Kopecky who lived in Santiago and now reside in Newport Beach.

Flo and I enjoyed the four hour bus rides from Buenos Aires to Rosario. Often there were severe storms on that journey which we both enjoyed. Martin and his mother took us in Martin's father's motorboat cruising the channels and islands of the mighty Paraná river. There are portions of that river six kilometers wide. I noticed I was the only male attired in a Speedo a brief bikini bathing suit, all the other men wore boxer trunks. I imagine that some might have had certain thoughts about my sexual orientation.

During the latter years Flo preferred to stay in Buenos Aires so as not to miss the tango dancing, which is far superior to that in Rosario. I always stayed at the small modest Hotel Embajador across the street from the main Rosario bus depot which made the traveling to and from Buenos Aires very convenient. There were also advantages in the depot such as all night eateries, pharmacy and shops. After numerous stays in this small hotel I became acquainted with the owner and friendly staff. I was also friends with one of the chambermaids.

I would often go on the roof to sunbathe in my bikini. I'm not sure that the management approved but they were kind in permitting me that privilege.

Me, Flo, Orlando Paiva, Graciela & Hugo Goñi, Martín and Susana. – Rosario

When Flo and I walked from the hotel to Orlando's studio we always stopped at a small cafe for a bite. It was run by a very pretty, athletic girl in her late twenties and her mother. The times I went there alone the girl would always ask me about Flo. One time I was talking to the girl about exercising I showed her my bodybuilding and balancing photos. I thought she would be really impressed. The following year in Rosario when I stopped by she showed me photos of her boyfriend who won some notable bodybuilding contests. He was much more muscular than I. Well, you can't win 'em all. When I met him during another visit we talked about bodybuilding. He was out of shape and explained to me that he gave up competing as the steroids and other supplements necessary to compete nowadays were too expensive for him.

I was chatting with an older women in the lobby of Hotel Embajador and went up with her in the elevator. I don't know why I refer to someone as older, when they may be years younger than me. We got off the elevator and chatted in the alcove before going to our respective rooms. There was no mention of tango. The next morning the concierge asked me if I knew who that woman was. I only knew she was from Buenos Aires etc. He said that she was María Graña one of the most famous female tango singers in Argentina that was performing here in Rosario. I was so disappointed that I didn't mention that I was a tango aficionado when I had the opportunity. I'm sure we would have had a long chat.

After my lesson with Orlando in his studio in Rosario he said he'd like to talk to me. He asked if I would be willing to take in Martín to live with me at my house in San Pedro and help him arrange classes to teach and I would get a percentage of his earnings. I said I would be delighted but refused to accept any money. It was like having a son and good friend all rolled into one. He gave me unlimited help with tango, Spanish and running the household. Martín was very capable, ambitious and a talented young man. He lived with me two years until he married Alyssa, a beautiful and very intelligent Chinese lady and moved to Costa Mesa. Martin graduated in Argentina in the field of cinematography which is his present occupation aside from a full schedule teaching tango.

Martín & Alyssa Vaccaro

I accompanied Martin, his mother, his brother and a few other female friends of their family to Villa Gessell (by the name it may be
obvious that the town was founded by a German), one of the small
beach communities south of Buenos Aires just before reaching the
famous resort of Mar de Plata. Martin and his family spend vacations there at a house on the beach with two rental units upstairs.
On the balcony there is a fireplace where we had asadas, the Argentine custom of grilling of meats and sausages. Being a beach
person, that's where I spent my time. It was only a few steps from
the beach.

I was playing with a large young dog on the beach and little by
little he became more rough and aggressive. I had a devil of a time
getting rid of him. I had to drag him into the surf before he would
release my left arm leaving me with angry looking welts and dark
blotches on my forearm. It took a few years before the blotches
disappeared.

On one of my more recent trips to Rosario, Martin's father, José,
a cardiologist, requested that I come to his clinic. Martín undoubtedly mentioned to him that I had a heart attack many years ago
and that I always seemed concerned about my cardiovascular condition. Doctor José, to show his appreciation for my efforts helping and watching over his son, said he would like to do a cardiac
work up on me. I was more than glad to accept. In his office he did
a thorough work up including a manual pulse examination from
head to toe, the most complete I've ever had. I was given a treadmill test at the hospital and passed with flying colors. The old technician monitoring the test said that in all the years he administered
this test he'd never seen anyone my age do so well. It's always a
great relief receiving good news. I was sorry to hear that Dr. José
passed away soon after.

Martín was an excellent cook. He could sew, iron and do almost
anything else. He would practice tango with me for hours. I should
have taken more advantage of his expertise but I wasted a lot time

that I could have spent learning to be a better tango dancer.

Martín and I started a tango class at the San Pedro Elk's lodge two blocks from the house. We had about 20 students. My friend Jo Ann Travis and Joe her dance partner for Lindy Hop were present. It was Joe who was interested in learning Argentine tango but Jo Ann wasn't interested and said she would just sit and watch while he took the class. At his urging, Jo Ann joined in. They picked up rapidly but after a few classes, for whatever reason, Joe dropped out and Jo Ann continued on and became an excellent tango dancer. Jo Ann never lacked partners. Apart from being a really good dancer she is a beautiful lady and the men would line up to dance with her.

One of the memorable performances was that of Martin and his partner Marina at the first International Argentine Tango Festival in Las Vegas. It was a four day affair of classes during the day and performances and milongas each night. Martin, Marina, Flo, Ann Shaver and myself used Woody's new van to drive to Vegas. Flo, Ann and I shared ,a room with an extra bed that was brought in for me.

I ran across my friends Ken and Nancy, a married couple of tango dancers, whom I invited up to our room for a snack. When I went to the room to tell the girls they were panicky and hurriedly threw all the scattered clothes and used towels in the bathtub and pulled the curtain. As always, we always had a great few hours chatting over bread, cheese and wine.

I have to admit that I thought Marina was one of the most gorgeous and talented dancers I have seen. It was a pleasure having her live with Martin and I for the period she was with us and being able to practice with her the all too short time she visited here. If I would have been twenty years younger, I would have been after her. She is now married and living and teaching dancing in Villa Gessell. Occasionally we communicate by E mail.

The Las Vegas International Tango Festival organizers were Marcos Cuestas and Hugo Latorre, two Argentine professional tango dancers, Marcos, the tango and Hugo, Argentine folklore. There were twelve Argentine professional couples performing, all internationally recognized as some of the best. Martin and Marina's performance was outstanding. They received a well deserved standing ovation with more applause than any of the other performers. As they were taking their bows Marcos got down from the podium and ran across the dance floor to congratulate them and offer them a contract for the following year. He didn't do this for any of the other couples while on stage. I took an excellent video with my camcorder and at the end of Martín and Marina's performance while panning the camera over the audience of a few hundred I paused a few seconds on Flo sitting in the front row with her legs crossed which Martín eventually erased. I thought it was showy and sorry that is no longer on the video.

Crossing the bridge over the Rio Manzanares in Madrid, a little before noon on a Sunday, a man approached me to ask directions. We began chatting and I mentioned I was going to a milonga. Actually it was my favorite milonga in Madrid from noon to 3 pm in Sala Cha 3. He mentioned that he was from Rosario, Argentina. We ended up gabbing in a coffee shop until I left for the dance. He asked me to look up Blanca Rovitti, a tango dancer and teacher when I was in Rosario,

Blanca teaches tango in Rosario. When she was in Buenos Aires we went dancing. I danced and stayed a few days with her in Rosario. We correspond now and then. She recently moved to Valencia, Spain where her children immigrated from Argentina.

Orlando Paiva's studio was built by him over his garage. Most everything was hand crafted by him. He was a master craftsman, a perfectionist. Downstairs, his older son Oscar did barbering. One day when I was taking a class from Orlando I asked if Oscar was around so I could get my haircut. He wasn't home so Orlando said he could cut it but I didn't bother him so waited for another time with Oscar. Since Orlando died Oscar took over the studio and continued giving classes in his father's unique style of Argentine tango. I understand from my tango buddies that Oscar is an excellent dancer and teacher. I wish the best for him.

Accompanying Orlando in Santiago on the subway from his class at Club Suizo to another class, we were going up a short flight of stairs when Orlando had to stop and catch his breath. I, being asthmatic could relate to that situation. We were 45 minutes late to the next class. All the students were there practicing while awaiting the maestro's arrival. This tardiness seemed to be not uncommon with many of the Latin teachers. I guess it's part of the culture.

Rosario is not a city that interests me. I would probably have liked it more had I spent more time there. Very few cities can compare with Buenos Aires. Rosario is Argentina's second largest city and known as the Chicago of Argentina. If it weren't for the mighty Paraná river, I doubt if Rosario would have ever existed.

Chapter XXIX
Return to California

I was waiting in the US customs line in New York coming back from Spain in front of an older, frocked Spanish priest who asked me if I would be so kind as to speak in his behalf when we arrived at the customs agent as he understood English but hesitant about his speaking ability. When I explained to the black lady at the customs booth that he didn't speak English, she said aloud that you could never trust priests, thinking he wouldn't understand. I was very apologetic and embarrassed for this cruel greeting to a guest entering my country.

— — — — — —

Returning to Los Angeles after my final departure from Formentera and studying for my new challenge to get certified in the specialty of electromyography, I began also working in physical therapy for a brief time to survive until I could incorporate electromyography together with my physical therapy practice. (electromyography and nerve conduction studies may be referred to as EMG or ENMG in the following pages).

In the beginning, at a conference I asked one of the noted therapists who taught electromyography at the University of Northern Arizona, as well as a few others, if they thought I could make a living specializing only in EMG. They all replied that one would have to do both in order to survive in our field. After a year, I believe I was the first physical therapist to dedicate myself wholly to my new field of electroneuromyography, giving up the practice of physical therapy.

Soon after I arrived back in the states, John Monlux, a physical therapy colleague and close friend, urged me to enroll in the first course in electromyography offered locally for physical therapists at Rancho Los Amigos Hospital. It was a three month intensive program and cost $500. I was resistant to spend the money which was more than I could afford at the time. I finally decided to sign up. The course was given by John, Arnie Tripp and Joyce Campbell. All fourteen students were physical therapists and all were recent graduates and a few with masters degrees. I hadn't practiced formally or been involved academically in the field for many years. I was overwhelmed by much of the material that I was rusty on or had forgotten along with the new techniques etc. My memory in anatomy was quite good but not in many of the other technical aspects. After a few weeks into the class I was disillusioned and told John that it was too difficult for me and I'm dropping out. He told me to stick with it and things will work out.

After the academic portion ended we were introduced to the lab with the intimidating electronic equipment used for EMG. I had absolutely no knowledge in this area. I didn't understand any of the terminology and was convinced I couldn't continue. The rest of the class appeared not to have those problems.

I had a sleepless night vacillating between continuing or forgetting about finishing. Finally I purchased a new EDX unit from Jack Hatton for $4,500 and committed myself come hell or high water. With time and intensive studying, in order for a physical therapist to be able to legally practice EMG in the State of California, one had to take a comprehensive test consisting of a written, oral and a practical exam lasting four hours. EMG examinations consist of needle penetration in many different muscles and electrical stimulation of nerves, not much fun, practicing on one another. One of the prerequisites for the license examination was to perform 400 hundred case studies with reports and 400 hours of study in courses related to EMG under the supervision of a physician specialized in that field before qualifying to take the state licensing exam. I was extremely fortunate in being able to do this under my best friend Dr. Luis Spamer who specialized only in EMG and neurophysiology. I managed to pass the exam sometime time later after failing my first attempt.

Aside from these difficulties too few applicants were able to pass the exam; therefore the California Board of Physical Therapy Examiners set up a committee with a few of us, in the presence of members of the state Board of Standards and Measures to rewrite the test questions and lessen the number of EMG tests one had to perform and the hours of supervision requirements to half the amount of the original requirement. This consisted of five or six meetings in hotel conference rooms in different cities in the state over the period of six months. It was an honor and privilege to partake in this endeavor and a great learning experience for which we were well reimbursed. I believe that California may be the only state or at least the first to issue physical therapists licenses to practice electromyography.

Stan Marks and I attended the California licensing EMG exam for physical therapists held at the naval hospital in the Camp Pendleton Marine Base. The testing was monitored by navy physical therapists Mike Skurja, Rick Nielson and a civilian PT/EMG, John Monlux

Doctors Mike Skurja and Rick Nielson after retiring from their military service were instrumental in seminars and developing and promoting EMG for physical therapists. They eventually formed the Rocky Mountain University of Health Professionals at Provo, Utah.

On the return drive to Los Angeles after the test, Stan's car engine died and I got out to push. The air was smoky from a nearby forest fire. Being asthmatic I immediately had an acute exacerbation and was ill for months before recovering. Since then I carry a gas mask with filters in my car, which I've never had to use. I am cautious about avoiding smoke, perfumes and other allergens as much as possible.

Stan Marks and I would study together at his house in Encino till the wee hours. One night at 2 am we ordered a pizza. When I went to pick it up the attendant asked me to wait as the cook wanted to see who ordered anchovies as he rarely got an order with anchovies.

I had a habit of palpating different muscles and anatomical landmarks to familiarize myself in preparation for the electroneuromyographic examination. I often did this unobtrusively in restaurants and other public venues. I can only assume what some observers may have thought.

Electroneuromyographics was my AKA business name. Some of my best clinics were with Dr. James A. Miller, a black orthopedic physician who gave me my first chance. He was a retired paratrooper physician and served under and was a personal friend of General Westmoreland. I worked with him for ten or more years until he passed away. The other was Dr. Jon Mc Lennan. It's been my experience that contracts are too easily broken and felt that as long as I performed well and was professional that this was more dependable than a formal contract. My services were billed and collected by my office with no financial incentive for the referring sources but rather providing them good service.

In early 1982 I decided to open my own office instead of working out of my car and my house. My next door neighbor Rudy Pearl, an attorney, had his part time office in a medical building just three blocks from our house. I asked him about the possibility of sharing the space which worked out well. After a few years he worked less and less in this office and eventually I had it to myself. I had a part time office lady, Betty Hodges and another office lady and billing clerk Louise Steele. I couldn't have had better help. After Louise passed away Betty stayed on a while before retiring. Except for Louise and Betty, I never had anyone that was honest and dependable at collections. It seems that I lost as much as I made, either through theft, inefficiency or both.

While performing EMGs at Dr. James Miller's office in October of 1982 I began to feel nauseated and a heaviness in both arms. I knew those symptoms were consistent with heart problems and should have told the doctor but foolishly I said I didn't feel well and I would finish the testing another day. I left my equipment and drove five miles to the emergency room at Gardena Memorial Hospital where I was put in the intensive care unit. I was told to lie down and remain lying. I still had a sharp pain in my right upper back but the heaviness and chest pain and discomfort were lessened. I did sit up and immediately the back pain disappeared. I'm convinced the pain in my right scapular area was incidental to the heart problem. The cardiac enzymes were positive and I was informed that I had had a heart attack. I was released a day or two later.

Following my discharge from the hospital I was very conscious of every little thing I felt in my chest. I complained of chest pain and was admitted to the same hospital three weeks later and was hospitalized for testing. I was given morphine before going to bed and had a miserable sleepless night with an excruciating headache and nausea. The following morning the nurse brought my morphine which I refused to take in spite of the nurse's insistence. I began feeling better from the outset and since then I list morphine as an allergy.

They performed an angiogram and the cardiologists present commented and showed me on the screen that all my coronary arteries were clear as a baby's and no negative findings. I requested and was given extensive testing, all results were negative. Nevertheless I became a part time paranoid hypochondriac with a vivid imagination. I went to different emergency rooms a dozen times within a six month period with no abnormalities found.

Many years later with a thallium nuclear scan treadmill test my cardiologist Dr. French, found a small area of decreased circulation in one of the heart septums, but the important thing was my heart function was one hundred percent. I make certain the I get periodic check ups and testing including a recent angiogram, treadmills, echo cardiograms, etc. Evidently my heart attack was due to an embolism or lose particle that temporarily blocked one of the coronary arteries. It's now been over 30 years and I believe my heart function, according to my cardiologist, is 100%.

In spite of the fact that we were just divorced Jill was kind enough to let me relax on the sofa and waited on me and helped me even though I was no longer living at home.

— — — — — —

I went to Honolulu in March of 1997 to celebrate John and Linda's 15 year renewal of their vows. I really enjoyed Honolulu going to the beach at Waikiki almost daily. As a member of the Elks I went to the Elk's club in Waikiki on the ocean near Diamond Head. Parking is very difficult along the beach but fortunately I used one of John and Linda's cars and parked in the Elk's club private parking. Belonging to another lodge, and not having a local membership doesn't entitle one to use the gym but they graciously let me work out in the gym and the use of a locker. I also danced there and ate at the restaurant. I didn't use their private beach as I didn't see anyone there nor did I use their pool, preferring the ocean beaches with people.

Jheri, Linda, John and me at their 15th anniversary renewal of vows in Honolulu.

I asked about nearby beaches and was told there was a nice beach about one hundred yards away. When I got to that beach I was not sure if it was the one they mentioned so I asked the young life guard if I'd gone far enough or should I go past the large concrete wall which was part of a marine aquarium. He was rather hesitant and finally said that he hoped he didn't offend me but that side was a gay beach. I replied, no problem I'm fine here. It was next to a large hotel and there was a small nook in the building that sold Hawaiian plate meals which were inexpensive meals to take out consisting of rice, meat and vegetables, a decent meal for four dollars. I almost always find interesting people to converse with or books to read, otherwise I find lying in the sun boring.

Some of the evenings I would go to George Garcia's milongas (tango dances) in the Honolulu Club. George is a friend and excellent all round dancer. I had many good tango dances with Elizabeth, a German lady painter who has her atelier apartment near the Elks club. I danced mostly with her both times I was in Honolulu and also bumped into her on the street in Buenos Aires and again in Niño Bien, a milonga in the same city where we danced. Hawaii's my kind of place. I'm sure I could adapt very easily to the life there in spite of the modernization and commercialism that eventually seems to permeate the desirable places in the world.

We later celebrated their twenty fifth wedding anniversary in March of 2012, on our Mexican Riviera cruise in February with David, Abbey and Penny.

— — — — — —

Before signing an employment contract with Lockheed, Yale requested a six month vacation. He told them that since a child he was always in school including most summers. They agreed to three months during which time Yale traveled abroad.

One day I received a call for Yale from Lockheed. I mentioned that he was out of the country and asked if she cared to leave a message. She said that they made an error thinking San Pedro was outside the Los Angeles area and they could not honor the perks in the contract such as a paid hotel, automobile and living allowance for one month. I was upset and phoned Yale to tell him about the call. He said not to worry. When he came home he called the office to see about the matter and was told that they couldn't set a precedent. Finally he went to the head office out of town to talk to the president of Lockheed to relate that the error was on their part. The company honored their original agreement and had the perks restored.

Yale since his childhood has always been assertive but not argumentative or aggressive and will stand up for what he thinks is right. I would have been afraid to rock the boat and would have given in. I've always admired Yale for standing up for his values.

Yale came to me after working eight years with Lockheed in Burbank and in Atlanta and said, "Dad, I'd like to go back to Spain to live." I said that I thought that was a great idea especially since we still had the house where my ex, his mother, was living. He's been working in Spain and other countries ever since. He was thirty one or thirty two at the time he left the US the last time.

We were worried about the children's transition adapting to our schools from the school system on the island. All teaching previously was in Castilian. Yale was always the studious one who was at the top of his class in Spain and maintained a top level in high school here and also at Northrup (Aviation) University where he earned a full scholarship and graduated on the president's list for academic achievement.

Upon graduation Lockheed Aviation offered him a job. He requested work in aircraft design but was told he has to work his way up from other basic departments. He mentioned that to his professor who put in a good recommendation and he was accepted in the aircraft design department.

David and Linda, like their dad, were not the greatest students. Linda came home with a test she took in Spanish and had three or four marked wrong. I went to the school and told the teacher, who was Mexican-American, that in Castilian these answers for telling time were correct. I think he felt a little subdued but I realize that many of the high school teachers may not be very proficient in certain areas.

David, after graduating high school, attended a school for graphic design, his present employment. He also plays harmonica and sings blues professionally. He and his group were invited twice to perform in the International Blues Festival in Switzerland and other European venues and David has recorded three CDs. He still does gigs locally. A few years ago I went with Flo and Woody, their daughter Becky, Jo Ann Travis and Vidal to the restaurant the Rusty Pelican in the Long Beach Marina where David performed periodically and we danced west coast swing to great traditional blues. At the time David was teamed up with Henry Carvajal, a first class guitar player and a few other musicians.

I received a phone call for San Pedro Slim and had no idea who they were referring to until he mentioned the person who sings blues and plays the harmonica. When I realized he was referring to my son David I jokingly said, you mean San Pedro Slime, there is an "e" at the end. I seem to have knack for sarcastic humor as long as it isn't directed at me.

Jill had grounded Linda for a month for some minor thing which was unreasonably long for a minor offense but Jill was quick to react and even if she realized that the punishment was too extreme she wouldn't admit it or change her mind. I believe Linda was sixteen at the time. She took off the screen and climbed out the window that evening. I was also told that I must have a talk with Linda. The following morning at breakfast I told Linda the least she could do was to put back the screen. Jill wasn't amused. I really never saw or heard that any of the three children did anything that called for a strong reprimand or punishment but realized that one of the parents had to take charge so I was the permissive one, the good guy. Jill did the hard part.

I and most of my family and friends realized that Jill and I had constant communication problems. I tend to avoid conflict and arguments which in turn upset Jill. We were probably both at fault.

I was getting more distant from Jill and we were both unhappy with the situation. It got to the point that we could never sit at the table and finish a meal without Jill getting upset and usually leaving the table. I wouldn't say anything or argue and the children were careful what they said. It seemed that Jill would get offended at a completely innocent remark believing it was directed at her. In any case one day the three children came to me and said, "Daddy, you gotta get a divorce." They weren't blaming anyone but they realized that it was not getting any better and it was no way to live.

Our divorce was final in early 1982.

On May 14, 1991 I was asked to give a course on ENMG to the physical therapists and as a consultant in Electroneuromyography at Martin Luther King Jr. Charles R. Drew Medical Center in Los Angeles by the chief of the Physical Therapy Department Austin Grigsby and assistant chief Tom Payne both certified electromyographers. This was the first such program for physical therapists in this large general teaching hospital in California. The course was an intensive two hour session of twelve classes consisting of lectures, discussions and demonstrations with specific goals.

MARTIN LUTHER KING, JR./CHARLES R. DREW MEDICAL CENTER 12021 South Wilmington Avenue Los Angeles, CA 90059 213/

EDWARD J. RENFORD, Hospital Administrator   JAMES G. HAUGHTON, M.D., Medical Director   JANINE ROONEY, R.N., Acting Director

May 24, 1991

Manley Kiefer, E.N.,P.T.
Certified Electroneuromyographer
2403 Moray Avenue, Suite #1
San Pedro, CA   90732

To Whom It May Concern:

The above named Physical Therapist was employed at this facility
from July 29, 1984 until July 31, 1985 as a Physical Therapy
Consultant in Electroneuromyography.

Mr. Kiefer was instrumental in establishing a Clinical Training
Program in Electroneuromyography for Physical Therapists at this
facility. This was the first such program for Physical Therapists
in a large general teaching hospital in California.

Mr. Kiefer developed specific topic areas in Electroneuromyography
to teach basic knowledge and skills to the therapists in the
training program. He set specific goals to be met by each trainee.
The methods used in the training were lectures, discussions and
demonstrations. In the end each trainee was expected to be well
versed in all topic areas.

The services provided by Mr. Kiefer were done in such an exemplary
manner that Physical Therapists are now performing Electroneuromyography Tests in a routine manner at this facility.

Sincerely,

Austin F. Grigsby, E.N.,P.T.
Certified Electroneuromyographer
Chief Physical Therapist

COUNTY OF LOS ANGELES/DEPARTMENT OF HEALTH SERVICES

Tom was a good friend. He invited Virginia, my wife, and me with his family group of about ten to the Plum Tree Chinese restaurant in Beverly Hills for dinner. Virginia and I where the only whites in our group. Almost without exception everyone in the group were professionals, doctors, lawyers, school principal, etc.

I also monitored Tony Hunthausen, PT. who has a masters degree in physical therapy for his preparation to take the state board exam in EMG. He was an adept student having passed on his first attempt. Few passed on their first attempt.

Ken Boak Strong, a friend and colleague, has been a San Pedro Elk member even longer then I in spite of his living in Hawaii the past many years. The past few years he has stayed with me for three or four months at a time. A few years ago he asked me if we could work together part time as physical therapists at a local rehabilitation center that offered us a contract. It worked out well for a month but the facility hired a full time therapist and terminated us. Actually it seemed strange that we two therapists in our eighties were treating old patients younger than us. Ken aside from being a physical therapist was a Marine vet and part time frustrated actor constantly emoting lines at home and when out with friends. Ken and his wife Sharon, until they moved to Hawaii, had lived a few blocks from our house when Jill and I first came to San Pedro in 1967. He passed away in 2012.

I skied periodically at Mammoth Mountain and thought I could combine that with my work, giving me tax reductions for many of my expenses. I stopped at a two doctor orthopedic clinic in Bishop and spoke to Dr. Jon Mc Lennan about the possibility of using my services. He agreed to refer a few patients for me to test and eventually that increased to up to a dozen patients in his new clinic in the medical center alongside Northern Inyo Hospital where I also provided services. Later I also performed examinations on patients referred by other local doctors including Mammoth Lakes and surrounding areas. I provided services for Dr. Mc Lennan's orthopedic clinic until the doctor closed his office and moved to another area.

I went at least once a month for a period of sixteen years. There were other physician EMG specialists who tried to get the contract to do the services but the office receptionist told me that the doctors claimed that I did better and more professional work. She added that they also mentioned trying other well known neurologists and physiatrists in San Francisco, Reno, Sacramento, etc. before they contracted my services but preferred my work.

One of the patients I tested in Bishop was brought in from a nearby prison with his hands and feet shackled. The sheriff accompanying him asked me to do the test with the shackles left on but I insisted he remove them.

Doctor Mc Lennan was in the process of building his own hospital clinic but due to pressure and legal problems with the local hospital and other medical entities, moved his practice to Southern California. I was very impressed with his ability to correctly diagnose neuromuscular and orthopedic problems, something many of the physicians that referred me patients were not very adept.

I contacted the gun club in Bishop and they permitted me to practice on their range with my revolver. Previously I did some target practice with the San Pedro Elk's gun club at the police range nearby. My friend Howie did reloading and furnished me with .38 caliber wad cutters for my Smith and Wesson .375 caliber magnum revolver with an 8 ¾ inch barrel. I also was given a Christmas present of a new Ruger 9 mm, 16 shot automatic by my friend and colleague Dave Arant. Later he offered to purchase the gun back from me but I made him a present of the gun and went to a local gun shop to re-register the gun in his name.

I almost always left for and returned from Bishop and Mammoth at night, avoiding the busy traffic times and weekend traffic, especially during ski season. I took advantage of stopping to rest or sleep at Coso Junction rest area that had facilities and was safe. I would often sleep in my van for a few hours. One rainy night with the rain beating on the metal roof I slept eight hours. I always gave myself ample time for traveling and scheduling my patients, otherwise I have a tendency to worry about arriving late or being under pressure.

I was sadly aware each time I passed Manzanares, "our national disgrace," between Lone Pine and Independence. I understand there was no evidence of any Japanese-American involved with spying for Japan. This relocation camp was located on US route 395 in the high desert the foot of the Sierra Madre, Mountains 230 miles north of Los Angeles.

During a ski trip many of the ski clubs gave Christmas parties at Mammoth Mountain Inn where many of us were staying. I happened to walk into the wrong club room but was invited to join in. I spoke to a group of three ladies for a few moments and then left to find my club's party room. After a few moments in walked the three ladies. The tallest was Dixie Bateman a shapely blond, probably my age. It was very flattering when she told me that she came to find me. We instantly hit it off.

Dixie was an outdoor person and loved nature. She was a member of the Sierra Club and like organizations. She was a police officer and investigator in her local station in Glendora. We went on trips together in my new 1984 Ford Econoline extended van, where we slept. We went to the top of the White Mountains to visit the ancient bristle cone pine forest. Bristle cone pines are the longest living trees known on the planet, some being five thousand years old. The heavy dense wood doesn't rot nor float.

Our first night in our ten day trip to Baja California in my new van was at San Quintín Bay. Before starting out early the next morning we noticed our left front tire was flat. I pulled into the nearest garage and upon examination we discovered a three pronged spearhead. San Quintín is a favorite spearfishing spot. The inside of the tire was completely destroyed and filled with burnt black rubber shreds. We had no spare for the remaining nine days traveling through cactus and rough roads to Loreto and back. Dixie and I are great traveling partners, both easy going, no disagreements.

Before we left for our trip to Mexico her police captain gave her an official letter in Spanish, sealed with sealing wax, to show the Mexican authorities if any problems arose. No real problems occurred but we were stopped on a few occasions by Mexican Federales and soldiers. Fortunately we had no trouble but it feels threatening as it invariably happens that you are stopped at night in deserted areas.

Dixie Bateman - Desierto Vizcaino, Baja Sur, Mexico

Bahía de Los Ángeles – Baja California

At Bahia de Los Angeles I was ready to go diving when I noticed that all the fishing boats were still in the harbor. When I inquired from one of the locals why they weren't out, he replied there was a large pod of orcas (killer whales) in the area. I stayed out of the water. There were some American military families camping nearby who asked us if we could use a ten gallon plastic container of water as they were leaving and didn't want to lug a large plastic bottle of water. This was manna from heaven, we had just been discussing that we were out of water and no water was available until we reached one of the sparse, distant towns or settlements, one does not travel in that region without water.

We stopped to prepare our supper in the middle of the Viscaino Desert. We dined on the few potatoes, the only food we had left, which we roasted over our fire amid the giant cacti with a full moon and coyotes howling in the distance. It was a lovely dinner and a pleasant, earthy experience.

If I can reach Dixie when I'm doing testing in one of the local medical clinics, we occasionally go out to eat when I finish with my patient load.

Dixie travels occasionally working for the state of California and also donates her services as a surgical nurse with the Flying Samaritans who donate their medical services to the poor in some of the remote areas of Mexico. Living conditions are very primitive, uncomfortable and sometimes dangerous. The participants pay all their own expenses including the flights in small private planes. She has traveled much of the world, usually on her own. She is a very knowledgeable and independent person.

— — — — — —

It was becoming more difficult to collect from most insurance companies for Medicare and Worker's Compensation, especially when attorneys are involved. Until 2010 I continued taking a few patients periodically at a chiropractic clinic in La Habra, California, from a very knowledgeable chiropractor, Dr. Betty Clayton. She always insisted that I do her testing. The last few years most of the monies owed me by the payers were never collected. I made some bad choices in using other billing agencies that robbed and also cashed many of my checks. I reported one collector to the police department. Even with the evidence I couldn't believe how difficult it was trying to recover funds or prosecute although the detective in charge of the case did help recover a small amount. Eventually I accepted that fact that there was too much red tape and aggravation to proceed legally and decided not to pursue the matter.

I really enjoyed my profession. Dr. Betty and I often consulted on cases, even on cases that others performed. I look forward discussing cases with such a knowledgeable practitioner. I was fortunate that the doctors in these three aforementioned clinics were very knowledgeable in their fields and more accurate in their diagnosing than many others I have worked with. It was an emotional act finally giving up my physical therapy and electromyography licenses and canceling my malpractice insurance after 58 years of practice with an untarnished (professional) reputation, I'm not too sure about the other.

In the meantime I enjoy and am content spending more time at home and locally. I've done work on the house and put in a complete new patio, planted more fruit trees and other plants. Seems that there is always something to do. Who ever said that one would get bored when retired?

It was difficult convincing referring physicians that physical therapists were qualified and legally able to perform diagnostic testing and few of the P.T.s were able to survive doing only EMG testing. I may have been the first to specialize and limit my practice totally to electromyography. Many of the physicians involved in the practice of electro-diagnostics were constantly trying to discredit our participating in their economic turf by trying to get legislation passed to rescind or limit the scope of our licenses. I believe for the most part they've more or less given up their opposition and have reluctantly conceded that we are competitors.

I am convinced that most of the physical therapists specializing in the field of electroneuromyography, on the whole, do much better examinations and reports than many of the physicians in the same specialty. At the same time one must consider that the physician has to deal with a much wider field, whereas I and many of my colleagues are dedicated and specialized in the one area.

All the doctors who used my services gave me carte blanche in the procedures I deemed as necessary. Usually the referring specialist orders specific procedures and areas to be treated and I was pleased that they had that much confidence in my ability. I may have mentioned that I scheduled a minimum of two hours per patient and am aware that most electroneuromyographers average a half hour or less per patient. Our fees are according to the number and types of procedures performed and not for the time involved. I have had lucrative offers from facilities for my services if I could do two or three limited examinations per hour but I wouldn't consider working in these medical malpractice mills doing substandard work. I enjoyed the challenge of my profession. More often then not one had to change the direction of the examination employing different techniques and procedures at different body sites or areas to arrive at an acceptable outcome.

— — — — — —

It was about midnight in the Outdoorsman Motel where I stay when in Bishop. I went to urinate but couldn't so I went to the emergency room at Northern Inyo Hospital a few doors from the orthopedic clinic where I perform my electrodiagnostic testing for Dr. Mc Lennan. No doctors were present so the nurses performed a urethral catheterization. I went back to the motel and after sleeping a few hours had the same problem. Back to emergency to repeat the procedure and back to sleep in the motel until six am when again I couldn't urinate. On the third catheterization that part of my anatomy was getting a little raw. I told the nurses to leave the indwelling catheter and give me a leg bag so I could go to the clinic and do my work. They refused because there was no physician present to authorize the procedure. I had them call Dr. Greenberg, my urologist in San Pedro, who gave his OK but said in no uncertain terms that I was not to do any testing but return immediately directly to San Pedro Peninsula Hospital and not to stop at my house before.

During the five hour trip I was very hungry but hesitated to go into any restaurant as my leg bag was leaking badly and my pants were wet. I finally did go to eat disguising my wet pants as well as I could. I disobeyed my doctor's orders and went home and showered before going to the hospital.

I requested the saddle block instead of the general anesthetic for the TURP or transurethral resection of the prostate commonly referred to as the "roto rooter" procedure. I was hospitalized for a few days.

— — — — — —

Skiing down the steep face of the back side of lift number three at Mammoth Mountain I had a bad fall hurting my right shoulder and was unable to get up on my skis for ten minutes but managed to slowly ski down without the use of my right arm. I drove to doctor Mc Lennan's office and he examined my shoulder. He said I tore my rotator cuff and if I didn't regain normal function within six months at the latest that the nerves would degenerate and surgery would be necessary. As a physical therapist I was able to take care of my own recovery without surgery. It was a long struggle lasting a year or two. I do notice at 87, about twenty years after my fall, that there is some post traumatic residual and muscular atrophy of my rotator cuff musculature.

— — — — — —

I was friendly with Ramona Uy, M.D. a Chinese physiatrist and her office manager and companion, John Martel. I believe I performed all their EMG procedures.

Entering their clinic on Wilshire Avenue I couldn't help observing the beautiful young Latina woman, Rosamaría Rivera, sitting in the waiting room. I am not timid about approaching beautiful women but professional ethics deterred me. I was anxiously trying to figure out a way to speak to her when fate stepped in and the doctor asked me to talk with her. After speaking with her in the consultation room, I invited her to lunch afterward at a nearby restaurant. Her diet was very limited. I was informed by her and her medical records that she was seriously effected by toxic chemicals in the place of her last employment. She was one of the most beautiful ladies I have seen, very intelligent and modest. We maintained an erratic communication by phone and e-mail throughout the 12 or 15 year interim.

Rosamaría e-mailed me that she would like to visit me. I mentioned that I really didn't look forward to driving to Oxnard. She said she would gladly drive to San Pedro to spend the day and stay overnight. It was very nice seeing her. She adamantly refused to accept the fifty dollars I insisted she take for gas. I know she does not have a lot of money and she is a proud lady. She is related to Diego Rivera the famous Mexican painter and Frida Kahlo, whom she remembered vaguely when she was a little girl.

We had the full day to talk and I am impressed, as I was when I first met her at her self taught knowledge in many areas, especially conventional and integrative medicine in relation to her pathology. I will keep in touch to check on her progress.

— — — — —

My cousin Marvin and his wife Sandy rented the Wrigley Mansion in Phoenix to celebrate their 35th wedding anniversary. There must have been between eighty and 100 guests mostly family, relatives and friends. My return flight to Los Angeles left at 11:30 pm, scheduled to arrive at LAX at 1:00 am. Due to inclement weather we were re-routed to Ontario airport near LA, landing at 1:20 am then taken by bus to LAX where I took the airport bus to the parking lot a mile away. It was raining heavily and after searching for my car without success, I realized that it had to be in another lot a mile away. At the exit gate of the lot I asked the attendant if there was any transportation to the other lot. There wasn't. It was now 4:00 am, three hours since landing. Fortunately at the exit gate one of the cars leaving heard my plight and kindly dropped me off at the other parking lot. I finally found my car after another half hour search in the rain. I plopped my drenched body in the car and drove, arriving home at 5:20 am, four miserable hours since landing. As an afterthought I would have rather driven to Phoenix than flown.

— — — — —

Until the advent of the September 11th Twin Towers attack, I was issued, at my request a pass from the US Department of Immigration at LAX permitting me to avoid the passport check lines upon arrival in many of the larger US airports by presenting the pass and putting my hand against a screening device at a special station at the airport. I never encountered anyone else doing this upon various arrivals. This was discontinued the day following the attack. I was able to qualify for this pass by stating that I traveled outside the US at least four times a year on business and since I owned property in Spain, that was acceptable.

— — — — — —

Jill, my ex, later married Billy and moved nearby in San Pedro. Billy was an alcoholic but seemed to be a likable person. Later they moved to Scotland where Jill bought a cottage. Billy's father died leaving him an inheritance. Suddenly without telling Jill, he returned to Oklahoma to remarry his former ex-wife leaving a charge of $8,000 on Jill's credit card, back rent of $5,000 owed me and $4,000 owed Mike Good's garage.

I suggested she file suit but she would have return to attend the trial in Ardmore, Oklahoma. She didn't want to come but finally agreed and I proceeded to contact Bill's attorney and set a trial date. Billy, knowing he would be going to court, sent a check to Mike Good for the $4,000 and me a sent me a torn, invalid check he owed me for back rent. Jill decided not to come and the trial went into default. Trying to help Jill I lost, aside from money owed me, an additional $3,000 for lawyers and fees.

Chapter XXX
Cuba

December of 2002 I took a Mexican bus line, Golden State out of Santa Ana, California to the Tijuana airport for a special semi illegal flight to Havana. I have taken other Mexican bus lines from Los Angeles to other places in the interior of Mexico and enjoyed the unique pleasure of no other gringo in any of the trips I did and none of the drivers spoke English.

We were herded into a deserted part of the airport and later confined in a room before our luggage was thoroughly searched and we boarded. Our government's ridiculous policy of boycotting Cuba and not permitting American citizens to enter Cuba makes this subterfuge necessary. I had already contacted and arranged to rent a room at doña Rosario's house in the Miramar Playa section of Habana.

I was especially pleased by my room, overlooking the ocean and the famous, old Copacabana Hotel. My room was 13'x 15', closet 4'x5', bathroom 8'x11', balcony 5'x13' with two chairs and a table, sliding glass doors to the balcony, double bed, five-drawer dresser, bed lamp, ceiling light with fan, 2 chairs, a large coffee table, radio, CD, cassette player and a private entrance. Breakfast and supper were included. Breakfast consisted of two eggs, ham or bacon, fresh tropical fruits, orange juice, toast, coffee or tea. Supper was a delicious, hearty meal. My cost was $30 per day. The two gracious maids were Nubia and Muni.

This is one of the more elegant districts in Havana. I have invariably sought out and stayed in inexpensive lodging and the same for restaurants, mostly in people's homes and in restaurants frequented by local workers. My purpose in traveling is meeting and living among the people, enjoying the music, dancing and their way of life. The neighboring Copacabana hotel is on the ocean and has two salt water pools on the spacious decks and one pool one and a half meters deep, three meters wide and twenty meters long on the ocean adjoining the seawall. This is mainly for swimming laps. There is another section for sport diving and fishing and my favorite haunt, a body building gymnasium. There was a daily charge of three dollars for the gym and five dollars for the pool area. Many Cuban ladies were at the pool with the express purpose of meeting foreigners or well-to-do fellow countrymen. It was common to see older gentlemen, primarily Spaniards, who found that sending a woman a relatively small amount of money, monthly, furnished the man with a lover and often free lodging.

One of the maids in the house where I was staying told me to mention her name when this particular groundsman was on duty at the hotel. He usually let me into the hotel pool area without paying unless a supervisor was present. I would go tango dancing at El Caserón del Tango in La Habana Vieja, probably the only milonga in Cuba, hosted by an ex-Argentine, don Emilio Álvarez.

Two blocks from my room in Havana there was a park with three restaurants. There was a pizza stand, another stand with sandwiches and a variety of other finger foods and salads and a Chinese restaurant where a full meal cost about the equivalent of a dollar and a half. The other two places I mentioned were about half as much for a light meal. I was only aware of seeing locals and no tourists the times I was there.

One night at the tango dance there was a group tour of American tango enthusiasts. I was dancing with a tall blonde of the group. We chatted and she said she was from Denver. I replied that I had lived in Denver before moving to California. She asked me if I knew Flo. I replied Flo was my good friend with whom I started dancing tango. When Cheryl Guay said that she and I had danced together before at a milonga in Denver then I remembered her. I've bumped into her with Flo in Buenos Aires since. I was also surprised to encounter two tango friends from California who were leaving the milonga as I entered.

I took Rosario, my landlady, to the milonga one night to satisfy her curiosity about tango dancing after she showed me around Habana Vieja, the old city.

Middle two, doña Rosario & Francisco Alvarez,
La Habana Vieja

After eight days in Havana I left the airport for Santiago on the other end of the island. The plane was an old dilapidated twin engine propeller Russian aircraft. Many of the backrests were broken and when the engines started, the roar was deafening. It seemed as if the plane would come apart. I was relieved when we landed in Santiago. Cuban aviation has one of the worst accident records in spite of their modern international fleet.

I found a room for fifteen dollars a night in a pension owned by a Dutchman. I found rooms in Cuba to be clean and often without their own bathroom. My room was simple but large and I could hear the beautiful music all through the night. The location couldn't have been better for me, one block from the park named after Manuel Céspedes a local hero and across the street from Casa de la Trova and Casa del Estudiante, both places for traditional Cuban dancing. It cost one dollar to dance at La Trova all night. On formal occasions the men had to wear either a jacket or a guayabera shirt. I didn't have either but they let me watch from a side balcony. I did slip out of the balcony to dance son, bolero, rumba and danzón with some of the black ladies. In the eastern part of the country, called El Oriente, most of the inhabitants are black. The park is surrounded by beautiful old traditional Spanish style buildings. Cuban and tropical music is also some of my favorite dance and listening music. It's difficult just to listen to those stirring rhythms without wanting to move. Santiago is the cradle of Cuban music and the revolution. Most of the famous Cuban musicians of the traditional music are from Santiago. Two of the esteemed older Cuban musicians from Oriente province are Ibrahim Ferrer of the Buena Vista Social Club fame and Compay Segundo.

I was sitting on a bench in Manuel Céspedes park only a half block from where I was staying. At a nearby bench a young husky black man was sitting. After awhile he walked over to me to ask if I had a light for his cigarette. I was a little dubious about engaging him in conversation but we chatted and he seemed pleasant. His name was Alcides. He was on vacation from working on a farm. He turned out to be a good dependable friend and spent his whole vacation taking me around to all the historical sites and telling me what he knew about the area. We went to Siboney beach, twelve kilometers from Santiago. It's small and rustic, not like a picture postcard beach one sees in the brochures. People sell coconuts, pineapple, watermelon and papayas to eat on the beach. I always look forward to eating green coconuts and drinking their sweet milk. One can scoop out the meat which has the consistency of yogurt or slightly firmer, depending on its ripeness. I was fortunate because being with him and speaking in Spanish we managed to pay in many of the local restaurants in Cuban pesos, the equivalent of one twenty-sixth of what the tourist peso cost. It's illegal for foreigners to pay in Cuban pesos except for items like gum, candy, etc. Good meals with meat, seafood etc. are expensive and scarce. Most people eat basic staples such as rice, beans, bread, chicken, eggs, pizza and pork. The national dish is called congri, consisting of rice, beans and small bits of pork and may have peppers, tomato and condiments. I don't recall if I drank bottled or tap water.

Alcides invited me to a party with his cousin, a tall, comely black lady of twenty two with a lovely young daughter. There were two other young men. They all lived in the outskirts of Santiago in an old dilapidated Russian built apartment building on the third floor. His cousin was paying a lot of attention and flirting with me but I wasn't quite sure if there was some sort of situation between the other fellows and the lady so decided to lighten our flirtation. We have corresponded and she always invites me to stay with them, maybe because I'm an American and also would be able to help financially. We all went to a communal party in back of the building with two pits and two roasting pigs of which we partook.

I was getting a haircut from a woman, in her house. She asked for five dollars and I knew the price for locals was one dollar. We settled for two dollars, tip included.

One problem in Cuba, as in many other poor countries, where even surviving is hard, the prostitutes are always hustling anyone they can. Walking in Céspedes park a young black girl approached and hung on to me and as much as I tried to get rid of her she wouldn't let me go until finally I dragged her toward a policeman which scared her off.

A strikingly beautiful mulatto lady was strolling in the park with a buggy with two babies. Whether they were in her care or were her children was questionable. I can only assume that she "belonged" to a very wealthy or important person. She had a body hugging, pink suit, matching high heels and cap and her voluptuous body that undulated with poise along the path. No one seemed to pay her any attention which I attribute to a sign of respect of her standing in the community.

Just before I was to leave by bus for the fifteen hour return trip to Havana, Alcides's vacation ended and he had to return to work in the fields. He refused any money so I offered him my wrist watch which he also refused. Finally I contacted his sister who worked in a hotel in Havana and gave her the watch to give him.

Points of interest for me in Havana were the seawall promenade, El Malecón and Habana Vieja. I don't usually have many special places of interest but go day by day doing whatever I want to do and going where I want to go. I always enjoy being with and chatting with the locals. Cuba was one of my favorite places. I've thought often of returning but it's doubtful. When the US lifts the embargo and US citizens are permitted to go, I believe the island will change overnight especially in the larger cities and tourist destinations. If that should happen I would have little desire to return.

I was careful packing so as not to have anything that would even hint that I had been in Cuba. I didn't even take any written phone numbers or addresses but then again I am probably too conservative or over cautious.

Chapter XXXI
Chalet

My decision to sell the chalet on the island revolved around the fact that I would not be living there anymore and I could surely use the money. Jill and Yale were against selling any of the property. My other children were very understanding and advised me to do what was best for me. When the original property was bought, there was no way to divide the land as I would have preferred and the way it worked out I was required to cede the major portion with the chalet, leaving the main house with a much smaller portion. Yale went to the municipal planning committee to see if we could obtain a re-segregation of the properties but to no avail. These things took place during 2006 through 2008.

After deciding to sell to a young Italian family I had the problem of a renter who was difficult to evict and some repairs to make before concluding the sale. To take advantage of a tax break for foreigners in Spain I returned to the island for a period of six months twice within a two year period to establish Spanish residency. I later found out that it really wasn't necessary as the statutes on selling property changed. I would have been very upset about this if I hadn't enjoyed life on the island so much. I still had to make a few journeys back and forth from Los Angeles in order to take care of all the inefficient bureaucratic red tape. All in all, when both parties agreed to the sale, it was still ongoing for another year or more. Then I had to keep pestering my Spanish bank about getting all my money transferred to my US bank. As luck would have it, I sold at the right time as real estate was high and the dollar-euro exchange was favorable. Both dropped in value immediately after.

Being that Jill was upset with me it was decided that when I was in Formentera I would stay in our adjoining, well furnished studio. I relished the independence. I took pleasure in making the studio more comfortable, putting up shelves, more cooking utensils, etc. I was not interested in the nightlife in the bars or other tourist hangouts like the beach at night. The beach during the day was my milieu.

I became very involved, spending three to five hours most nights writing my autobiography. My son Yale was kind enough to charge my computer in the house and to send and receive my e-mails. Yale always offered help whenever I needed it. He was more adept at getting things done especially when there were technical or legal aspects to resolve.

— — — — — —

I had already signed the contract of sale, collected the money and transferred it to my bank in San Pedro when I was informed by the authorities of Formentera that according to Spanish law the release and signature from Virginia, who was my wife at that time, was mandatory. I immediately phoned Virginia who said she would be happy to comply and I set up an appointment for us at the Spanish Consulate in Los Angeles for ten the next morning. Since I didn't hear from her by evening I phoned and asked her husband if I may speak to Virginia. He curtly told me that Virginia was not to sign anything and not to bother them or call in the future. I tried to explain but was immediately cut off. During the following months I sent three letters but to no avail. This nightmarish dilemma hung over me day and night and was on my mind constantly for the next few months. I really couldn't see any way of satisfactorily resolving this matter.

With the limited dealing I've had in Spain and other counties especially Latin countries, I for one, would be very cautious about buying property or making other financial transactions. Spain has been very stable in regard to foreigners owning property in spite of the inefficiency and bureaucratic red tape and delays in most transactions.

— — — — — —

I met Beverly Berg when I went with Norm Oakvic, who was visiting me at the time, to watch the California Swing Dance finals in the fall of 1986. I had a cast on my left leg for a tennis ankle strain and was ambulating on crutches.

I noticed this very attractive lady and we just seemed to click. She danced Go Go and dances almost any dance. She looks twenty years younger than her age. We have been friends since we met but didn't go steady and had other relationships through those years but we've kept in touch. I think we would be together more if it weren't for the driving. She lives in La Habra.

I only met Penny a few times briefly when she was married to Neil Hankin. I knew Neil through tennis and Virginia Cuffel all at the Palos Verdes Mobile Home Park near my house. When I found out that Neil died, I called Penny with my condolences.

I don't recall how we got together but I was attracted to this lovely, intelligent lady. Through the five years we've been friends she has been the most pleasureful company.

Penny and Suzi Wong

I taught Penny Tango for two years, She was an adept partner with whom I enjoyed dancing. Unfortunately she developed a foot problem and has discontinued dancing.

Penny invites me over to watch one of our favorite programs, Bill Maher on HBO which I do not have. Suzi Wong, her lovely Persian cat is usually around to entertain us or distract us. Suzi likes to get up on the counter when I come in and rub noses for my greeting. Along the way Penny has managed to take in two other stray cats. Penny has recently retired and has been doing more painting. She is very good but she is a very modest person.

Two blocks up the hill from our house is our local Elks lodge #966 with panoramic views of the San Pedro harbor, south along the coast to Dana Point, the downtown buildings in Long Beach to the east and the Los Angeles downtown skyscraper complex to the north. When the setting sun is just right it imparts an awesome. golden bronze reflection of those building in Los Angeles and Long Beach. I was sorry not having my camera at those fleeting moments of beauty.

We have one of the larger Elks Lodges with an Olympic size swimming pool enclosed in a large tiled sunning deck lined with sun lounges and chairs, three adjoining tennis courts, horse shoe pitching, a well equipped men's gym with sauna and steam bath, pool room, large domed lodge meeting room, restaurant, formal dining room, bar, three large salons for parties, dancing, weddings, large parking areas, etc. Great place to eat and take guests. I am a 35 year life member and make frequent use of the gym. Years before, I played tennis there often and tanned at the pool.

I was working out at the gym at the Elk's lodge speaking with my friend Dan Sanchez in Spanish. I happened to mention my predicament of a blocked sale of some of my Spanish property. He asked me about the details and to bring in any pertinent documents and paper work and said that he would look into the matter when he had time and get back to me. He told me not to call at his office as they would charge his fee of $600 per hour but to contact him at home if I didn't hear from him in a week or two. I wasn't aware that he was an attorney of international law. I said I would be willing to pay the fees with the hopes that it might expedite the matter. Dan said, as my friend, he wouldn't charge me. We got in touch two weeks later and he informed me that under California law there was no need for my ex-wife Virginia's signature and gave me a copy of the California statutes which I translated into Spanish and forwarded to the officials in Formentera. They rejected my petition. I then contacted and sent the documents to an attorney that I knew from Formentera who practiced in Barcelona, who in turn contacted the lawyer and agency in Formentera and convinced them that California law supersedes Spanish law in this case as we are both California residents who married in this state. My nightmare was over and I could return to the living. When I profusely thanked Dan he said it was nothing. "I replied it may have been nothing for you but there is no greater favor you could have done for me."

Dan's parents were from Galicia in the northwest corner of Spain. I am impressed with his achievements. Dan was an amateur boxer and has sparred with many champion fighters, one being Rocky Marciano. He was a Los Angeles County life guard, part time movie actor, author, twenty nine years with the LAPD, reaching the rank of commander and until his recent retirement and an attorney of international law. He has given lectures, both in legal and police subjects in many countries and has taught at the University of Badajoz in Spain. Five years ago he developed a very serious heart problem, "the widow maker" and was near death a few times but fortunately has improved and has been able to start exercising again. I'm looking forward to spending more time with him.

In October of 2013 I lost my Elk's Lodge membership card. I was informed duplicate fees for lost cards were fifty dollars. I refused to pay what I think an exorbitant fee and opted to wait till the new year to renew my membership card without any penalty payment, only the dues. I've been a member of this lodge for 35 years without any previous incidents.

I previously was a member for a few years before and during a membership drive, at the encouragement of the membership committee I suggested a new neighbor, a military officer and his family. I didn't realize that at the time our fraternal organization the Elks, didn't accept blacks. I immediately canceled my membership and didn't rejoin until years later. Presently all races and genders are accepted.

Chapter XXXII
My First Cruise
(at 84 years old)
(A once in a lifetime adventure)

Rotterdam Dining Room   ms Veenda 10th December 201

Penny and me

Penny and I boarded the Holland America "ms Veendam" departing from Buenos Aires on December 8, 2010 at 8 pm with planned stops at Montevideo, Uruguay and Port Stanley, Falkland Islands. We were scheduled to cruise around Cape Horn, up the Beagle Channel to Ushuaia, Argentina, through the Straits of Magellan to Punta Arenas and Puerto Montt, Chile, and disembark in Valaparaíso, Chile (port of Santiago) on December 20th at 7 am.

The cabin Penny and I shared, number 765, was located fortunately on a lower deck amidships. We were pleasantly surprised at the spaciousness and furnishings with a large unobstructed view window. Penny, who has taken quite a few cruises said it was much better than her previous accommodations on other cruise lines.

We boarded at the new steamship terminal in Buenos Aires at noon. The boarding procedure was fast and efficient. The ship departed on schedule arriving at Montevideo the following morning.

We strolled the streets, plazas and the port area for a few hours before returning to the ship. Penny purchased a tango painting from a street vendor with whom we had a delightful conversation about the tango milongas in Montevideo in contrast with the milongas in Buenos Aires, along with some local tango history.

I had hoped to use my bathing suit to sun bathe at the pool before we were too far south where it would undoubtedly be too cool or the weather bad even though it is the beginning of summer south of the equator. No such luck, although some used the indoor pool and spa, chlorinated pools are not my thing.

I did take advantage of the gym except for the two days that it was impossible due to the heavy seas. It was an eerie sensation of lifting weights when the ship is really rolling. When the ship rises on a swell a weight feels heavy and when it falls suddenly the weight feels almost weightless. The gym is located on the 11th deck toward the bow, higher off the water and the further from the center, exaggerating the ships movement. The center and low parts of the ship move less than the bow, stern and higher decks.

Needless to say, as probable on many cruises the friendly service was unsurpassed, the cleanliness immaculate, along with the unlimited, delicious food and varied menus, always a treat.

The most interesting and exciting aspect of the voyage, at least for me and many other passengers we met aboard was, believe it or not, having sailed through the worst weather imaginable. Our first day started out sunny, cool and windy with moderate swells and whitecaps. A few hardy souls attempted to sun in their swimsuits or shorts in areas protected from the winds but soon went inside as the weather slowly worsened. The second day was cloudy with intermittent rain, gale force winds and rougher seas. We were informed that a storm was forecast which eventually turned out to be three times worse then predicted. The captain said if he'd known what lay ahead for us he would have returned to port. The Italian MCS cruise ship following a few hours behind, after two days returned to the port of departure canceling the entire cruise because of the storm forecast. We were informed by radio to be on the lookout for a French yacht and a Portuguese yacht that were reported missing in the area. It was later reported that both were lost at sea and all presumed dead. Two of the bodies were later found washed up on the rocks. Survival in those icy waters is a matter of minutes.

Tierra Del Fuego, December 2010

30 meter waves – Veendam, Cape Horn, December 2010

The tenders carrying passengers from our ship on the excursion in the Falkland Islands barely were barely able to return to the ship through the high swells and rough seas. For awhile, they thought that the tenders would have to remain in Port Stanley to await calmer seas, but after some delay the last three tenders chanced returning and finally made it back after a scary hair raising, roller coaster ride half of the time under water. Later that afternoon and night the storm increased and was rated as a class two hurricane. All entertainment, activities, etc, were canceled and passengers were confined to their cabins until the following morning. The cabins with portholes had to be protected during the hurricane with metal shields, obscuring any view. Our 3 by 4 foot window was large compared to the portholes but it held up during the constant bashing by waves that completely covered the window. There were moments looking through our window that we appeared to be underwater.

Regressing to our second night out, Penny and I went to the "Crow's Nest" lounge for Latin dancing. I asked the DJ if he had any Argentine tangos and was surprised that he had some very danceable tangos. We danced our first tango being the only ones on the floor. When we finished there was much applause and requests for encores. We danced two more tangos until I was worn out (naturally we threw in some showy stuff). Some asked if we would dance the following night so they could film and we agreed. I'm reminded of a Spanish adage "En tierra de ciegos, el tuerto es rey" (in the land of the blind, the one-eyed man is king). The following night dancing was more difficult with the constant rolling and pitching so we decided no more dancing unless there was less movement and that didn't happen.

The seas became rougher with huge swells and the wind increased to 80 miles per hour. On our fifth day, December 13th we were in the brunt of the storm with waves of 30 meters (98 feet) and a wind speed recorded at 118 miles per hour until the wind sensor, docking radar, antennas, life rafts, working lights, etc. were swept off the fore deck into the sea. It's likely the wind speed went even higher than we recorded. The highest mid-ocean wave recorded in the Guinness Book of World Records is 34 meters, not much higher than we experienced. Our recorded wind speed was classified at the maximum level on the Beaufort scale. We were in the midst of a class two hurricane.

Waves constantly broke over the twelve story bow. This data is recorded on the ship's log. The ship stopped for some hours when the port anchor was torn loose and made a frightening, continuous noise as it ran out the full 1000 foot length of chain. The winch was unable to retrieve the anchor. Luckily the navigation department's sonar sighted a sea mount nearby and was able to drag the anchor to a shallower area permitting the winch to recover the anchor avoiding cutting the chain and losing the anchor. The ship was listing on the port side and sea water was taken into the hold to serve as ballast. When we finally got underway we were at three knots instead of the usual 18-22 knots. It was estimated the loss of dishes and china was $180,000. Many of the statues, artworks etc. were thrown to the deck along with many occupied chairs. I have been on various ships and vessels and often get queasy or seasick but I didn't take anything or feel bad on this voyage except a little light headed now and then. Long ago I read or was told that to avoid "mal de mer" one should not refrain from eating or have an empty stomach to which I wholeheartedly adhered to religiously with no problem. I normally eat continually anyway but not in large quantities.

We did not get much relief from the inclement weather until entering the Beagle channel two days later and the Straits of Magellan both protected on either side by continuous mountain chains. Weather was cold with increasing number and size of ice floes. At one point it seemed as if we were going through solid ice. Interestingly enough our ship had ice breaking capabilities. We also experienced much rain, drizzle, hail and a half hour snow storm. There are many isles and glaciers in these channels and straits. The scenery is magnificent. On entering the Pacific Ocean once again the sea was rough for a short time but soon we were protected from the winds and heavy seas by the many fjords as we sailed north along the Chilean coast.

We were now more than 24 hours behind schedule which necessitated not being able to stop at certain glaciers and our day stop in Puerto Montt. I had no intention of leaving the ship and wasn't concerned about seeing the town as I've been to Puerto Montt twice, two years ago, when I took the 8 hour catamaran trip form Puerto Montt south to Chaitén to join my friends Jack and Patty Schmitt at their cabin on the River Yelcho.

We eventually became dining room buddies with four other couples, two from Florida, one from northern California and one from England. After a few days we all decided that we would change our open dining and reserve our table at the late sitting till the end of our voyage. We enjoyed talking and joking and were the last to leave the dining room. The passengers were mostly adults with many seniors and very few children. We five couples still maintain contact, having shared a common bond.

At our table María Concepción Gonzalez-Santos and her husband Tom were seated. I really enjoyed speaking Spanish to her but limited myself in deference to the others who were non Spanish speakers. She was from Colombia, a retired lieutenant colonel from the US army and presently a Spanish professor in Santa Clara University. Tom is also retired and an ardent salmon fisherman.

Our other friends at our table: Dick and Barb. Barb loved to sing Karaoke and was always the dominant singer at the Karaoke sessions. She also won a fair amount of money at the gambling casino on board. David and Barbara were from Florida. The English couple were Conrad and Diane; he an experienced yachtsman.

One of our favorite pastimes was sitting in the lounges and watching the mesmerizing panorama of mountainous seas and the various storms through the large windows.

I also met a gentleman traveling to South America who claimed to be a missionary. He was seasick so I gave him a half dozen meclizine tablets that I always have available. The next day, after taking one tablet he said he felt fine.

At one of the tables at the cafeteria one of the group was a very nice looking flirtatious Korean woman who was quite openly plain spoken.

At voyage's end the captain announced that in his 27 years of sailing he has never experienced a voyage as rough and as difficult. It was evident that the crew and especially the officers in charge had some worried moments. Before the end of the voyage there was an interesting session in the amphitheater for all with the Captain, chief engineer and the head of service and personnel discussing the crisis we went through and answering questions from the passengers.

Other problems arose during and after the hurricane which can be seen on the article "Weather Permitting" in the Cruise News of February 2011 of the magazine Pacific Mariner. There are also various videos, blogs, and comments on You Tube, ms Veendam storm December 10, 2010.

When the ship docked at Valparaiso it was discovered that the stern plates had been so heavily pushed in that the main deck had buckled breaking the overlying teak deck strips and causing bow damage and buckling of the forward port doors. Repairs were made at the ship's next dry docking before sailing again.

The company announced that due to the conditions that we endured and the wonderful cooperation of the passengers that all would be eligible for a 25% discount on any future Holland America cruise booked before the end of 2011. We took advantage of this offer and booked two cabins for an Alaskan cruise in February, 2012.

Our Captain Rik Kronbeen deserved and received many commendations and thanks from the passengers for his able handling and for getting us safely through a precarious situation.

Late during the last night of the voyage, Penny wasn't feeling well with a very rapid an erratic heart beat. We went to the ship's doctor who immediately put her on a gurney and connected her to the oxygen, heart monitor and an intravenous hookup. Her pulse was up 170 beats per minute. They gave her an injection of magnesium sulfate. It looked as if she might be allergic and was in anaphylactic shock. We were all scared including the attending medical personnel. She was quivering and could barely talk and later said at the time she thought she wouldn't make it.

The next morning we were debarked first to a waiting ambulance that rushed us to the Valparaíso Clinic. The physicians except, for the older head doctor, were young female recent graduates. I did all the translating as their English was limited. Everyone was pleasant but it took much longer than it should have. We entered at 10 am and left at 6:30 pm in a special taxi for an hour and a half drive to the airport at Santiago where Penny caught her flight to Los Angeles. She was stabilized and had no problems on the flight home. Penny received medical care upon arrival. She recovered completely with no residual effects.

A seaman's adage I ran across while seeking information about Cape Horn (named by a Dutch explorer for the town of Hoorn, in Holland) which, translated from the original Spanish refers to the southern latitudes around the southernmost tip of South America. Our southern most latitude was 56 degrees south latitude, less than ten degrees south to the Antarctic Circle.

Debajo de los 40 grados, no hay ley. (Under 40 degrees, there is no law.)
Debajo de los 50 grados, no hay Dios (Under 50 degrees, there is no God.)

In the same article, a poem also in Spanish, by Sara Vial published in 1992 on a plaque in the Cape Horn area reads as follows:

Soy el albatrós que te espera en el final del mundo. Soy el alma olvidada de los marinos muertos que cruzaron el Cabo de Hornos, de todos los mares de la
tierra, pero ellos no murieron en las furiosas olas. Hoy vuelan en mis alas hacia
la eternidad en la última grieta de los antárticos.

(I am the albatross that awaits you at the end of the world. I am the forgotten
soul of dead mariners that crossed Cape Horn from all the seas of

the earth, but
those didn't die in the furious waves, today they fly on my wings
toward eternity
in the last crevasse of the Antarctic.)

Penny and me

I returned to Santiago by taxi after seeing Penny off. I remained in Santiago for four days before returning to California. Patty Schmitt's friend, Nani, was supposed to be awaiting my arrival at Jack and Patty's house but she wasn't there. I went to Patty's sister's family house next door and waited two hours until Nani showed up. She expected me earlier and did an errand before returning. She took off four days from work in order to take care of me. It was almost embarrassing having her wait on me hand and foot. There was nothing that she wouldn't do for me. She is a loving, caring lady and I do appreciate her taking off from work for my benefit. I told her that I could do my own things and she could read or crochet. I don't like someone fussing over me all the time.

September 11, 2010 (Patriot's Day, in commemoration of the destruction of the Twin Towers). I had a patio party with more than twenty tango friends along with David and Abbey and Linda and John. It just happened that it was a convenient date and nothing to do with that tragic event. It was perfect weather and all commented on the extensive patios I recently put in and the view of Catalina island and the sea. We all had a good time and I received many thanks at the party and for days afterward. I made a large amount of Spanish alioli which basically consists of crushed garlic and olive oil and very heavy on the garlic. One of my favorite tango dancers, Sheryl Johnson, really had quite a bit and really enjoyed the pungent flavor. When I make a batch, I usually put some aside for her. It's probably a good idea not to eat it for a few days before being with people, unless they are also heavily into garlic.

On September 17, 2011 Penny and I flew to Anchorage for an Alaskan cruise. I invited Linda & John and David and Abbey but David and Abbey were unable to come due to their work commitments. We booked a cruise for them for the following February for a week with the six of us on the Mexican Riviera.

Linda and John left a few days before and rented a car to sight see before meeting us in Seward aboard the Statesdam in she afternoon of the 18th. It was our second cruise on Holland America. The weather was lovely for the two and a half hour bus trip from Fairbanks to the port of Seward. Great scenery and wildlife. We saw moose, Dall sheep, bald eagles and Humpback whales.

Upon boarding we were advised that there was a storm in the Gulf of Alaska and our departure was delayed 38 hours resulting in being able to make a stop only in Juneau and have to forgo scheduled stops at Glacier Bay, Hubbard glacier, Skagway and Ketchikan. The first day out brought heavy seas, wind, rain and fog. The remaining days were the same except the sea was less rough. Even so the decks were closed except for a few hours during the last two days. Fortunately the day in Juneau was nice and we were impressed with the Mendenhall Glacier and the nearby glacier gardens, the shoreline, fjords and many islands that were visible were shrouded in hues of black and gray. In spite of not being able to see many of these beautiful sights at sea we did enjoy the cruise. It was especially nice to spend time with Linda and John. The more time I'm with them the more impressed I am with both of them but again I feel the same about all my children and their spouses.

Other benefits were the luxurious lifestyle of cruises, dancing and meeting interesting people. We always request a large table in order to enjoy the company and get to know others. The cafeteria is often crowded so we normally share a table. One breakfast I sat with a middle aged man who had a rugged appearance. He was an outdoor type from British Colombia who loved camping and hunting big and small game with bow and arrow. We almost always chatted at length with whomever we met. Many and possibly most of the passengers who booked passage departing and returning to Vancouver were from the area of Vancouver/Seattle environs. The second day we saw two couples dancing to an American tango to a trio in a lounge. It was evident that they weren't very advanced but we enjoyed their company and conversation. Naturally we stopped and became well acquainted with them and the musicians. At his request I loaned the band leader a CD of Argentine tangos, oddly enough American or Continental style tangos are absolutely the worst music for dancing Argentine tango. Although they were unable to play Argentine tango we did manage to dance a tango waltz to "Sunrise, Sunset" from Fiddler on the Roof which worked out very well. My only problem was my lack of stamina which limited the amount of my dancing. We all enjoyed watching John and Linda perform various dances. They dance well to any music and make a handsome couple.

There was a classical string quartet of lovely young ladies from one of the Balkan countries. I am not a fan of classical music but must admit that I enjoyed the music. It was frustrating hearing selections that I would have loved to dance tango in the small space on one side of the stage knowing that Penny my companion being a very proper person couldn't conceive of dancing or rather performing in that dignified ambiance. By comparison my friend Flo would have been difficult to dissuade. The older couple dancing in the lounge was from British Columbia. The gentleman was impeccably dressed but had poor eyesight. His wife would assist him. The other couple from the states was younger. Both couples questioned us about tango.

We were impressed with the quality of Holland America compared to some of the other cruise lines. I marvel at the efficiency, including transportation to and from the ship and airports. On our return to LAX John rented a car but exchanged it for a larger vehicle in order to get in all the luggage. A lot nicer than taking a shuttle home.

— — — — — —

Friday, November 19, 2011 just after midnight Saturday morning my closest friend and ex-partner George Patten passed away. A month later my dear friend Howard had a severe exacerbation of his Alzheimer's and circulatory problems. He was taken to the emergency room at the hospital then to a nursing home where he had to be tied to his bed. It was just a week after we went to visit Howard and his wife Sandy, where we meet with Joe and Addie Liss for our customary get together a few times each year. It was very obvious that Howard's mental condition was deteriorating and he really wasn't to aware of what we were talking about. Both George and Howie have been my friends for 68 years. Howard passed away a few days later.

During some of my visits to Minneapolis, I usually stayed with George and his wife Lee or in latter years when George and Lee had moved to a smaller condo, I stayed with Norman Oakvik. On my most recent visit Marisa Riviere invited me to stay with her at her large manor like house one block from Lake of the Isles. Marisa and her husband were from Buenos Aires. He was a professor of mathematics at the University of Minnesota. She also worked at the university. He died at a relatively young age. They bought and she still lives during the summers in her house that originally was owned by Walter Mondale, politician and 42nd vice president of the US. We spent much of the time at the beach at Lake Calhoun which adjoins Lake of the Isles.

George Patten had a habit of giving me the grand tour of the Twin Cities whenever I visited. One time he parked in front of our home on Xerxes Avenue. The house looked the same as I remembered. I went to the door but no one answered. We waited a while and I noticed that on the other side of the street facing Theodore Wirth (Glenwood) Park there were quite a few new homes where none existed before when we had a pristine, panoramic, unblocked view. After a brief time a car pulled up and parked in front of the house. When the three black passengers got out of the car and started up the steps I told them that I used to live there. We chatted a short while and they invited us in but George was due home so we didn't go in.

— — — — — —

I went to the Los Angeles West Coast Swing Dance Club at the Golden Sails Hotel on their scheduled alternate Sunday dances. I hadn't danced west coast swing for 15 years and decide to take the free beginning lesson given before the dance taught by Paula McHam.

Paula said to me, "Don't I know you, you look familiar?" When I mentioned that I used to go to the swing jam sessions at Bobby Mc Gee's Restaurant on Pacific Coast Highway and 2nd Street in Long Beach and some of the other old haunts, she then recognized me.

I got together with Paula who wanted to learn Argentine tango and arranged to help her with tango in exchange for helping me with swing. She picks up very fast. She is an accomplished dancer of all the ballroom dances. I'm sure I got the better deal. I haven't been confident enough in my swing dancing to ask many of the ladies even though there are worse dancers there than I. Just my own hang up and my own fault.

I recognized many of the old timers, Frankie Rodriguez, little Annie Hirsch and Jack and others. I haven't attended the swing club dance of late but with good intentions of going more often. Like many of my other good intentions that haven't as yet materialized.

I bumped into Lee Laitz and his wife Nita at the West Coast Swing Dance Club dance. I don't think he recognized me immediately in spite of almost continual contact through the seventy years we've known one another. Nita recognized me immediately and I've only seen her once four years ago when they married. I'm afraid his memory is deteriorating. Nevertheless we are able to talk on the phone about old times. Another tango friend, Bill Boyd, passed away the day after the new year.

Lee Laitz danced Lindy and Balboa, competing in California, New York and other venues in the 40's and 50's. I don't remember much of his first wife. His second wife Lucille, who passed away and his present lovely wife, Nita. All three were excellent dancers and beautiful, lovely women.

When I was dancing with Virginia, Lee and Lucille gave us free lesson in their home. I also attended a series of classes of Balboa by Maxie Dorf in Lee's garage studio. We were about fifteen west coast swing dancers, many of whom were very accomplished and well known dancers.

Chuck Beltran and Phyllis, my friends in San Pedro, were excellent swing dancers. Chuck's brother Bill Moreno also danced swing. Eddie Pierson, a sought after swing dancer also from San Pedro recently passed away. Most were either members of the Los Angeles West Coast Swing Dance Club or non members who often attended the club's dances.

I saw an announcement that mentioned at a certain time and channel on TV there would be a program of the West Coast Swing Club of Southern California. I noted the time and when that day arrived I anxiously tuned in awaiting seeing my old cronies on TV. When people were being presented I didn't recognize them, thinking that since I've been out of that circle for almost twenty years there may be a few that I didn't know. More and more were being presented and still no recognition on my part. After I heard a few of the comments it dawned on me that this was not a dance club but a wife swapping club of "swingers" and I had unwittingly notified many of my dance friends beforehand to tune in and watch.

— — — — — —

David and Abbey, John and Linda, and Penny and I went on a seven day cruise to the Mexican Riviera February 25th through March 3rd embarking on the Princess Sapphire from and returning to San Pedro. I originally booked a cabin with a view window for Penny and I and another for David and Abbey. The day before leaving I was just about to go out when the phone rang. It was the travel agency. Princess offered us an upgrade to a two bedroom suite with a large balcony. I said I would like to consult the others but the cruise line was also on the phone line and they had to know immediately so I accepted their generous offer. It included many special perks and privileges that regular passengers don't receive. We were able to arrange that many of those perks were available to all instead of just to Penny and myself. Another perk that I always get when Linda is around is a great haircut. I intentionally brought special scissors along for that purpose. Both David and I had her cut our hair. She always gives me a better haircut than any of the barbers I've had. Could I be prejudiced?

I was not as active as the others and not interested in many of the things they all did. I attempted to work out in the gym a few times but my shoulder didn't permit me to do much and I didn't have the energy. I was looking forward to dancing but Penny forgot her dance shoes and I don't think she was in the mood for dancing. Our cabin was far forward and we had to do a lot of walking on board. The weather was fair and the sailing smooth except for the last day or two. We made two stops first at Puerto Vallarta and second at Cabo San Lucas. I didn't leave the ship but the others visited both ports of call. I have no desire to visit many of the ports that are full of tourists and I often lacked the energy for some activities and shore excursions.

Next to the last night at sea the wind rattled the deck chairs in our balcony incessantly which constantly interrupted our sleep. We each made an attempt during the middle of the night to move them but the wind was so strong that after stepping into the balcony we hurriedly shut the balcony door and suffered the constant rattling through the rest of the night. The next day I arranged the chairs so they would be OK for our last night. I spent quite a few hours during two or three days tanning on our balcony under the hot, radiating Mexican sun. I don't tolerate the heat as I did in my younger years and it leaves me too tired for other activities afterward. Suntan, the price of vanity.

As on our previous two cruises the food and service were good. We all had a great time. It was delightful being with family. Penny couldn't have been a better companion for all of us. I hope in the not too distant future we can do a similar get together. John, Linda and Penny all bought paintings from the many art exhibits on board. One of Penny's pictures tripled in price after the Israeli artist died.

I can only compare this cruise to the two previous cruises both on Holland America. First of all because of the larger size of this vessel with eighteen decks, two hundred seventy feet longer and double the passenger capacity of two thousand six hundred plus compared to one thousand twelve hundred sixty wasn't as homey and low key as the other Holland America cruises. I wasn't as impressed with most of the shipboard activities or presentations. Unfortunately all the Princess ships are similar in size and capacity. It's like being in a large metropolis rather than a smaller community.

Spoke to Tricia from Perone Travel Agency to inquire about the value of our upgrade and future cruises. Checking with the cruise line that suite would have cost us $9,000, more than double what we paid.

— — — — — —

At nine one morning last year I arrived at Harbor General Hospital for three sessions of clinical trials for persons with chronic obstructive pulmonary disease (COPD) for the purpose of evaluating a new device for those who use oxygen. Supposedly it was for three sessions, one each week for six hours each time. This consisted of various tests, examinations and prolonged exercise. After completing the exercise I was informed that I did so well and my oxygenation was one hundred percent throughout that I wouldn't qualify as a subject. I feel the bike testing was too strenuous and detrimental to my condition. My maximum heart rate is 135 per minute and they took me to 141 per minute. It's not recommended to have the heart rate more than 90% of the maximum for beneficial aerobic exercise. I was exhausted for days afterward and wasn't about to continue with clinical trials after this experience. I was elated at the favorable results and saved copies of the data printouts that I received.

As I was leaving I was approached in the same department by a young Dutch lady doctor who asked me if I would be interested in doing clinical trials under her supervision and monitoring for six weeks duration consisting of three days a week on a bicycle for three weeks followed by three more visits of testing other parameters. I decided it would interfere with my exercise regimen and other activities. Aside from being paid for these studies I appreciated the information I receive including copies of the clinical data and the benefit of the exercise involved.

Kris Brust, RN is in charge of the Better Breather's Club of Providence Little Company of Mary Medical Center in San Pedro, California. Her husband is a psychiatrist who has his office in the same medical building near my house that I had my office,.

I am impressed of Kris's management of their extensive program of all phases of pulmonary function. I have had the pleasure of attending many of their varied activities and plan on periodically continuing to take advantage of this marvelous organization.

Chapter XXXIII
Linda & John

On March 16, 2012 Linda informed me that she spoke to Yale who just received his Spanish citizenship after his ten year residence requirement and four more years of bureaucratic red tape and waiting. He now has dual citizenship. I'm very proud of him and his accomplishments. He deserves them all. He sent me a copy of his new Spanish passport and identification card. I was surprised to receive an e-mail from him asking if I would like his company if and when he visits Israel. I hope that works out. I've never been to Israel.

Linda and John arrived this year again on the twenty second of July and left two months later. What's nice about Linda and John and Patty and Jack from Chile when they stay with me is that we each do independently what we want to do and at the same time we do many things together. Linda and John convinced me to re-place all the floor carpet with wood laminate. She said it would be a healthier environment considering my asthmatic condition. For that same reason I had the carpet replaced with the wood laminate flooring in my bedroom six months before and decided to go ahead with their suggestion of re-flooring the rest of the house.

We purchased the flooring and padding on sale at the local Lowes with the help of John's brother-in-law Pentti, an ex-marine who does construction. He showed them how and what they had to do, then John and Linda finished the flooring the rest of the house themselves. Pentti did come a few days and we couldn't have done it without his help. He wouldn't accept payment for his labor and John said their family does that for one another. I did give him my unused sea kayak and equipment.

I fully intended to really get into kayaking and looked forward to using my new kayak. I bought a top of the line ocean kayak thirteen years ago that has been suspended from the rafters in my garage for all those years. An apt name had I named it, would have been The Sea Virgin. My intentions were to use it for pleasure, skin diving and spearfishing. I have free access and parking at Cabrillo beach, but rationalized through those years the reasons I never launched it. Actually it was too heavy and cumbersome for me to have handled alone during the last five years.

I didn't think they would finish the flooring before my party coming up shortly but early one morning the two of them began ripping up the carpeting and the insulation base that was stapled and nailed into the concrete slab floor. When all was removed we swept up a pail full of sand and whatever else was accumulating under the carpeting through the years. They didn't want me exposed to the dust or do any work but we had face masks. I felt guilty watching them work non stop and helped pull staples and nails. It was tedious work pulling up all the trim. They worked every day and to my surprise and joy it was finished the day before my party. The only cost I had was for material and a few beers and meals. There remained two bedrooms and closets to re-floor which they did finish the following summer.

They also installed ceiling fans in two of the bedrooms, a security screen door in the front entrance, and they replaced the rear door screen that had both plastic wheels broken preventing it from sliding and kept it constantly falling off the track. John and Linda tried to remove the two wheels without success and finally they took the screen door to Home Depot. There were four employees trying to remove the wheels but also failed. John, being the excellent negotiator that he is, told them that if he were in charge seeing three men working for fifteen minutes it would be cheaper to give away the sixty dollar door than pay the labor involved. They charged three dollars ninety five cents for the new wheels and made us a present of a new door.

I hung my bike on overhead hooks in the garage. I have an old rotator cuff injury to my right shoulder putting more of a strain on my left shoulder which now made it painful lifting the bike up and getting it down. John suggested an overhead bike pulley attached to the rafters as he has in his garage. We received delivery in two days from Amazon and John and Linda installed it the same day. They work together on almost everything. I am surprised at how handy John is but I'm really impressed about how much my daughter is able to do. She repainted her bedroom, the living room and the dining room. She asked my permission as I really wasn't going to do anything with the house. After they left I ordered and had my gardener and handyman Silverio, install a special horizontal chinning bar on a rafter and move my large heavy commercial Total Gym and apparatus from the den into the garage. I hope I'm not too optimistic on being able to do chins again for exercise. I recently was able to move my Total Gym back into the den by myself. I didn't think I could do it alone and planned on getting someone to help but I took it in sections. It's a professional model which is three times heavier than the home model advertised on TV.

I kept procrastinating about cleaning out the garage for as long as I can remember. It was overwhelming just looking at the unholy mess. I was actually ashamed to let anyone see it. With my permission (and gratitude) I let Linda do her thing. I didn't even want to be around. It took her three full days and when I went in and saw everything neatly stacked and labeled I could even put my car in with room to spare. I'm sure that my car can't remember the last time it saw the inside of the garage. I'll be embarrassed if it's messy when they return this summer.

— — — — — —

Sunday, September 9th, 2012, I gave my second patio party with about 25 tango friends including David and Abbey and Linda and John. I enjoyed being able to get to know my friends better. At the milongas because of my poor hearing and the din of the constant chatter and music I rarely understand what people are saying, which is frustrating to both parties. The shindigs were a great success both years. Some of my friends helped prepare things and Linda was especially helpful. I don't think I could have done it without her and John. I don't plan on doing more parties. Been there, done that.

Six days later Linda and John had a family get to-gether that John arranged. We had much food and drink left over from my party six days earlier that they were able to use. His family is very close and I really enjoy them. I am so glad that Linda is close to them and part of their family. I've been away from home starting from when I was single and through the many years living abroad with Jill and the children. That distanced us from family and friends until we returned and re-established relationships.

Linda and I went to one of David's gigs at Red Men Lodge here in San Pedro. David is very popular and has many friends in this area. I'm only sorry I didn't see anyone present that danced west coast swing. When I hear good blues, tangos, or rumbas, they make me want to get up and dance. The scene was that of a typi-cal off beat, San Pedro waterfront biker ambiance of artists, long-shoremen, boozers and broads.

Linda and John visited me for three months the summer of 2013. They stayed two months and we had a great time. Looking for-ward to next summer if they are able to come. Meanwhile Jack and Patty came to visit from Chile earlier that year. I welcome the company and companionship.

May 10th 2013, John and Linda flew to Madrid where they met Yale coming from Portugal at the airport and the three went to Formentera in time to spend Mother's day with Jill.

John enlisted in the Air Force as an Airman Basic and retired twen-ty two years later as a major. Linda and John eloped a year after John enlisted. I was happy about their elopement. It was a year or so after my heart attack. I was just starting to get back on my feet financially.

They were stationed in Honolulu twice then in Montana, Spain, Germany, England, Florida, Texas, and South Korea. Since his retirement he has become vice president of a company that deals with military bases. Both John and Linda still travel extensively for business and pleasure throughout the world.

David is very modest. He never tells me where he's playing unless I ask. He had another gig at the Fire House Grill in San Clemente. Linda and I went with Penny. Other friends of mine that I informed and met there were, John and Betty Tice, Fernando and Laura, another lady whose name I don't recall, Woody and Flo and my cousin Bob. We all had a marvelous time, good friends, good music, good food, and for the others, drinks. I'm the tee totaling designated driver

— — — — — —

My cousin Bob and Nancy have had me over for Thanksgiving and have invited me often, but I just don't like driving that far on a busy freeway for more than an hour and a half each way in case there is traffic or worse, an accident. I did accept Penny's Thanksgiving invitation this year with her family at her house five minutes away. I believe it was the year or two before that we went to her daughter Lisa and Jay's house for a lovely Thanksgiving dinner and evening. Also present was Jay's father, Megan their charismatic eight year old daughter going on twenty and Bob, their musician son. A very smart and talented family.

Marvin Wolfenson is my oldest cousin six months older than I. He and his wife Sandy have been living many years in La Jolla Shores, a stone's throw away from Scripps pier. They are also from Minneapolis where Marvin and his former partner Harvey Ratner were in business. From owning only one house they became builders ending up with eight large condominiums and apartment buildings, eight complete health spas and the professional basketball team the Timberwolves for which they built the Target stadium. Each of these facilities occupied a full square block.

Marvin returning home on the troop ship after the second World War had saved the money he won playing cards on the ship. He was an excellent card player and also a top baseball, basketball and tennis champion.

In the last few years he had health problems. Before that time they gave a lavish yearly party in December for family and friends often numbering a hundred guests. The past few years there were fewer and much smaller parties.

Sandy, after raising their three children, studied art at the university and became a well known talent in abstract art. For the past decade Sandy has been taking care of Marvin who's had a series of small strokes and been at death's door a few times. If not for Sandy's insistence and demands on the medical staffs involved in his treatment Marvin wouldn't be with us today. I was surprised that he seemed much improved from a few years ago. Unfortunately he passed away on December 21, 2013 at 87 years of age.

— — — — — —

My friend Penny has season tickets for the Long Beach Performing Art Center. She usually goes with a family member and was scheduled to go with her daughter. Her daughter was unable to go and since it was a Spanish artist she invited me. The concert was Spanish classical repertoire with the Spanish guitarist Pepe Romero. I didn't see one of my very favorite selections on the program but was pleasantly surprised when he played that very song, Recuerdos de la Alhambra by Tárrega, for his encore. I have listened to the flamenco music of the Romeros, the father Celonio, and sons Pepe, Celín and Ángel, for years. This quartet is also known as The Royal Family of the Guitar.

The large remodeled Cabrillo Beach bathhouse and complex is two miles from my house. This complex contains our Cabrillo Beach Polar Bears club room, shower room and gym room with a large beach area enclosed in sprawling, park like areas with miles of very wide sidewalks and roads and parking lots for large hotels and marinas. Our Polar Bear club has unlimited free beach access and parking, a monthly pot luck at the beach and a restaurant dinner paid by our modest annual dues. The outer beach that we frequent is sand extending one half mile from rocks to the breakwater. Most of our members swim daily to the buoys and further. I rarely swim unless the water is calm and the temperature over 67 degrees Fahrenheit, which is unusual. This outer beach has one of the cleanest water ratings of the South Bay beaches in contrast to the more enclosed inner beach which has a poor rating. Going along Paseo Del Mar, a half mile before Cabrillo Beach, in Angel's Gate Park atop a high hill overlooking the ocean is the beautiful Korean friendship bell dedicated by the Republic of Korea.

Margaret Van Daalen & Christine Lewis - Korean Friendship Bell

Instead of biking along Paseo del Mar where I previously rode for years until recently when a large portion of the the cliff slid into the ocean making the road impassable. Now I only bike in the safe Cabrillo Beach complex and out on the fishing pier.

Since January 2013 my routine on sunny days has been Cabrillo Beach where I ride my bike for an hour then walk along the beach barefoot for two to three miles. Unless it's cold, I'm in my Speedo. On non beach days I may go to the Elk's gym to work out. I go dancing twice a week and try to rest and not exercise one or two days a week. I'm not consistent but usually manage to get in from five to eight hours of low impact aerobic exercise weekly. I do have my periods of bronchitis and asthma along with minor injuries at which times I exercise lightly or not at all. I allow my body to dictate what I should or should not do. I feel after all the years I've been involved in physical culture I am a better judge of my exercise needs and tolerances than the doctors, except for critical or emergency situations.

I took my first bad fall on my bike in 25 years without any major incidents. For a moment lying flat on my back, I wondered if I'd broken anything or if I'd be able to get up. I was making a tight turn at the end of the Cabrillo pier and pitched forward somersaulting over my handle bars landing on my back on the cement. I had two lacerations which were treated and bandaged at the lifeguard station. My left hip was painful to walk on and the gluteal muscles on that side were flaccid and non responsive. I had X-rays of the hip but no fracture was found. After two months the only residual is a painful left shoulder. I'm even more cautious biking now but not ready to give it up as yet.

Today was special. I found a large live Pismo clam on the beach. Before I got back to our club area Mary Samaras and Mike Schaat, the curator of the Cabrillo Aquarium were talking precisely about Pismo clams. Mary said since the storm of 1968 there hasn't been any seen locally. I was told that John and Muriel Olguin transplanted some Pismo clams at Cabrillo Beach brought back from Pismo Beach many years ago where they were once plentiful. I was thinking that if I had had two or more I would have made clam chowder. But Mike said he would put the clam in the sand at the surf and hoped it would live. I am glad I didn't cook it but gave this increasingly declining species a chance at life.

It's not unusual to find interesting things washed up on the beach. Aside from interesting shells and stones I have found three coconuts, different fruits, net balls, wood, etc. By a strange coincidence, "Snorkel" Steve a fellow Polar Bear, found a large pismo clam by the breakwater at the edge of our beach just a few months later. Maybe there's hope for the pismo clams in the future in our beach.

— — — — — —

A sad note, recently I received a call from my neighbor's daughter that Roger her father had passed away. Roger and his wife Diane have been our next door neighbors since we moved here 45 years ago. He was in ill health for the past few years with kidney and other problems going three times a week for dialysis. He was a good neighbor and friend. I'll miss him.

— — — — — —

I look forward to the times when my dear friends Jack and Patty Schmitt come stay with me. Jack's complete mastery in all forms of Spanish is there when I need help. Both Jack and Patty have been dancing tango for more than twenty years. Orlando Paiva, when in Santiago. stayed at their house and practiced with Patty off and on for a period of eight years. Jack is very knowledgeable in Orlando's style and he and Patty have often practiced with me. It's especially nice when Patty is available to dance with at the milongas.

The first time I went to visit them in 2003 they arranged a room for me with their neighbor Mari Cordete. There was another voluptuous lady from Brazil staying with us in Mari's house. She would come into my bedroom when I didn't feel well and soothe me. There was a common wall between their rear outdoor patios. Jack said, when I hear the tango music to come over and we would practice in their patio. I stayed at Mari's two different times and then on the following visits, I would stay in Jack and Patty's home.

Patty & Jack Schmitt.- Santiago Chile

Jack is six years younger then I and Patty twenty years younger than Jack. It is obvious that they are very attentive to each other and appear to have a very happy and fulfilling marriage. Jack is a Teutonic looking, tall, erect, handsome gentleman with gray hair and light blue eyes while Patty is short and lithe with black, curly hair, olive complexion and sparkling dark eyes. She is rarely without a smile and laughs at anything humorous. She is always in great shape. She walks daily five miles and is strong as well.

Jack's origin is from my part of the country, Minnesota and Wisconsin. Consequently, we have a similar common background. After and during his military service he was constantly studying and eventually entered the field of education with doctorates in Spanish, Portuguese and French, teaching in various high schools and later in various colleges and universities. Jack has done many translations of important and classical literary works in the aforementioned languages. He is an avid and knowledgeable outdoorsman, camper and fly fisherman. They have a summer home on the river Yelcho in the Chilean Patagonia near the town of Chaitén. A deadly volcanic eruption on May 2nd, 2008 buried the town and much of the surrounding area up to a depth of forty feet of ash. To this day they are still digging to clear the town. It was believed that the town would never return, but slowly it is being revived. Ash fell as far a Johannesburg, South Africa.

My first trip to the area was with Patty. We took a fourteen hour bus ride from Santiago to Puerto Montt then a catamaran ferry for seven hours to Chaiten where Jack awaited us in their Volkswagen '69 van with a million miles of service. I was lucky on the ferry to pay half fare as a senior. The passage is similar to the Alaskan coastline with volcanic, snow capped peaks and countless fjords and islands.

Their house is twenty yards from the river which is almost white due to the glacial waters and fairly wide with a strong current. Jack, being an excellent fly fisherman, catches many king salmon which he shares with neighbors who in turn supply them with eggs and other supplies and services. His record is a 56 pound salmon. His neighbor downstream caught an 85 pounder. They are really Chinook salmon but called king salmon because of their size. Much of the salmon is frozen and some is smoked.

Naturally we ate a lot of salmon and always a large salad of fresh vegetables. One can't help noticing the difference in eating all fresh foods with no additives or coloring. It seems so much of the world and even the poorer countries eat more wholesome and natural foods than in the US. I slept in the cooler of the bedrooms where all the food was stored.

Jack, often with Patty, have visited me three or four separate times over the past few years for periods of two to four months each visit. I always look forward to their visits. One couldn't ask for better guests and better companions. They do most of the shopping and cooking and I must say I eat better and more varied when they are here.

Since we have many common interests we have long, interesting conversations. He is extremely knowledgeable in many subjects. Our mutual friend Flo said, Jack doesn't converse, he lectures. This is undoubtedly a carryover from his many years as an educator in schools and universities.

Jack has been fighting lymphatic cancer for the past fourteen years. He is treated at the Veteran's Hospital in Long Beach for the various, intense and specialized treatments. Many of these procedures etc. are not available and/or are unbelievably expensive on the open market. Very often the treatments and tests are very debilitating such as the chemo and the radiation therapy that he has had to endure numerous times. They all take their toll.

After the first month of almost continuous treatment and weeks of hospitalization he spends most of the time resting and recuperating. When he feels better they load their car with camping equipment and travel around the country mostly in the west including Canada. It is uncertain if they are able to do any serious camping each visit. It all depends on his strength and health. If I have other guests or family visiting, Jack and Patty would stay with their other close friends and colleagues, Paul and Brigitte who live less than a mile from our house.

After my first trip with Jack and Patty returning from Chaitén and

Puerto Montt alone by bus, a Chilean woman named Ruth boarded at one of the bus stops during the night. Ruth was going to Santiago to celebrate Michele Bachelet's winning the presidency. We were sitting together chatting for a few hours. She reclined her seat and invited me to do the same. I really wasn't interested in any possible intimacy, if that was her agenda, and mentioned that I saw an empty double seat toward the rear where I could sleep.

— — — — — —

Saturday, May 25th, 2013 was the night of my favorite milonga. My passengers were Jack, Patty and Jo Ann. As soon as I began driving I noticed a sharp pain in my left scapula, a fullness in my chest and an uneasy feeling. Had I been alone I would have gone to the emergency room at the local hospital. I sat most of the evening watching the dancers and sitting and chatting with friends. I went to sit in the car for periods to rest. My friends suggested we leave and go to the ER but I wanted them to enjoy the dancing and waited until 11:30 pm to leave. They did have two and a half hours of dancing.

My pain and discomfort were getting worse. By the time I arrived home the pain was excruciating so I drove to the hospital emergency room at one am. They offered to go with me but I felt I could make it and didn't want them staying up to keep me company that late. From the ER I was hospitalized until five that afternoon before being discharged. I had a cat scan, many X-rays in the cervical area, left shoulder and chest areas. I won't go into detail but had constant severe pain, in spite of heavy doses of different pain medication intravenously.

In spite of the pain medicines administered in the ER the constant intense pain continued, tolerable during the day but much worse at night. The first time I was able to lie down, and only on my back only for short periods of an hour or less, was sixteen days after the onset. Twenty days from onset I was still unable to stay in bed the full night. The previous nights I tried to sleep sitting in a comfortable armchair. Consequently I got very little sleep some nights only dozing off now and then usually in the wee hours.

Have had two excellent physical therapy treatments with Der How the therapist at Harbor Physical Therapy Center and an MRI that was requested by the neurosurgeon, before I could arrange a consult with the neurologist.

Twenty eight days later, after dancing for the first time in five weeks, I felt no pain and was able to sleep the whole night. I really needed the sleep. The nights before my improvement I slept little sometimes hardly more than dozing a few minutes.

— — — — — —

Jack and Patty left on June 5th. to go camping. The following morning I drove to LAX to pick up my brother Dick who arrived from Denver to spend the week with me while Sharon his wife flew to Seoul, South Korea with their granddaughter Kayla to Join Kayla's mother, Susan who went on ahead to visit their Korean mother and family.

Unfortunately, a week after leaving, Jack came down with a fever and was ill necessitating returning to my house and going to the VA emergency and being hospitalized for a week. This time when they returned he was hospitalized with pneumonia for three days. As of this writing, we don't know when he will be released to come home and recuperate. He really wasn't in good enough health and was too weak to have undertaken those camping trips even though Patty did the driving and most of the work. According to his wife Patty, when he feels recuperated he will probably want to resume their trekking for a month or more, living out of doors in the wilderness.

On my first trips to Santiago, Chile before I knew Patty and Jack and Miro and Elizabeth, I stayed with a young tall blonde lady who was and ex-airline stewardess and presently employed in the

Chilean Embassy in Santiago. I keep in contact with most of my old friends even if it's only once or twice a year.

— — — — — —

I've known Jo Ann Travis for twenty years. We frequently share rides to the various milongas. She was in the process of having her house redone by a contractor who failed to do the work as designated and she just received a judgment in her favor. After the hearing, the contractor threatened her in the courtroom and followed her and her girlfriend in their car for many miles. I let her sleep in the spare bedroom for the week until she made arrangements to stay at her sister's house. Unfortunately, the sister was the one who recommended that contractor who knows both houses. Jack and Patty were also staying here but left about the same time as Jo Ann, so I had one day alone until my daughter and her husband arrived.

My dear friend María Eugenia from Buenos Aires came to stay at the house awhile ago. I don't get a chance to be lonely these past few years. We fixed up a bedroom in my dance studio adjoining the back den and patio for her. I always enjoy María's company. She is very independent and one of my few vistors who is valiant enough to use the L.A. public transportation system.

Fourth of July, 2013. The third consecutive year Penny and I were to attend Ken Brassard and his girl friend Jocelyn's party. Later the party was canceled due to inclement weather. Ken is my friendly computer technician. He has a lovely house two miles from my house with large various level patios with a panoramic view of the whole city and surrounding areas. One can see the countless firework displays from San Pedro, Long Beach and the San Fernando Valley. There's always abundant delicious food prepared by them. Jocelyn is from the Philippines and makes many tasty dishes from her native land. There have been from eight to twelve people in attendance, many whom we know. Aside from the computer, Ken also volunteers to fix my other electronic and mechanical equipment including my car. Thanks Ken.

I enjoyed the 2012 holiday season in touch with Linda and David although they were physically absent and two special holiday milongas, one on December 29th my favorite with John and Betty Tice and on the 31st with my dear friends Martín and Alyssa.

New Years eve of 2013 David made a bouillabaisse, whole grain toast with butter, and a few sips of white wine making it a lovely dinner with him and Abbey. By eight thirty I was in bed. I really enjoy spending time with my children and family, which for many years has been too seldom.

July 5th, 2013 Linda and John arrived and stayed till September 22nd. Jack and Patty left the day before. In the interim Jo Ann and shortly after María Eugenia. A full house lots of activity although I don't participate in all the activities with the energetic younger generation.

John and Linda have been a boon staying with me. They help with everything and convince me of things I should do and items I should have in the house. As an added attraction, my beautiful friend María Eugenia Yanzón, tango dancer from Buenos Aires, stayed with us for the month. Needless to say, I've never had it so good, with three gourmet cooks and house cleaners including my son-in-law John. I'm living high on the hog.

They all help me with my computer. John is able to fix, remedy and repair things is seconds. They are also assisting me in the intricacies of Facebook and my iPod. I notice many photos of Facebook users taken anywhere from a few years to decades ago. I know we all want to appear at our best, but come on! My humorous son David who is 44 has recently put a photo of himself on Facebook when he was four years old. That got me to thinking I might be narcissistic enough to post older more flattering photos of myself and wait for the insulting comments from the readers.

Patty and Jack returned to San Pedro and stopped to say hello, pick up their mail on the way to Paul and Brigitta's house where they stayed while Jack continued with his treatments at the Veteran's Administration Hospital in Long Beach. That same night María and I were going to the milonga at Club One in Costa Mesa. Patty and Jack had an appointment at the hospital at eight am the following morning. They were both tired after driving and had to be awake at six that morning. Patty hadn't danced in quite awhile and decided to join Jo Ann and myself driving to Costa Mesa. Just on the far side of Long Beach my engine warning light went on and the car was running hotter than usual. I pulled over to see if we could see what the problem might be. I decided to turn around and backtrack the few blocks to the Arco station on Ocean Boulevard. I thought this would be a more convenient and illuminated place for the Automobile Club emergency service to locate us, rather than in the dark street where we were parked. When I phoned the AAA, I mentioned two or three times that we were three passengers and needed more room than the standard tow truck. Sure enough the tow truck arrived without enough room for all. I had the driver call in and finally he went back to his garage and came with a large double cabin flat bed truck. We were comfortable driving and chatting in Spanish with Carlos the Spanish speaking driver who let us off at Zibi's garage on the corner of 25th and Moray, a few blocks from my house. I phoned my son-in-law John who picked us up to drop Patty off first and then take us home. So much for our tango dancing that night.

— — — — — —

My daughter, Linda tutored me how to transfer my music CDs to my iTunes and iPod. I don't know any of the neighborhood children but they could probably do the job. I've been wanting to be able to do this for two years. John my son-in-law is a whiz at solving anything on computers. I am inept and leery of experimenting with my computer.

I don't want to neglect mentioning my granddog Cisco. Although it's their dog he is always at John's side. He is a ten year old hairy Chihuahua. He is very obedient and well trained. He performs many tricks on command. He's extremely easy to take care of and quite content if left alone. He lets us know when he wants to go out by one bark, if a stranger is at the door, three barks and if he feels threatened, a warning whimper. He shies away from strangers.

— — — — — —

I received a call from my friend Jo Ann Travis. She fell stepping out of her house and badly fractured her left wrist. I drove her to the ER at the hospital where she was interned for six days. She had to wait two days for an available surgical amphitheater.

me, Pat Stein and Craig Smith

At the request of two of my dear friends, Pat Stein and Craig Smith, I went with them on a three day, four night cruise on the Carnival Inspiration December 2-6. We went with Jon Gatyas's dance group. We stopped at Catalina Island and Ensenada. I had no desire to go ashore in either place so stayed aboard.

I shared a cabin with Kish a congenial Indian gentleman originally from Mumbai. I did enjoy the company and as always managed to have in depth congenial talks with many other passengers but would probably not use the Carnival Line again.

I took advantage of the gym each morning for an hour and a half daily and a sauna afterward the first day, after which, neither the sauna nor steam room were functioning. Did little dancing. Wasn't my kind of music nor dancing but I enjoyed watching the others. I wasn't much interested in most of the activities or entertainment offered but enjoyed engaging the other passengers in conversation.

Pat and Craig were kind enough to pick me up before the voyage and take me home afterward. They also offered to take Kish, my cabin mate, to his car which he left at a friend's house near my house. On the way home I invited the three of them for lunch at one of my favorite restaurants, the Long Beach Cafe. It is patronized by retirees, longshoremen and others who appreciate the large portions at a reasonable price. It has an extensive menu and specializes in Greek food.

I enjoyed the company of Pat and Craig so much on our three day cruise that we planned another cruise a few months later on the Holland America ship "Veendam" to the Mexican Riviera for seven days. That was the same ship as my first cruise at the end of 2010.

I was very pleased that Paula, who I dance tango and west coast swing with, agreed to join us. Again, Craig drove up from their home in Fallbrook to pick me up first, then to pick up Paula at her son, Sean's home in Santa Ana, on to Fallbrook to pick up Pat and finally to the dock in San Diego. We arrived at the dock in the nick of time and consequently didn't have to stand in line to go aboard. We booked an inside cabin but accepted the offer, for a few dollars more, of an upgrade to an outside cabin with a window.

I spent time and was very impressed with an Iranian couple, Abbass and his lovely wife Jamilah. They have lived in the US for many years. He was an OB-GYN physician, recently retired . We happened to have the next table in the dining room and also talked during our gym sessions. They are both in excellent shape. I will maintain contact with them and hopefully meet them again on another cruise.

On one of my walks around the deck I noticed a well built, muscular good looking young man in a tight tee shirt and brief trunks, accompanied by a petite Oriental lady. I crossed their path a few times on deck and in the health spa. I spoke to him commenting on his athletic appearance. He Was from Paris and only spoke French but his companion spoke fluent English and translated. From then on, every time we crossed paths, he would give me the thumbs up sign.

I didn't go ashore at our two ports of call, staying on board as I did on a previous cruise with Penny and my children, who did go ashore at both stops.

Before they drove us home from San Diego at trips end, we stopped to see Pat's beautiful house and property.

— — — — — —

About 3 am on April 15, 2014 I was awakened by loud sirens driving nearby. A fire that destroyed our beautiful lodge, two blocks from our house, was purposely set by one of our members, a 78 year old man who was later arrested for arson. Huge clouds of black smoke filled the sky, with three fire engines on the scene battling the blaze. It was verified that he purchased gasoline and a lighter at a nearby gas station around midnight and his car was seen on the club's video surveillance camera, leaving the scene at 2:30 am, before the start of the fire.

This was a great loss to our members and the community. They finally are scheduled to commence removing the debris and reconstruction the middle of this April, 2015, which is estimated to take a year and a half, of which I am doubtful.

Chapter XXXIV
Israel Journal -- Travels With Yale

I had decided and told the world that I had no plans to travel by air any longer. I eat my words. Yale, my oldest son living in Spain, contacted me and asked if I'd like to go to Israel for a few weeks with him. I'm looking forward to spending the time with him more than with the trip to Israel. I haven't seen him since traveling together in Mexico four years ago.

I've been vacillating back and forth saying that I didn't feel well enough but have finally decided to go. I don't look forward to the airports or the long flights that lie ahead, but will try to think more positive.

Going to Israel is a coveted Jewish thing. Every Jewish person I know has been to Israel at least once and some I know have been to Eretz Yisrael, the Promised Land, many times. I always intended to go but put it off the many years I lived in Formentera on the opposite side of the Mediterranean Sea. I finally took my first trip to Israel at age 87

Up at 3 am Friday, May 9th, 2014, for the shuttle to LAX. Six hours later to JFK, a two hour layover and then nine hours later I arrived at Barcelona where Yale was waiting there for me. He was easy to spot, a head taller than any of the crowd awaiting the arriving passengers. I was disappointed that on the JFK to Barcelona flight my seat was not an aisle seat as I requested and that my travel agency had supposedly arranged.

Doesn't anyone talk anymore? I was aware of the lack of conversation and human contact among the passengers, especially the younger ones who were completely absorbed in their electronic gadgetry of i pads, computers, smart phones, head phones, etc. A few of the older passengers would converse at times, but even they are members of the electronic age. These activities seem to be prevalent on the street, in restaurants and just about everywhere. It difficult to get someone's attention when they have devices in both ears. Is this the sign of our times and our future?

Yale mentioned that his transport to and from the airport only cost him one euro in contrast to the 35 euro taxi fare. Seeing I was tired after the long, grueling journey, Yale was about to hail a taxi when I said I'd like to return to town his way. The object was for the experience of having done it more than for the economy. With a lot of walking, buses, trains and other conveyances and with Yale carrying my baggage, we arrived at Yale's shared apartment, our destination. Climbing the six sets of narrow stairs in an already exhausted state, I was ready to crash.

By now I should know better than to push myself to that point, knowing that my fatigue syndrome often follows with days of lassitude. I was lucky this time.

I readily accepted his suggestion of a taxi to the airport the following day for our El Al flight to Tel Aviv. BCN is a large airport requiring a lot of walking. Yale was very patient suggesting we go slowly and rest whenever I felt tired. He offered to do everything.

It was a pleasant, short four hour flight with Yale for company. I tried reclining my seat but then I realized it wouldn't leave enough room for the large tall gentleman in the seat behind me. He requested that I not recline my seat and it was evident that if I did it would be extremely uncomfortable for him. I assured him that it was OK and he thanked me. Our departure was delayed as was our arrival at the Tel Aviv airport. We decided to take the train instead of a taxi to our reserved apartment in town, knowing it would take much longer. Again I felt it was more adventuresome traveling as the locals.

We sat opposite a pretty, smiling young Greek lady and immediately started a pleasant conversation. After a few minutes our conversation was rudely interrupted by a brash American lady who assumed the Greek lady might be able to give her directions at what station to get off. The Greek lady couldn't quite comprehend and the American lady rushed off to find another person to tell her where to get off (the last six words of a common quote).

The Greek woman told us that she has been in Israel the past six years with the Greek Foreign Ministry and was soon returning to her home in Athens. We only spent 10 or 15 minutes before we got off, at which time I kissed her on the cheek and Yale followed suit. I felt this was a nice gesture to a nice person who seemed to have been pleased with the attention. We got off at Hashalom Station from where we did take a taxi, our driver a large, older man with a heavy beard and moustache garbed in a turban and Arabic style clothing, to our destination.

I was really surprised at the size of our clean, modern two bedroom apartment, at Tchernichovski 21, with all the modern amenities of any upscale American home. I'm not accustomed to this luxury in my traveling.

We went out to eat shwarma, hummus and falafel, Middle Eastern delicacies at Hacarmel, a large, local, open air market. It was jammed with humanity, fresh local produce and food booths. As we were leaving the popular local hummus eatery there was a line extending out of the entryway and down the block. We were in luck not having to wait more than five minutes with only four or five people ahead of us. Before we go again we'll ask what hours are the least crowded.

We did buy food items in Hacarmel market to make salad in our apartment and fruits for desert. We ate on our patio with its abundant tropical foliage. I can finally find the kinds of home baked breads of whole grains that I prefer in the many specialty bakeries, shops and markets.

I always prided myself as a salad maker but Yale does a much better job than I with salads and all cooking. While Yale was out running errands to the bank and the car rental agency, I decided to eat breakfast at home with the items I had available, consisting of tea, toast, Persian cucumber, olives and cherries - - a healthy meal.

I was concerned about being able to rent a vehicle as we didn't seem to have the correct documents according to what we had read in the guide books and on the internet but Yale was confident and a great problem solver and I, a worrier.

If I can remember not to repeat myself too often, I want to say that Yale did everything. If I was tired he'd run out and bring me anything. He was a real spoiler. I haven't traveled much of late, whereas Yale travels extensively and is very confident of himself, a trait of his I admire. Things were much simpler in my traveling days. One dealt more with people in lieu of mechanical and electronic devices and apparatus.

We walked the six blocks from our apartment to the beach. Tel Aviv is known for its lovely, extensive beaches. My Cabrillo Beach Polar Bear buddies would love the mid seventy degree water temperature. I spoke to a lovely young Jewish lady and her mother from Johannesburg, South Africa, who were here visiting parents who immigrated to Israel years before. We took a few photos with them. I joined some boys or young men doing exercises and gymnastics on the bars. I really miss being able to do these things. In my youth this was my forte.

I now had better luck with the acceptance of credit cards. Each day we drove all over as Yale loves to explore. It doesn't interest me much, but then again I just don't have the interest nor the energy. We spent an hour and a half on the beach. Seems the latest beach athletic activity in this country is paddle ball. Men and women, young and old play on the hard packed sand near the water.

Yale had been looking forward to a fish dinner at Jacko's, a well known landmark restaurant. It was very low key, no one dresses. On Friday early evening they have musicians with some of the people singing and dancing to the Middle Eastern music. I assume many of the patrons were originally from those regions. The proprietor is from Turkey. Jacko's closes at 8 pm.

Ever since I arrived in Barcelona I noticed my right ankle and foot were swollen. With the continual walking both my feet and ankles swelled. That night my left ankle began to hurt with some swelling. I was worried that if this condition worsened, my walking would be limited or maybe I would not able to walk at all. Fortunately it felt better in the morning and I decided to stay in, rest and take care of myself. I would have preferred going out to see the sights with Yale, but tomorrow is another day. I cannot recall ever having had this condition before, but I wasn't 87 before.

Yale and I were trying to figure out the possible cause or causes of my ankle and foot problems and arrived at the conclusion that the onset was due to the long hours of flight followed by the long walks on hard surfaces and taking the long way, previously described, back to Barcelona, in addition to the long walks our first two days in Tel Aviv. What luck having us two good diagnosticians available.

Yale went out and brought back falafel, which we ate in our patio. A few of the small local food booths charge the equivalent of $9 each and yesterday we found a place that made the same for half the price. It didn't take long to realize that Israel was an expensive place for travel compared to the countries I've traveled and lived in.

May 16th – Left our apartment at 11 am. We rented a car from the agency Aldama on Hayarkon Street and proceeded north on freeway number 2 along the Gold Coast making many side trips wherever we thought might be of interest. Our destination was

Haifa where Yale made our reservation for tonight and tomorrow. The reservation stated that we would not be able to get in until 9 pm. We drove around the Haifa port area (on the lower level of the city's three levels) and having many hours to spare before we could occupy our new apartment, decided to go further north to Akko, close to the Lebanese border. We spent much time walking and driving through the port area mazes, narrow serpentine passages and often dead-end streets. As usual, Yale did all the driving which he does beautifully and with relish. I was tense when both sides of our vehicle passed inches away from obstacles and other vehicles, both stationary and moving. I was amazed how well Yale was able to get around, find places and look at maps while driving. I am continually disoriented and was absolutely no help whatsoever as a navigator or as a reader of maps at a glance. I was surprised that the road signs were only in Hebrew and Arabic and not English, as there is so much tourism and English is international.

We were impressed with this Arabic appearing region, its architecture, inhabitants and cuisine. We ate on the patio of an Arabic style restaurant enclosed in a large old, high walled, fortified plaza. Yale ordered lamb skewers and a salad for the two of us. One by one, small dishes of different vegetables and salads, including tabbouleh and various Middle Eastern sauces and other specialties totaling a dozen different plates, were set before us on the table. Though we were hungry, not having eaten much breakfast six hours before, we could not finish the huge quantity of food. Then out came two wooden platters, each with four lamb shishkabobs with beet slices, yam slices and small potatoes on the side. We only ate one of the skewers each and had the rest in a "doggy bag" to go. The skewers were actually long, thick rods of cinnamon. I understand that it is a Middle Eastern custom to leave some food on the plate so your host won't think you're still hungry. I don't know if this also applies to eating in restaurants.

Leaving Akko, we continued driving around the countryside and other villages and towns until it was time to return to Haifa and look for our new apartment. It was rush hour and we encountered heavy traffic.

All buildings and houses in the area were a beige color, probably to match the stony countryside and undoubtedly to conform to a municipal code or ordinance. Many homes are built on steep hillsides making a lovely scene to behold. Yale and I ventured a guess that the elevation of the high section of the city of Haifa was 500 meters above sea level.

At 9 pm the rental agent met us a the entrance, explaining that she would find us another apartment for the first of the two nights as there was an error and the gentlemen occupant would not leave until the following morning, at which time we could move in.

I won't go into the details as the three of us discussed, argued and finally decided. Yale cajoled an additional discount and she agreed to accept payment by credit card. Many refuse to accept and are not set up for card transactions.

Saturday, May 17th – Yale went to climb the 19 tiers of stairs of the Baha-i Gardens. I decided that with my limited breathing and swollen feet, I would stay in and do some exercises and packing. We planned on leaving about 2 pm, heading inland and would not see the Israeli coast again.

At 2 pm we left Haifa, heading east and north through the Upper and Lower Galilee and the Golan Heights north to the Israeli, Lebanese borders near the Syrian border. Heading south we drove along the east shore of the Sea of Galilee (Lake Kinneret) to the O halo lodge just past the town of Kinneret, where we spent two nights. A few miles before we arrived at the town of Kinneret, heading south we could see in the distance columns of black smoke, later passing through miles of burning countryside and the thick billows of smoke. Most of the wildfire was partially controlled but there were flames popping up all through the area and many trees still burning along the highway. Fortunately some special fire air-craft were being used to scoop up water from the adjoining lake to extinguish the blaze.

Sunday, May 18th – Today we drove up the west side of the lake and spent most of the afternoon in Safed, a center for orthodox Jewry. My guess is that the great majority were Ashkenazi. It appeared that everyone, including the children, were clad in Hassidic vestments, the male children with yarmulkas and the girls with their long braids. A sight to behold.

— — — — — —

Monday, May 19th – We left Kinneret early in order to return our rented auto, a Fiat Panda, by 11 am in Jerusalem. It was a pleasant ride on the highway 6 toll road through the pine forests of the Judean Hills. Slowing through the highway reconstruction zone, we arrived at the rental agency in Jerusalem a half hour late but they didn't charge us the late fee of an extra day. We still were unable to reserve lodging. We toted our luggage, or should I say, Yale carried almost all the bags, the few blocks to a large, modern mall where we sat in a coffee shop. We had some drinks and lunch for more than three hours with Yale using his computer and was finally successful in arranging a place to stay. He spent much time on his computer for our travel information and reservations as we went on a day by day basis so we could vary or change our itineraries at will.

I spent the time observing the people, a mixture of tourists, Jews and Arabs, walking by - - a kaleidoscope of colors. Very few were dressed up, most women in slacks or ground length skirts, black being the favored color. I get the impression that many Israeli and Arabic women tend to look dowdy and unattractive. This may be a chauvinistic cultural trait in many cultures to purposely make the women look undesirable and less attractive to other men.

Our lodging was an old Arab underground cistern converted to living quarters consisting of three levels, the bottom floor and a loft on each of the upper two levels. The furnishings were quite basic and novel. The place was immense and could sleep six to eight people. Yale slept on the bottom level and I on the top of the three levels. Neither of us could hear any snoring with so much distance between us. We both got a good night's sleep. At first I was dubious as the mattresses were quite hard. We must have been tired.

According to the manager, an Argentine lady, the edifice was the Polish Embassy years ago. This was the Russian Compound.

Tuesday, May 20th - We walked to the old walled city with its separate gated, divided sections. Our lodgings were just a few blocks away. I was tired after four hours of continual walking through the bazaars, tunnels, alleyways and mazes, up and down countless stairways in this historical, ancient Jerusalem. One of the most popular sites in the old city is the Western "wailing" Wall in the Jewish Quarter.

Overlooking Jerusalem's Old City from a high vantage point along with others. I had a chat with a young Israeli soldier sitting with me on a bench. Interestingly, he, like most sabras (Israeli born), had parents or grandparents who were not Israeli, the majority being Ashkenasi Jews originating from the regions of central and eastern Europe.

It's a reassuring sight in these times of unrest and danger seeing the omnipresent uniformed and armed young men and women of the IDF, Israeli Defense Forces.

What was very noticeable is that the Israeli sections of the country are modern and actively building, while the Arabic sections appear old and not well kept.

My breathing was good all the time we were in Israel in spite of some of the higher elevations. Jerusalem's altitude is 2,500 feet above sea level. Days have been warm and the nights cool.

As I wrote this, Yale was out getting us some supper at 10 pm. I don't like eating so late and going right to bed, but didn't want to ask him to go earlier especially for me. If I didn't go to eat with him, he went out and brought me meals. How good can it get?

Wednesday, May 21st – Another good night's sleep. After a few days following my exhausting flight to Israel I slowly regained my energy but I noticed the start of an infection on my left eyelid and a minor irritation in my right inguinal area. The following days the symptoms of both increased, the inguinal pain probably due to the extensive walking and stair climbing. The swelling of my feet was much less.

Today I decided to stay in and rest, although I climbed our three flights of spiraled stairs at least a dozen times, a total of 400 steps up and the same down.

Thursday, May 22nd – Yale is very much into seeing and learning about things. I didn't accompany him often as he walks fast and I didn't want him to have to slow down for me. Yale asked me if I wanted to accompany him on a bus and go to the West Bank for the day. I was indecisive and decided not to go. I'm somewhat repentant that I didn't take advantage of these adventures and opportunities that I probably wouldn't have again.

Friday, May 23rd – Yale went to rent a Kia Forte from one of the few rental agencies that have vehicles permitted to enter the West Bank. We left Jerusalem through Judea and Samaria (the West Bank), back into Israel. The Israeli border guard enjoyed speaking to Yale in Spanish. We had another day with Yale's non stop driving through the highways and byways for seven hours except for lunch in a Palestinian restaurant in Hebron and photo stops. We enjoyed another meal or two in West Bank Arab restaurants and were trated exceptionally well by the hosts and others.

Yale climbed the Herodion, a hundred meters high. I stayed down below. The Judean desert continues south to the Negev Desert and the scenery was different from what I expected. There were areas that were extremely rugged and looked impassable by any means. The Dead Sea is bordered by high, rugged hills and cliffs.

Yale would often pull over, off the road, to take photos of scenery, camels and once he followed an Ibex to get a better photo. I'm certain he took more than 200 photos during our trip.

Our apartment for two nights in Arad, in the Judean Desert, was very clean, new and modern. The charming hosts made us feel at home. We were told that this city developed in 1960. It's quite modern with wide streets and well planned. Arad is a half hour driving to the Dead Sea ,

I am weary of riding in a car and welcomed resting and a shower before I fell into the arms of Morpheus. I'm already dreading the long, tedious flights to LAX.

Saturday, May 24th – Drove through to the west entrance to the Masada. The only way up is walking, so I stayed below while Yale climbed to the top. Later in the afternoon we drove to the main east entrance of the Masada. Again Yale climbed to the top where I met him. We were told at the entrance that the climb to the top is rated from a half to one hour for someone in good physical condition. Yale made it in a fabulous 20 minutes. I met him on top riding the cable car both up and down. I'm huffing and puffing while Yale either waits for me or leaves me to rest and returns for me after he's seen more sites.

We've come across many Argentines working and living in Israel and a few other Spanish speaking people.

A few miles further, along the Dead Sea, we finally found the spot where people go to swim and cover themselves with the black mud found nearby. We enjoyed swimming or should I say float-ing. Yale actually swam quite a distance in the salty water (one third salt, ten times saltier than most oceans) and then we covered ourselves completely with the black, greasy mud. The Dead Sea is composed of different salts, some of which are toxic. A few of the minerals are bromides, iodine, potash and magnesium. There are numerous warnings regarding swallowing the water, which would require immediate medical attention. The atmosphere has about 10% more oxygen and gases emitted from the various elements that filter out much of the ultraviolet rays, with less danger of sun-burn.

I won't go into much description as there are many good sources available. This area of the Judean desert, the Negev, Masada and the Dead Sea has impressed me more than most of this country I've seen. Not to discount the many other numerous marvels in Israel.

Yale and I look forward to seeing the European Soccer Cup cham-pionship match between Atlético de Madrid and Real Madrid to-night at 9:45 pm on TV. I watched the game from the comfort of our apartment but Yale preferred the camaraderie of joining the ardent soccer fans gathered in local bars, watching, commenting and arguing constantly during and after the match.

Sunday, May 25th – Left our luxurious apartment in Arad, back-tracking along the Dead Sea, past the Masada and the mud beach to Jericho where we spent a few hours. I wandered off and got lost, not able to find our car. I knew Yale would eventually find me if I waited in a nearby plaza. Back in Jerusalem we turned in the rental car, took a train to the bus station, a bus to Tel Aviv and a taxi to our apartment rented for tonight only as we have to take a taxi to the airport at 6 am.

Monday, May 26th – A short sleepless last night. Our El Al flight from Tel Aviv flight was less than half full, so we each had a whole middle row to ourselves. I haven't seen a plane that empty for many years. Had a tasty Spanish meal in one of Yale's favorite local Barcelona restaurants. How good it is, being able to enjoy the cuisine in this country. I really miss that.

One thing I always said about traveling: Away from home you don't have to think and have your mind dwell on things that you have to do the following day and there's not a damn thing you can do about it. I'm certain that is the reason I sleep better and longer when away from home.

I can't thank Yale enough for doing all the chores, taking care of all the details and arrangements, being my personal travel agent, guide, porter and wonderful companion. I am grateful and appreciate his efforts on my behalf, making this trip a reality and wonderful adventure.

Me & Yale, Dome of the Rock, Jerusalem's Old City, May 2014

Chapter XXXV
One More Chapter

I was relieved after finally having my book printed after almost nine years. My initial thought was wondering if I'd have the perseverance to complete the task and when nearing completion hoping I would get it published before anything happened to prevent publication.

Although I am pleased with my book, I regret not having reviewed the final draft and proof copy before the final printing. I have decided to do a revision, mainly for my benefit, by correcting typos, errors, adding text and more photos and updating some of the chronology.

I have began the dauntless task of re-reading the complete text of this revision of my first published edition, having read before many of the sections umpteenth times.

A few friends suggested doing a more commercial style, but if I followed all their suggestions I feel that it wouldn't be true to my style (or lack of style).

I was devastated to find that shortly after starting the revision all my fifty plus files became encrypted and consequently destroyed, many containing all the items pertaining to my book, even my back up drive files were also contaminated and of no use in recovering any files. I was fortunate that my son David had the ongoing format of the book in his computer which saved the day.

— — — — — —

On Sunday, September 7th at 9:30 am I picked up my friend Cherie Magnus in her new apartment in Koreatown after finally arranging between Cherie, Inesita, Stamen and myself a get together at Inesita's studio to watch her and Stamen's rehearsal. We enjoyed their marvelous traditional flamenco and the chatting after and at the two hour lunch at the local Marie Callender restaurant. Later, Cherie surprised me after she talked wih Inesita, that Inesita was 95 years old and I thought she was younger.

Howard Barsky, me, Cherie Magnus & Rubén Aybar - Maipú 444, Buenos Aires

I invited Cherie knowing that she had extensive dance experience including belly dancing, flamenco and Argentine tango. She performed these aforementioned dances professionally in Europe, North and South America. Cherie had been living in Buenos Aires and teaching and dancing tango with her partner, Rubén for the past 14 years before returning to her beloved Los Angeles.

— — — — — —

I have been looking forward to favorable conditions of the ocean to practice swimming now that my shoulders are better. I'm awaiting calmer and warm waters. Due to a series of constant hurricanes off the Baja California coast for the last ten days, the surf has been very high with waves, during the worst day, reported at the Cabrillo beach lifeguard station to twenty feet from trough to crest. The water temperature has been exceptionally high, up to 72 degrees. This high surf and warm water is something I've never experienced here in all the years I've lived here. There is still high surf with crashing breakers and many rocks on the bottom making it risky entering the surf.

— — — — — —

"I'd love to come but I'm sorry I won't be able to make it." As I grow older, more and more, this is my reply to most invitations that I receive especially ones that are distant. I just don't often feel that driving long distances is worth the effort. There are special invitations from family and very close friends that I may or may not attend.

My daughter Linda and I received an invitation for the 90th birthday for Henry Hunter at their ranchito style home, La Madrugada, in San Marcos near Escondido, California. Linda did me the favor of driving the two hours there and three hours home. I hadn't seen Henry, his wife Helen and others, including my dear friend Ze and his lovely Persian wife, Behin, for many years and at this stage in the game, under the circumstances, there is every possibility of not getting together again.

Fifty to sixty attended, many of Henry's relatives and friends from England, India and Canada. Helen out did herself with a delicious Spanish Paella and salad preceded with appetizers and flan for dessert. I had three large helpings at Helen's sister Linda's insistence.

Chapter XXXVI
Alone With Myself

As much as I enjoy people, I also value my solitude. My hearing deficiency makes it difficult for me even with my hearing aids when there is loud background noise, music, chatter, etc. When this happens I frequently withdraw from the conversation. As most hard of hearing persons, I find it much easier to understand when facing the person speaking. People with hearing deficits unconsciously lip read.

Lying in my patio I was enjoying watching two hawks soaring effortlessly high in a blue spring sky. While tending the new avocado tree I planted I came face to face with a tiny humming bird that hovered a foot from my face for six or seven seconds and in a flash disappeared in the distance. A few days later dozing in the patio I felt something on my forefinger. It was a humming bird. A second later it was gone.

Nature, what beautiful creation. I recalled a few of the places that impressed me, thinking how nice it would be to share those adventures with a very special friend. Lightning, thunder, rain and storms fascinate me and sometimes put me in a very romantic mood. I would hope to be in the right company for these occasions.

It's a nice feeling to be able to go out and pick my oranges for juice in the morning along with limes, figs, kumquats, loquats, lemons, greens, chard, etc. Considering the time, effort and expenses involved, I resent sharing some of the efforts of my labor with the squirrels, birds and other creatures who feel this is their domain. I will plant one last tree this fall a dwarf type A avocado as I have two young fuertes type B. After a year my fuerte seedling failed after having produce two small avacados and the other one also died, so I decided to give up planting the dwarf type A and give up any idea of future avocados plantings. There is enough work involved maintaining the fifteen fruit trees, five other trees and plants crammed into the limited space available, aside from caring for the worm trays and compost bin. I'm seriously thinking of cutting back on the vegetable gardening once the young trees and seedlings are established. I relish watching the newer plants develop.

I have a special policy never to make any New Year's resolutions. I think they're usually made on the spur of the moment and are easy to break.

I wonder if many of us, as we reach the golden years, enjoy reminiscing of the past and getting a more introspective awareness of the past and the present and enjoying the times we lived in that will not come again in ours or anyone else's lifetime. I'm certain this doesn't necessarily apply to all, but to those of us fortunate enough to have experienced a good and fruitful life. I've come to realize in latter years that almost everyone I've ever known was a very special accomplished person in one way or another.

I've often thought that sometime during my thirties I would have liked to have taken off on my own for anywhere from three to six months with a knapsack, travel down the west coast of Mexico all the way to the Patagonias and return along the eastern Atlantic seaboard stopping at interesting places along the way in small fishing villages, staying as long as I like with no time limits. I would choose to stay in a rented room preferably with a local family and travel as cheaply as possible mostly by bus, auto, rail or ship. I enjoy mingling and getting to know the people.

I've had to curtail many of my physical activities primarily due to an increasingly progression of chronic bronchial asthma (COPD) and other related problems of normal aging. I do feel fortunate in having been able to lead a relatively normal life, more so during my youth and middle age, when I was more able to cope with this condition.

After vacillating the past few years I finally donated my ski equip-ment and my skin diving and spearfishing paraphernalia, knowing that in reality in spite of my fantasies that era has ended for me, leaving only fond memories in its wake. Sometimes the changes that occur with the passing years range from hardly noticeable to rather sudden and drastic especially when one decides it's best not to continue some of the activities that have been dominant in one's life.

It's been more than eight years since I began this odyssey and I want to finish it while I'm still here. I seriously doubt that what-ever adventures I may have in the future would enhance this story.

—to control my own destiny as much as possible.

While I am alive and of sound??? mind I would expect my children to let me make decisions about my life and death whether they agree or not but feel welcome to discuss any situation. One stipulation being, that if I'm hospitalized or in a board and care or convalescent facility under the limited Medicare coverage, I demand leaving before any of my property, estate or funds are used to pay for those services. I want the money that I don't spend to go to my heirs and I definitely do not want anyone else to contribute to my care.

If I am unable to indicate in writing or speak for myself and have a disabling condition with a poor prognosis for a decent, relatively independent lifestyle and, when in my opinion, my life doesn't seem worthwhile, I hope there will be a painless non traumatic method legal or otherwise to leave the living and hope for a rapid termination

When I am gone my children will inherit and share whatever they want, other items can be given to friends or donated for a tax write off to charity to one that can itemize.

If you wish to have a get together to celebrate my life, please make it as happy and joyful as you can. I wouldn't have changed my life for anyone else's life. Mine was beautiful and adventurous with three of the best children I could possibly have any right to hope for.

I hope that my children will always love and respect each other.

I have now seen Israel as I wanted as would most Jews. Being a secular Jew and not religious I still feel a strong emotion and connection with Israel. Unless some unforeseen power or eve changes my perspective I'll probably remain an atheist. Though my children aren't legally Jewish I would hope they could go to Israel if possible and or learn some of the marvelous things the Jewish people and Jewish culture has produced. They can be anything they want to be, I have no preference.

I enjoy living in my home and hope that David & Abbey on my demise can arrange to inherit my house if they so desire. I give them that option. Otherwise John & Linda may want to take advantage or whatever they mutually agree upon.

I would love to spend some time even if it is brief with all of us together at the same time while I'm still functional. The cruises we took together were great.

I wish you well and hope your lives have been and will be full and interesting.

I love you all.

Postscript

I have taken license in employing many terms, items, names and places in their original Spanish.

I am sorry if I have not mentioned or included the names and photos of many of my friends and acquaintances.

I sincerely hope that no one is offended about anything they read in this text as I certainly did not intend to belittle or demean anyone. These were my remembrances and my interpretation of them.

I hope my children, although they may not approve of some of my choices and life's experiences, won't be uncomfortable or offended. I cannot excuse myself for any of my misgivings as I was fully aware at the time.

Much of the content will be of interest to only a limited number of people primarily family members and friends who may have known the people and have shared the events mentioned.

A self analysis:
I am not an extrovert and try to avoid being the center of attention.
I'm self confident, primarily, when I feel competent in a situation.
I am frank and open with people. I do not exaggerate my status.
I am comfortable speaking with all and confident when engaging women.

I am aware of some of my faults and weaknesses but also my strengths and never have desired to make any major changes in who I am. I, like many, have deviated from some of the norms in our society, desiring more of a simple uncomplicated life with more emphasis on pleasing myself and loved ones and of less importance, the quest for material objects. I am frugal in many aspects but also generous in others. It is my choice and no one else's. I feel I've lived my life more or less as I've wished and done most of what I wanted to do. Some things I would like to do better and still hope to improve. Nevertheless, I am content. I don't believe that my nature is very competitive except maybe with myself. Life has been good to me. I still live an active, adventurous life. From the very beginning and to the this day I have always been interested in the natural world and sciences, later in girls progressing to women, strength, health and body, Hispanic language and culture, living abroad, dancing, friends, my children, and enjoying whatever remains of life.

Regarding travel, the lasting pleasure I get is being able to relate to people of different cultures. I have had the most memorable times of my life raising a family in a different culture under basic rather primitive conditions living with, relating to and participating wholly with the local populace. Our three children attended the local schools and played with their schoolmates and neighbors. My fluency in Spanish has made this possible. Being bilingual has been of immeasurable value for myself and for my children.

I, unlike my parents and grandparents who immigrated to America for various reasons and couldn't afford the luxuries of travel or leading a leisurely carefree life. I was able to take advantage of the opportunities I had because I was single and without many responsibilities until later in life. I tried to make my life as I wanted to live it. Things didn't always work out as planned, nevertheless I was fortunate that things turned out well for me.

I am not an extrovert nor an introvert and try to avoid being the center of attention.
I'm self confident, primarily, when I feel competent in a situation.
I am frank and open with people. I do not exaggerate my status.
I am comfortable speaking with all and confident when engaging women.

SYNOPSIS of achievements

From the age of sixteen I began and dedicated myself to physical culture throughout my lifetime.

I began studying Spanish at 25 years of age till the present and consider myself bilingual.

In high school I added gymnastics and hand balancing to my body-building regimen.

I studied and became a registered physical therapist and later certified and licensed to perform electroneuromyographic examinations and testing in California. I am proud of my work performance and have saved a half dozen of my favorite EMNG reports to use a samples for recommendations, etc.

I have lived in Spain a total of 21 years. I acquired property and helped raise our three children in addition to having traveled in Europe, Cuba, Mexico, Argentina, Chile, Hawaii, Alaska and the US. Through my employment with the US military Mission, our act Manley & Jyl and pleasure travel in Spain, I am certain that few people have traveled as extensively and constantly throughout the Spanish peninsula and Balearic Islands as I during those many years.

Favorite sports and activities: gymnastics, handbalancing, body-building, downhill skiing, tennis, free diving (skin diving) and dancing. Although I've never received accolades, fame, trophies or medals for any of my pursuits, I have enjoyed the self challenges that have opened new worlds for me to explore and become part of.

Made in the USA
San Bernardino, CA
20 August 2016